Women Talk

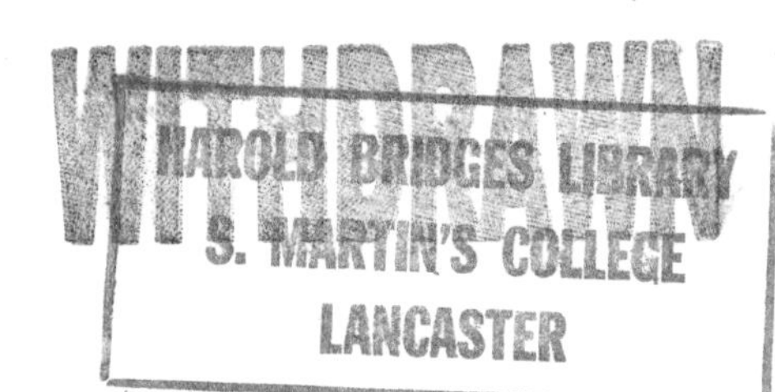

This book is dedicated to the members of the Oxton 'Ladies', past and present – Ann, Anne, Caro, Carol, Margaret, Moira, Rhiannon, Roslin, Rossanna, Sue – in celebration of over twenty years of friendship; and to Gina, in celebration of over forty years of friendship.

Women Talk

Conversation between Women Friends

Jennifer Coates

First published 1996

2 4 6 8 10 9 7 5 3 1

Blackwell Publishers Ltd
108 Cowley Road
Oxford OX4 1JF
UK

Blackwell Publishers Inc.
238 Main Street
Cambridge, Massachusetts 02142
USA

British Library Cataloguing in Publication Data

A CIP catalogue record for this book is available from the British Library.

Library of Congress-in-Publication Data

Coates, Jennifer.
Women talk : conversation between women friends / Jennifer Coates.
p. cm.
Includes bibliographical references and index.
ISBN 0-631-18252-7 (alk. paper). — ISBN 0-631-18253-5 (pbk. : alk. paper)
1. Women—Language. I. Title.
P120.W66C6 1996
302.3'46'082—dc20
95-49251
CIP

Typeset in 10½ on 12½ pt Palatino
by Graphicraft Typesetters Ltd, Hong Kong
Printed in Great Britain by Hartnolls Ltd, Bodmin, Cornwall

This book is printed on acid-free paper.

Contents

Acknowledgements

The research that underpins this book took over ten years to do and has involved many people in many different capacities. Firstly, I owe a special thank you to all those who allowed their conversations to be recorded and used in the research, and also to those who allowed me to interview them about their ideas and feelings about friendship: Alison, Ann, Anna, Anne, Caro, Carol, Catherine, Celia, Christine, Diana, Eleanor, Harriet, Jenny, Kim, Laura, Moira, Morag, Naomi, Naomi S., Rhiannon, Susan, Susan H., Susan P., Susan T., Vanessa. I'm also highly indebted to Christine Cheepen and John Wilson who gave me access to all-female conversations they'd recorded.

These conversations and interviews would never have found their way into a book without the help I received with transcribing the audio-tapes: from Brigitte Frank, Kate Hudson, Tam Richmond, And Rosta (who worked on the conversational data); from Emily Coates and Emilce Rees (who transcribed some of the ethnographic interviews); and from the COBUILD project at Birmingham University, which provided me with transcripts of some of my recordings in return for adding this material to their database.

I'm also indebted to those institutions which supported me in various ways to write the book. Writing became a possibility after I was awarded an Arts Faculty Visiting Fellowship by Melbourne University, beginning in August 1994. This allowed me to spend eleven months based in the Linguistics Department at Melbourne University, an environment which turned out to be ideal for my purposes. I'm very grateful to the University, to the Arts Faculty, and to my colleagues in the Linguistics Department, especially Nick Evans, Lesley Stirling and Jean Mulder, for providing me with this opportunity and for helping me to have such a fruitful stay. I'd also like to thank other Australasian universities that supported my visit through grants for travel and accommodation: the Department of English, University of Queensland (Brooks Visiting Fellowship); Faculty of Education, University of Technology, Sydney (Visiting Professorship); Departments of Linguistics and Women's Studies, University of Western Sydney; Department of Linguistics, University of New England, Armidale; Department of Linguistics, University of Victoria, Wellington; Department of Linguistics, Monash University; Department of Linguistics, LaTrobe University, Melbourne. Going to Australia only became a reality when my own institution, Roehampton Institute, London, granted me a year's study leave: I am grateful to the Institute, and to the English Department in particular, for their support.

I'd like to express my gratitude for the following research grants: grants awarded by the Research Committee, Roehampton Institute, which freed me from some of my teaching to work on the project, which allowed me to employ research assistants to help with transcription of the data, and which provided me with the necessary word-processing and transcribing machines; a British Council Travel Grant, which contributed towards my travel costs to and within Australia; a British Academy grant, which supported my attendance at the Symposium on Conversation, University of New Mexico, July 1995, where I presented and discussed a version of chapter 6.

I'd like to thank those who read and commented on drafts of the chapters: Mike Baynham, Jenny Cheshire, Christina Eira, Norma Grieve, Mary Ellen Jordan, Alison Lee, David Lee, Jean Mulder, Mary Porter, Cate Poynton, Joanne Scheibman, Amanda Sinclair, Lesley Stirling. I feel very lucky to have found so many willing readers; I appreciate their help more than I can express. I'm particularly grateful to Norma Grieve, who read chapters as I wrote them and gave me immediate feedback: her comments and support throughout my time in Melbourne were invaluable. I'm also very grateful to Janet Holmes, who read the manuscript for Blackwell in its entirety and whose comments and queries have been a great help in the final revision of the text.

I'm grateful to those who asked questions and made comments at the lectures and seminars I've given over the last year – in Melbourne, Sydney, Brisbane, Armidale and Wellington – for enriching my understanding of my data and for directing my attention to new points or to research by other scholars.

I'd also like to thank my friends and colleagues in English Language and Linguistics at Roehampton Institute for the many stimulating discussions we've had over the last ten years on issues dealt with in the book: I am indebted to them for listening to me and for challenging me. I'm also grateful to friends and colleagues in Australia and

New Zealand who discussed the ideas presented in this book with me. I am sure much of what I say derives from such discussions, and in that sense it is nonsense to claim that this book is my own unaided work: all I can say is a heartfelt thank you to all my colleagues and friends. I'm grateful to my publisher, Philip Carpenter, for his intelligent comments and suggestions throughout the writing of the book, and for his constant support for the project.

And last but not least I want to thank my women friends for their support over the years: it is my relationships with them which have been the inspiration for this book.

Notes on the Transcription of the Conversations

The examples in this book come from two sources: interviews and conversations. While interview material is relatively easy to transcribe (because it consists of a series of questions and answers), conversational material is much more difficult. The transcription of spontaneous conversation involves taking important decisions which have significant consequences for the ensuing analysis. After all, in a very important sense, transcription is theory.[1]

I have had to decide between timing pauses and using symbols which indicate 'short pause' or 'long pause'. Since pauses of any length seem to be such a rare feature of women friends' talk, I adopted the simpler system, distinguishing only between longer pauses – more than 0.5 of a second – and shorter ones. I have also had to decide whether to include prosodic features of talk (intonation patterns, rhythm, stress, etc.). In the end, I decided to exclude such features, except in the chapter on questions, where I have marked intonation patterns in key utterances. I have also taken the decision to mark all utterances that I am going to count as questions with a question mark, irrespective of intonation.

Most critical was the decision about how to set out speakers on the page. I had several options: I could adopt the conventions of the playwright (speakers alternating on the page); or I could put the words of the person who was 'the main speaker' at any point in conversation down the middle of the page, with other speakers at the edges; or I could experiment with an adaptation of the musical stave.[2] Because of the collaborative, all-in-together nature of women friends' talk (to be discussed in detail in chapter 6), I have chosen to use a musical-stave-type notation for the conversations, to make the relationship between different voices easy to grasp. This method of presentation is not easy to read at first sight, but is the only method capable of representing the data accurately. (However, in chapter 1, where one or two examples from the conversations are used to illustrate a point, the stave notation is not used.)

Because much of the interview data is less conversational in nature, I have presented this in the simpler play-like form, with speakers alternating on the page. But there are exceptions to this practice: where I interviewed more than one woman at the same time, the interviews were much more conversation-like, and as a result, some extracts from these interviews are presented in musical-stave format.

Transcription Conventions

The transcription conventions used for the conversational data are as follows.

1 A slash (/) indicates the end of a tone group or chunk of talk, e.g.:

 she pushes him to the limit/

2 A question mark indicates the end of a chunk of talk which I am analysing as a question (see chapter 8), e.g.:

 do you know anyone who's pregnant?

3 A hyphen indicates an incomplete word or utterance, e.g.:

 he's got this twi- he's got this nervous twitch/
 I was- I was- I was stopped by a train/

4 Pauses are indicated by a full stop (short pause – less than 0.5 second) or a dash (long pause), e.g.:

 he sort of . sat and read the newspaper/
 why doesn't that creep – *start to go wild/* <LAUGHING>

5 A broken line marks the beginning of a stave and indicates that the lines enclosed by the lines are to be read simultaneously (like a musical score), e.g.:

- -

A: the squidgy stuff that they put on pizzas/
B: Mozarell [a/
C: [Mozarella/

- -

6 An extended square bracket indicates the start of overlap between utterances, e.g.:

- -

A: and they have newspapers and [stuff/
B: [yes very good/

- -

7 An equals sign at the end of one speaker's utterance and at the start of the next utterance indicates the absence of a discernible gap, e.g.:

- -

A: because they're supposed to be=
B: =adults/

- -

8 Double round parentheses indicate that there is doubt about the accuracy of the transcription:

what's that ((mean))/ gayist/

9 Where material is impossible to make out, it is represented as ((xx)), e.g.:

you're ((xx))- you're prejudiced/

10 Angled brackets give additional information, e.g.:

- -

A: this is on tape you know
B: <LAUGHS>

- -

They also add clarificatory information about underlined material, e.g.:

why doesn't that creep – start to go wild/ <LAUGHING>
I can't help it <WHINEY VOICE>

11 Capital letters are used for words/syllables uttered with emphasis:

she BEAT him/
it's in MExico/

12 The symbol % encloses words or phrases that are spoken very quietly, e.g.:

%bloody hell%

13 The symbol .hh indicates that the speaker takes a sharp intake of breath:

.hh I wish I'd got a camera/ <LAUGHING>

14 The symbol [. . .] indicates that material has been omitted, e.g.:

Tom [. . .] says there's a German word to describe that/

15 The symbol ----> indicates that the line to the right of the arrow is the one to pay attention to.

as a dance might   so the speaking or as
circling   to and fro you   and maybe me
                                        a movement
an about around
heel   light footfall   toe light taps it
is womantalk   and wanderthrough
                    laughter and friends
the choreographies

Extract from Helen Kidd,
The Bower Meadow

1

'This is on tape you know': The origins of the book

In this book I want to celebrate friendships between women and to affirm the importance of talk for women friends. The talk associated with women is often given derogatory names: gossip, chit-chat, natter. These names demonstrate society's low evaluation of women's cultural practices. Women's talk is seen as trivial at best, tale-telling or 'bitchy' at worst. I want to make clear from the outset that gossip, chit-chat, natter – that is, the everyday talk of women friends – is what this book is about. I hope to demonstrate that women's talk is far from trivial, and that the label 'bitchy' betrays a fundamental misunderstanding of the way stories about absent others can provide a focus for discussing and re-evaluating social norms, and for the construction and maintenance of our personal identities, our 'selves'.

For many of us, talk is our chief form of recreation: we meet our friends to talk, and our talk is a kind of play. The conversations of women friends can be described as 'jam sessions': women's voices blend to create complex patterns, patterns which it is my aim to describe in this book. Women are well aware of the value of the talk we do with each other. Vera Brittain wrote as follows about the conversations she had with her closest friend, Winifred Holtby: 'Neither of us had ever known any pleasure quite equal to the joy of coming home at the end of the day after a series of separate varied experiences, and each recounting these incidents to the other over late biscuits and tea. Our conversations were irradiated by Winifred's delight in small, absurd trifles. She used to sit on the floor in front of the tiny gas fire . . . eagerly imploring: "Tell me some more!"'.[1] Like Vera Brittain, the women whose talk is the subject of this book are adamant that their conversations with each other are fundamental to their friendships, and that these conversations give them a very particular sort of pleasure. One of them said to me: 'I mean, you know at the end of the evening [spent in mixed company] you feel, yes, dissatisfied . . . whereas when I [spend an evening] with Anna and Liz I come home and I feel like we've talked about what we wanted to . . . it's undescribable'.[2] Another woman described conversation with friends as 'absolutely fundamental . . . the blood of life'.

The book is based on a corpus of twenty conversations between women friends and a set of ethnographic interviews with fifteen women about friendship. In the early chapters, drawing on what was said in the interviews, I hope to demonstrate the significance of talk in friendships between women. I want to build up a picture of what friendship means to (some) women in Britain in the late twentieth century, and to show how important friends are in women's lives. I shall extrapolate from these women's accounts of talk with their friends to sketch an outline of the shape of this talk. This sketch will be fleshed out in the six central chapters, where I look in detail at the twenty conversations, focusing on some of the conversational strategies typical of women's friendly talk. In the final chapters, I will take a broader perspective, looking at the ways in which women's talk constructs and maintains friendship, and constructs and maintains gender (in the case of girls and women, this means femininity).

Doubtless there are people who will view this book as trivial and unimportant, by association with its subject matter. But we need to challenge the negative social values placed on women's talk and to assert that such talk is as culturally significant, and as deserving of attention, as any other talk.

How it all began: Birkenhead, 1983–1984

In 1983 my marriage had broken up and I was looking for a full-time university post in linguistics. In retrospect, I realize that these circumstances had two very significant effects: the first was that I was forced to see the importance of my friendships with women, since without the support of my women friends I don't know how I would have survived that difficult period of my life. Secondly, I was galvanized into getting to work on the manuscript of *Women, Men and Language* (which was eventually published in 1986), since another book on my list of publications might make all the difference in terms of finding a lecturing job.

Writing the book *Women, Men and Language* changed my life in several ways. First, it was an intensely politicizing experience. Although I already considered myself a feminist, I was unprepared for the extent of sexism in linguistic practice which my reading uncovered, and for the strength of my response. Most importantly, however, I became increasingly uncomfortable about the ethics of writing a book which claimed to be (briefly at least) the last word on Language and Gender (or Language and Sex, as the field was quaintly known at that time) when I myself had done no original sociolinguistic work in the field. I decided that I would start a research project focusing on all-female talk, as I was unhappy at the extent to which Language and Gender research denoted research involving mixed-sex talk. Beyond this, I was vague about details. My main thought was that I must start collecting data, and that things would fall into place. It's probably a terrible confession to admit to, having had no clear research goals. Though it may be foolish of me to lay myself open to criticism in this way, I do so because I can't believe I'm the only researcher who's started a project in this way, and by speaking out I hope to draw attention to the question – how do we go about 'doing research'? I also want to challenge the notion that there is necessarily one right way of doing things.

The Oxton 'Ladies'

At this point, the germs of a research project and my support network of friends on Merseyside came together. Over several years (since 1975 to be exact), some of us had established a pattern of meeting once a fortnight at each other's houses. We would meet in the evenings, around 8.30 or 9.00 (when with any luck we had got our children to bed) and sit round and drink wine and talk. Later in the evening we always had something to eat, though this varied from simple bread and cheese to more elaborate home-made soup or pizza, depending on the whim or energy level of whoever was the host. Over the years, we came to call the group 'the Oxton Ladies' (since we lived in an area of Birkenhead called Oxton) or just 'Ladies', which is ironic, considering that we all loathe the word *lady* as a term for adult women. The name was initially a joke, parodying those polite but empty all-female Tupperware-style evenings we'd all experienced at some time or another. But the name was also a kind of smoke-screen to allay the fears of those (male partners) who feared that we were setting up a consciousness-raising group. In fact, this was very much one of the functions of the group, particularly in the early years, when we were all feeling constrained in various ways by the demands of small children. But I think we also gave ourselves this jokey name because we wanted to assert the frivolous side of our meetings; we didn't want to feel that we *had to* discuss serious things unless we chose to.

Starting to record

The initial group consisted of five women, all with young children, two with newly-born babies. The composition of the group has altered over the years as some of us have moved away and others have joined, and on any one evening there can be a different combination of people, since not everyone can make every meeting. In the autumn of 1983 – incredible as it may seem in these days of Ethics Committees – I took the decision to start recording these meetings surreptitiously (I will return to this issue). Initially, I intended to record each meeting, moving from one house to another as the fortnights rolled by. My first attempt was a disaster: we were meeting at Helen's house, so I took her into my confidence and rigged up some unsophisticated machine behind the sofa. The resulting tape was unusable for various reasons. First, not surprisingly, the recording quality was appalling, and, although I already knew that I was more interested in conversational features such as questions and repetition than in the minutiae of phonetic variation, these recordings were not good enough. This meant that I had to use better recording equipment. Secondly, the stress of managing the tape-recorder meant that I was distracted all evening: I began to realize that my awareness of the recording procedures was a methodological problem that had to be addressed; I needed to find a way of reducing my awareness to a minimum.

I decided that a solution to both problems lay in restricting recording to meetings held at my house. This had several advantages. First, I felt much more comfortable about recording my friends on my territory. Secondly, I could use the in-house hi-fi equipment which was in the living room where we always sat, coupled to my son's microphones. My elder son, Simon, was in a rock group and therefore had some reasonably sophisticated microphones: he reorganized the hi-fi system to become a recording system, with two microphones judiciously placed one on each side of the fireplace. Thirdly, I negotiated with Simon that, on the pretext of scrounging a glass of wine, he would come into the room during the evening and turn on the recording equipment. These new arrangements worked well: the recordings were of reasonable quality (apart from unexpected interference from the two-way radio of our neighbour's minicab firm) and, to my surprise, I was often so immersed in conversation that I barely noticed Simon's brief interruption of proceedings, and forgot for most of the time that recording was in progress. The only snag to these new arrangements was that meetings in my house only occurred at quite long intervals – after all, there were six or seven of us, and we met once a fortnight, with breaks for major holidays such as christmas and in the summer. So there were often three months or more between recordings. At the time this didn't worry me, but in the event I was offered a lecturing post in London, starting in September 1984. This meant that I had to move away from Birkenhead, away from my Oxton friends, with only four recordings completed.

Coming clean

At this point I chose to tell the group that I had been recording them for nearly a year. I was staggered by their reaction: they were furious. In retrospect, I'm amazed by my own naivety. Recording people talking without their consent is a gross violation of their rights. These people were my friends; they had come to my house in a spirit of trust. But I would ask readers to bear in mind that at that time, surreptitious recording still seemed methodologically acceptable. I had worked since 1968 as a research assistant for the pioneering Survey of English Usage, at University College London (initially full-time, then part-time after I moved away from London). The Survey was a pioneer in that it included spoken as well as written language in its corpus. Many spoken conversations collected for this corpus were recorded surreptitiously; that is, those recorded did not know they were being recorded (with the exception of the speaker connected with the Survey who was responsible for the recording). Working for the Survey was a formative experience: I admired the work done there and realize now that I adopted Survey practice uncritically as a model for my own work.[3] Major sociolinguistic work that I knew about – the research of William Labov in the United States and of Peter Trudgill in Britain, for example[4] – deployed the sociolinguistic interview as a tool for gathering data. While this method avoided surreptitious recording, it resulted in talk that was constrained by the asymmetry of the interview situation (the interviewer and the interviewee are not equals) and which was often relatively formal. It was not a method that could be used to collect the spontaneous talk of friends.[5]

The long, and sometimes painful, discussions I had with my friends after my revelation that they had been recorded have informed all research I have carried out subsequently. I have never recorded anyone surreptitiously again. I have had to think carefully about research methods, and am grateful to my friends for challenging me. Fortunately, they gave me permission to use the tapes, and are now pleased that we have a concrete record of our friendship. They are in fact rather amused that the talk of 'the Oxton Ladies' is the subject of academic articles and now a book.

Devising new methods

Over the two summer vacations following my departure from Birkenhead I started to transcribe the tapes I'd made. Anyone who has done any transcription of spoken language will know that it is an extremely difficult and time-consuming task. When you are working on recordings of conversations involving five or six speakers (as I was), you need to allow at least thirty minutes to transcribe one minute of conversation. But listening over and over again to my recordings, attending to every detail of what was going on in these conversations, proved to be an invaluable experience: it helped me to clarify my research goals. As I became aware of the richness of my data, I also became convinced that single-sex talk among women and girls was what I wanted to work on, more specifically, the talk of female friends in single-sex groups. I started to look for other existing groups of friends who would be willing to record themselves. Since I was no longer prepared to record people surreptitiously, I had to devise a new methodology: exactly how was I going to get at the talk of women friends? The corpus which I ended up with was arrived at by a hodge-podge of means. I use the word *hodge-podge* deliberately, to draw attention to the fact that this was not a carefully planned exercise, and to underline the serendipitous nature of the resulting corpus.

I decided first of all on what was criterial for my research. The recordings were to be made by groups rather than pairs of friends. (I chose groups of friends because I was particularly interested in patterns of conversational organization and believed – wrongly, it turns out – that the patterns typical of larger groups would not be found in the talk of dyads.) Secondly, these groups must already exist – I was not interested in artificially created groups. I also decided that groups should be given responsibility for recording themselves: in other words, I explained to them what I was doing and asked them to turn on a tape recorder when they met. (I explained to them what I was doing in the vaguest terms to avoid making them self-conscious about particular aspects of their talk.) This method had the advantage of excluding me from the conversations (where my presence would have been intrusive), but meant I had no control over recording quality (which was therefore variable) or over whether recording was carried out at all. (Many more groups offered to record themselves than actually did so.)

Speakers and self-consciousness

Because I no longer recorded speakers surreptitously, I had the problem of risking that the talk recorded would be distorted by the women's awareness of the presence of the tape-recorder. I hypothesized that the normative pressures of the group would overcome any self-consciousness over the recording equipment.[6] In fact, it's clear that participants in this research frequently forgot that the tape-recorder was on; this was demonstrated by comments such as *you do forget that's on actually, don't you?* and *ooh I'd forgotten that was on* (both coming at moments when a move to a different room focused attention on the tape-recorder); and exchanges such as the following between three girls:

BECKY: is it recording Hannah?
HANNAH: yes/
CLAIRE: bloody hell/
BECKY: oh no/

In the interviews I carried out with women who'd participated in the research, this was confirmed. Sue, for example, commented, 'Well we forgot it, we forgot it was on in the end'.

Occasionally, a chance remark will reveal that at least one of the participants is sensitive to the presence of the tape-recorder. In the first example below, Anna has arrived in a state from work and suddenly realizes Sue has the tape-recorder on:

ANNA: when d'you start [((like that thing- like that recorder))?
LIZ: [she's got that thing going/ all her tapes going=

SUE: =oh yeah/ we're doing our stuff/

In the following example, it's not clear whether Emily *was* thinking about the recording or not, but Gwen's question alerts all four girls present to the fact that recording is taking place:

EMILY: I'm a bit disappointed we aren't talking about sex or boys/
GWEN: for Jennifer?

When speakers *do* remember that they are being recorded, they sometimes direct jokey remarks at me, the researcher (thus acknowledging my presence as an invisible audience to their talk). The following is an example. (Note that this example also illustrates that taping has become such a normal accompaniment to talk that the friends can't always remember whether particular conversations have been recorded or not.)[7]

CLAIRE: this is on tape you know/
BECKY: <LAUGHS>
HANNAH: oh yeah/ well they- this is meant to be natural what we talk about/
JESSICA: <LAUGHS>
BECKY: must think we're a bunch of perVERTS/ no I mean PERverts/
JESSICA: not- not perVERTS/ <LAUGHS>
HANNAH: everybody saying 'Up your bum'/
BECKY: <LAUGHING> oh no/ the tape wasn't on when we did that/
CLAIRE: it WAS/ at di- dinner time/
BECKY: it wasn't/
JESSICA: it wasn't when we were eating our-
CLAIRE: it was/
BECKY: it was/ i- finished/
JESSICA: it wasn't when we were eating our fruit salad and stuff though/
CLAIRE: oh yeah cos we came down/
BECKY: goodoh/ <LAUGHS> I- I would- I would never have submitted that/ I'd be too embarrassed/
HANNAH: what?
CLAIRE: no they'll probably listen to it and they'll wonder what-
----> JESSICA: dear tape person/ that was a joke/
HANNAH: <LAUGHS>
BECKY: what was a joke?
JESSICA: 'up your bum'/ <LAUGHS>

John Wilson was struck by this phenomenon when he recorded conversations among adolescents in Belfast. His paper, 'The sociolinguistic paradox',[8] focuses explicitly on these kinds of jokey asides produced by research subjects. Wilson's subjects were all young, and, in my recordings too, remarks addressed to the researcher were produced only by younger participants. Adult participants sometimes remember the tape-recorder is on, but they don't exploit this knowledge to address me. This may be a function of age, or it may be the result of the younger generation's casual familiarity with recording technology.

Building up a corpus

Having decided who I wanted to record, I built up a corpus using a variety of strategies.

- I recorded my own friends (surreptitiously) – this resulted in the four recordings I've already mentioned.
- I asked girls and women I knew to record themselves when they were with their friends.
- Women volunteered to record themselves with their friends or volunteered to get their daughters to record themselves with their friends.
- I wrote to linguists I knew who had conversational data and asked them if they had any recordings of women friends, and whether they would be prepared to swap their data for some of mine.[9]

As a result of these strategies, I collected twenty conversations between women friends, involving in total nineteen hours and thirty minutes of talk. This summary does not give an adequate impression of the random nature of the collection process. For example, I gave a paper to the annual Women in Libraries Conference about women's ways of talking, and over lunch one woman said that she thought I would be interested in her daughter's group of friends. This has happened to me before and since, with no tangible result, but as usual I took her phone number and said I would contact her. To my surprise, when I rang she said that she had opened negotiations with her daughter, and invited me to tea to complete the negotiations. In the event, this group recorded themselves over a four-year period, from when they were twelve until they were fifteen, and provided me with invaluable developmental data. Another time, I mentioned idly in an introductory exercise with a group of first-year students at Roehampton Institute that I was doing research on the talk of women friends. One of the students stayed behind at the end and said that she and two women friends met to talk regularly, and would I like her to record them? I said I would, but was astonished and delighted when I came into college to find two audiotapes in an envelope with a message asking if I wanted more.

The grand total of nineteen hours and thirty minutes of data conceals the fact that the conversations varied in length from some very short stretches of talk recorded by the twelve-year-old girls (fifteen or twenty minutes) to a conversation lasting three hours recorded by a group of three women. I'm using the word 'conversation' rather loosely here, to mean part of a conversation as well as a whole conversation. The three-hour conversation just referred to was in fact unusual in being a recording of an entire evening's talk: most of my recordings are of parts of conversations. This is for several reasons: in the case of my early surreptitious recordings, I was only able to use one side of a ninety-minute audiotape. In the case of later recordings, different groups interpreted my request for material differently: some recorded one side of an audiocassette at a time; others recorded a whole evening's talk. In the case of material given to me by other linguists, I had no control over the length of recordings. (They too seem to have been constrained by the limits of the audiocassette: the conversational extracts they gave me all last either one or two sides of a cassette.)

Although I intended to collect only multiparty conversation between friends, I ended up with four dyadic conversations (conversations involving two women) as well as sixteen involving three or more speakers. The corpus includes groups of two, three, four, five and six women, with eight of the recordings involving groups of four.[10] Altogether, twenty-six girls and women were involved in the conversations on tape. They range in age from twelve years old to early fifties, come from a variety of geographical locations in Britain, including London, Belfast and Merseyside, and from a spectrum of social class backgrounds, from upper working to professional middle class. They are all white. (I deliberately excluded women of other ethnic backgrounds as it seemed to me likely that friendship patterns would vary with ethnicity.) In terms of sexual orientation, participants were all heterosexual or celibate (this category is not relevant to the youngest speakers in the corpus). I regret that lesbian women are not represented in this corpus. As I've explained, the collection of data, and, in particular, finding groups willing to participate, was a very hit-and-miss affair – one group who, after long consideration, refused to participate explained that, since some of them were lesbian, they felt uncomfortable about the possibility of revealing intimate aspects of their lives. There was certainly no intention to exclude lesbian women, nor did I at the outset consider that female friendship might differ depending on sexual orientation. However, the latter is a debatable point, which I shall return to in subsequent chapters.[11] The final sample, then, is reasonably homogeneous, apart from age differences and some minor class differences.

Because I wanted to give the women and girls involved in my research the opportunity to express their views on friendship and on the role of talk in friendship, I conducted a series of ethnographic interviews with them to complement the conversational data. I contacted the groups once recording was finished and asked individuals if they were prepared to be interviewed. They had the choice of being interviewed on their own or with a friend. I preferred the latter option, given the topic of the interview, but one or two women were interviewed alone (these were close friends of mine, who treated these interviews more as a rather strange kind of friendly conversation with me, than as a formal interview).[12] I supplemented these interviews with others involving women who had not been recorded in conversation with their friends (some of these women were lesbian). In all, I carried out interviews with fifteen women, nine of whom were involved in the primary research. It was important to me, as a feminist ethnographer, that my research subjects should add their voices to mine in describing what was going on in friendly conversation. Although I take responsibility for the final analysis, I wanted to check my (academic) judgement against their personal accounts and to strengthen the generalizability of my claims by grounding them in their insights.

'Balancing' the corpus

During the research period (1984–93) I gave papers from time to time arising from my work. In the early years I was challenged several times about the absence of boys' and men's talk from my corpus. I was intimidated by such challenges: it is hard doing woman-centred work when academic institutions are still male-dominated and when such work is not regarded as 'serious' by the malestream. I also managed to convince myself that there might be some merit in doing a more comparative study. I therefore began to collect data from groups of male friends as well. This was also collected by a mixture of means, not all identical with the methods I've listed above. In particular, there is no central set of conversations to parallel my original set of recordings of my own group of women friends. One new stratagem was to use data collected by students whose work I supervised or was closely involved in.[13] I was also helped by (male) linguist friends who volunteered to give me tapes of recordings they'd made of themselves talking with their friends.[14]

The corpus including the tapes of male friends' conversations consists of forty conversations in all, twenty from all-female groups and twenty from all-male groups.[15] I am embarrassed by the meretricious appearance of scientific balance that these figures give: my main aim throughout has been to collect good quality data, in particular the spontaneous talk of women friends. The fact that I have ended up with equal numbers of conversations involving male and female speakers is a freak statistic. In terms of the amount of talk in hours, the total corpus consists of over thirty-seven hours of recordings, with the women's conversations constituting more than half of that total (nineteen hours and forty-five minutes).

Setting the record straight

I have only included the information about male data to avoid falsifying the record. In other words, I don't want to give the false impression that I only collected all-female talk. However, in this book I will be concerned only with the conversations involving women friends, and with the friendship interviews I recorded with women (I have not interviewed any men). In the end, I realized that if I wanted to write a book that concentrated only on women, that was my choice. So I have chosen to write about women, about their friendships and the talk that goes with friendship. Feminist researchers are now beginning to insist on the need 'to address the many questions we all have about women, the way they talk, what they think, and how they think and talk about the world they inhabit'.[16] It's taken me a long time to fully understand the significance of friendships with women in my own life. It's taken me even longer to understand that the talk of women friends is what I want to explore as a researcher, and that women's talk is a legitimate area of study for a linguist.

What kind of researcher am I?

My background is in linguistics – that is, the formal study of language. I was trained to describe language in terms of syntax and morphology (grammar), semantics (meaning), and phonetics (sound systems). But as I've grown older, I've become less interested in studying language as a phenomenon in its own right, in isolation from its social and cultural context. I've become more and more interested in studying language as a (crucial) component of human interaction which both shapes and reflects our lives. What this means is that I've moved away from the 'scientific' study of language and away from the notion of myself as a dispassionate investigator, to the study of language in its social context, where my own standpoint, as a white middle-class woman, as a feminist, has to be taken into account. In other words, and to put it at its most simple, I've moved from linguistics to sociolinguistics.

More specifically, I would describe myself as an *ethnographer of communication*. Ethnography is part of anthropology, which is the study of human beings and human societies. (For the record, readers may be interested to know that anthropology is virtually always described as 'the study of "mankind"', a habitual usage which tells us a lot about the androcentric traditions of anthropological scholarship. For reasons which are, I hope, self-evident, I shall not adopt this usage.) In traditional anthropology, the study of human societies was understood to mean the study of more 'primitive' social groups. Thus, nineteenth-century anthropologists went off to document the lives of 'exotic' communities much as botanists documented exotic plant species in far-flung parts of the world. This kind of scholarly activity was part and parcel of the colonial enterprise.

Ethnographers developed a research paradigm which involved collecting data through intensive fieldwork: the ethnographer lived as a participant observer in the community they were investigating. At the beginning of this century, ethnographers would carry out their fieldwork in the colonial areas of Africa and South-East Asia, then return home to write up their findings. It was only with the collapse of empire that ethnographers have had to reorient themselves and look for new areas in which to carry out fieldwork. Now, in the 1990s, many ethnographers do ethnography in their own society. For example, a British ethnographer may do fieldwork in a working-class community in the East End of London; an Australian ethnographer may work in the Northern Territory with an Aboriginal group. But as these examples illustrate, it is still the norm for members of more privileged groups (typically, well-educated white males) to do research involving groups who are less privileged.

The phrase 'the ethnography of communication' was coined by Dell Hymes to widen the already existing (but not very well known) field known as the ethnography of speaking.[17] The phrase articulates the belief that if we, as linguists, are serious in our aim to describe language in its social context, then we need to become ethnographers. The phrase also captures the fact that much of the data collected by ethnographers is linguistic: since the invention of the tape-recorder, ethnographers have been able to record the daily activities of the group they are working with.[18] But ethnographers trained in the anthropological tradition are not interested in language as language, but as material which provides them with evidence about specific social rituals, such as marriage or death. Sociolinguists like Dell Hymes realized that anthropologists had devised a methodology which was ideal for getting at everyday linguistic usage. The term, the ethnography of communication, can be defined as the study of 'the norms of communicative conduct in different communities', which also 'deals with methods for studying these norms'.[19] Research in this field seeks answers to the questions: 'What does a speaker need to know to communicate appropriately within a particular speech community, and how does s/he learn?'[20]

Feminist ethnography

While I consider myself to be an ethnographer of communication, I would describe myself, more precisely, as a *feminist ethnographer*. What do I mean by this? I mean, first, that I put women at the centre of my work. Secondly, it means that I do not pretend to be 'objective' but acknowledge from the beginning where I'm coming from. There is an enduring belief in the academic world that 'truth' (whatever that is) can only be arrived at via impartial research. On the contrary, I believe that all researchers are necessarily partial and that all research is subjective and political. I would argue that being 'interested' rather than 'disinterested' is a strength, not a weakness: it means that I am engaged in what I do. One of the claims of feminist scholarship is that 'knowledge generated through engagement offers greater insights . . . than that generated through detachment'.[21] Thirdly, it means that I am sensitive to the potential for exploitation in the relationship between the researcher and the researched, and want to challenge methodologies which treat those researched as objects. In my own research I want to portray women as social actors, as agents in our own lives, not as victims. I want to be explicit about my relationship to those who participated in my research, not to make that aspect of the research invisible. I also want to emphasize that without the cooperation of a considerable number of women I would not have been able to gather this data. This cooperation was only possible because of the relationship of trust that we established, a kind of 'female social contract', to use Teresa de Lauretis' words.[22] De Lauretis argues that woman-centred research must start from honesty about asymmetry in the researcher–researched relationship in order to move on to trust. While the researcher may be powerful in terms of expertise, it also needs to be acknowledged that she puts herself at the mercy of her research subjects in the quest for data: this is their power. Feminist research tries to avoid the arrogance of malestream work and to encourage mutual respect between researcher and research subjects.

Women researchers, from Margaret Mead onwards, have frequently chosen to work with women. This is something I chose to do, both because I felt comfortable working with women and with friends, and in the hope that my insider status meant that I could bring a wider understanding to bear on my data. In this book, I want to celebrate women's everyday lives and to oppose the routine trivialization of what women do. Because ethnography is not detached, it can be a subversive activity, challenging accepted wisdom and normative values. As Diane Bell, a feminist ethnographer, puts it: 'Ethnography at its best opens a discursive space in which the silenced may speak. It empowers and validates everyday experience. It brings to the threshold of consciousness the routines, rhythms and rituals of everyday life, allows us to savour the ordinary, map the mundane . . .'.[23]

In the chapters which follow, I've tried to give space to women's voices and to validate women's everyday experience. I hope this book will allow you to savour the ordinariness of their friendship and their talk, at the same time as celebrating the extraordinariness of these friendships – their strength, their enduringness – and the extraordinary complexity and creativity of their talk.

2

'She's just a very very special person to me': Women and friendship

Whatever has happened to me, or has not, with lovers and husbands . . . , continuity and security have been built on the excellence of friendship; and when I look at [my mother]'s life I can see that this was so for her too. Yet these connections between women are taken for granted, a backdrop to the real business of life: husbands, children, jobs. It takes only the slightest change of focus to see that these neglected intimacies, independent of more passionate demands, can offer the terms on which we best learn to be ourselves. (Drusilla Modjeska Poppy, *page 309)*

In her strongly worded account of women's friendship, Drusilla Modjeska raises key questions about the place of these 'connections between women' in our lives, questions which this chapter will try to address. Right through our lives, friendship plays an important role for most of us. It's a strand that remains constant, alongside the flux of the rest of our lives. As small children, we form loose friendships that can change from day to day. Later, as we move into adolescence, our friendships become more intense; one or two of these friendships may survive into adulthood. It's often said, too glibly, I think, that female friendship in adolescence is a dry run for later, heterosexual relationships. In my view, the more straightforward claim would be that female friendships in adolescence are simply a dry run for later close relationships of all kinds, and that they constitute the first episode in the saga of female friendship which runs through our lives.

When we are children, our lives are divided into two camps: the world inside the home known as the family and dominated by parents, and the world outside the home. School is an important context in this outside world, and teachers have an important role in our lives, but outside the home the key figures are our friends and other significant contemporaries. (This division is often more abstract than real, since girls in particular tend to bring their friends into the home.) As adults, we go on having friends – this is a constant, while taking on the new domestic roles of partner, wife, mother, aunt, as well as new roles in the public sphere, in paid or voluntary work.[1]

The last paragraph may seem to be stating the obvious. But the point I want to make is that while the two worlds of childhood are discussed openly and uncontroversially by sociologists, educationalists, social psychologists and so on, adult women, until very recently, were only recognized in their domestic role. Women's friendships, like the rest of women's lives, remained unexplored and, in the academic world, it is hard to escape the idea that the topic of women's friendships was systematically ignored.[2] In some quarters it was even claimed that friendship was an important aspect of men's lives, but not of women's.[3] But in the last twenty years, there has been an upsurge of interest in women's lives in general and in women's friendships in particular. Women's friendship has become a topic of interest to historians, literary critics, philosophers, theologians, sociologists, anthropologists, folklorists. Social historians have discovered the lost history of women's friendship and have demonstrated that, while it may take different forms in different periods of history, it is a permanent strand in the social tapestry.[4] Feminist philosophers and theologians have discovered in female friendship a source of inspiration, a model for good human relationships.[5] Sociologists have carried out research on, and have thus made visible, the friendship patterns of young women, older women, working-class women, middle-class women, heterosexual women and lesbians.[6] Anthropologists have explored the ways friendship varies from culture to culture, but at the same time have demonstrated the key role female friendship plays in women's lives, whether on Crete, where the harshness of women's circumscribed lives is made bearable by friendship with other women, or in Central Australia, where solidarity and mutual support are vital in the maintenance of Aboriginal women's traditional practices.[7] Folklorists have asserted the value of women's culture, the collaborative folklore enacted in the privacy of the home, among women friends.[8]

In this chapter my aim is to allow the women I interviewed to describe what friendship means to them. (These descriptions are inevitably affected by the discourses available to the women concerned: I will discuss at a later stage the discourses which shape these descriptions, and, more generally, the way our everyday practices –

including talk – reproduce gender identity or 'gendered subjectivity'.)[9] As I've explained, the core of my interview sample was made up of women who had taken part in the primary research – that is, women who had allowed me to record their conversations with their friends. With these women, the interview had a double purpose – to give them feedback on what the whole process had been about and bring it to a conclusion, and to allow them to feed into the process by telling me their views on friendship and on the role of talk in friendship. I also interviewed another six women to broaden the sample. The overall interview sample is more heterogeneous than the conversational sample. Ages ranged from twelve years to mid-fifties. Social class background (as far as it is possible to assign) ranged from upper working class to upper middle class. Of the fifteen women interviewed, eight were married, or in a stable relationship (these included heterosexual and lesbian relationships), and seven were single, though this latter group embraces both the younger participants and also divorced and separated women.

I interviewed these women in their own homes (apart from one, who came to my home). We sat at the kitchen table, or on comfortable chairs in the living room, or even (once) in the garden, with a cup of tea or a glass of wine. The interviews were loosely structured around a set of twelve questions and lasted between thirty and ninety minutes, with most clustering around sixty minutes. They were as informal as I could make them. This meant that my role was ambiguous: I played a dual role, acting as the person with responsibility for making sure a certain set of topics was dealt with, and also as a woman discussing these topics with one or more other women. In many of the interviews, another woman's self-disclosure would trigger mirroring self-disclosure from me. The term 'interview' is therefore being stretched to the limit here, since these 'interviews' were much more like informal conversation than they were like formal interviews. But unlike everyday conversation, and like formal interviews, there was a set agenda.[10] In the rest of the chapter I will give an account of what these women said in the interviews, and will explore the ambiguities that emerge from what they said.[11]

Length of friendship

There can be no doubting the seriousness which women accord to friendship as a subject. I made no stipulations about which friends they should talk about: in the case of women interviewed with a friend or friends, they talked about each other; in the case of close friends of mine who I interviewed alone, they chose another friend to talk about when I asked for concrete examples. I asked each of them to state how long they'd been friends with the woman friend they'd chosen to talk about. The shortest friendship brought up by participants was five years, and many had been friends for a much longer time, with thirty-two years being the longest. While age is inevitably a factor in this – the oldest women in my sample (women over fifty) reported the longest friendships – it wasn't necessarily a factor. Becky and Hannah, two girls from one of the younger groups whose conversations I'd recorded, have been friends for fifteen years now (since they were three years old). The actual figures are in themselves unimportant and obviously unrepresentative. But what does emerge from these answers is a strong feeling the *it takes time* to become close friends. In other words, the lowest figure given (five years) is significant: no one mentioned brief relationships in the context of friendship.

The other inference I draw from the length of some of these friendships (specific examples are: eleven, fourteen, fifteen, twenty-four, twenty-five, thirty-one, thirty-two years) is that women's friendships are durable in nature. Such durability is no mean feat, give the vagaries of any ten-year period in a woman's life today: we move house, we have children, we get a job, we go to college. These external factors will mean, for any pair of friends, that living close to each other for long stretches of time is the exception rather than the rule. On top of this, the chance of major life events (such as childbirth, divorce, a new job) occurring in parallel is highly unlikely. When our lives do synchronize, it can be a great joy, and many friendships take shape, come to fruition at such times. But over our lifetimes, we have to work hard to keep our friendships going, and the fact that we are prepared to do this work tells us a lot about the value we place on our women friends.

How often do we see our friends?

It is probably only in our teens, when our friendships are most intense, that we see our friends every day. Friendship for young people ties in with the routine of their daily lives: we go to school every day; we see our friends every day. For some young people, this pattern continues after school, at college. But after that, friendship needs to be more consciously worked at, as we become involved in work and/

or child-rearing, and as we become more autonomous and more mobile. But the evidence of my interviews is that when women friends live close to each other they manage to see each other very regularly:

- 'at least once a week' (Becky and Hannah)
- 'probably once a week or once a fortnight' (Mary and Gianna)
- 'about once a week' (Jo and Miranda)
- 'every couple of weeks' (Meg and Bea)

How often we manage to see our friends depends in large part on factors completely external to the friendship, such as where we live. Some of the women I interviewed talked about friends who no longer live near. They said that this means that they may only see each other two or three times a year. But the pattern can be unpredictable. When asked how often she managed to see her friend Cathy, who lives twenty miles away, Val said: 'high days, holidays, sometimes not for six months, sometimes we live together for ten days, two weeks – very movable'.

How much this matters seems to be a moot point. On the one hand, the women I talked to were adamant that real good close friendship did not depend on frequent contact. Val, whose description of erratic contact with her great friend Cathy is given above, said, 'No, not at all' when I asked if frequency of contact mattered; so did Mary, Jill, Rachel, Meg, Bea, Anna, Sue and Liz. Sue and Liz formulated it like this:

SUE: I think once you've got a friend, whenever you see them you pick up . . .
LIZ: you just pick up where you left off, it's not a problem.

Rachel said: 'I mean, once you've made that connection it's like you can- you don't have to see somebody very often, but then once you get into [. . .] the two of you somewhere [. . .] you can go back to it very quickly, it's like a given between you'. Anna introduces the concept of 'sure-footedness' to explain why frequency of meetings is unimportant: 'If you're friends on that old sort of sure-footed basis, it doesn't really matter'. This is because, in Becky's view, 'If you've established a relationship, it can stand sort of bashing'.

For the young women in my sample, this issue was something they were just beginning to give some thought to, as school and living close to each other had guaranteed regular contact so far in their lives. Becky and Hannah are optimistic that they have established a basis of friendship which absence won't harm. (This extract, and one or two others in this chapter, is presented with the speakers arranged in staves, like instruments in a musical score. This is more difficult to read, but is essential to show how speakers' words link with each other and overlap. This method of transcription is discussed in notes on the transcription of the conversations, pages ix–x, and the whole issue of co-constructed and overlapping talk in women's conversation, will be dealt with at length in chapter 6.)

BECKY:	I think we'll probably be like that for the rest of our lives/

BECKY:	[like . we might not see each other for YEARS/ and then-
HANNAH:	[yeah I mean you could-

BECKY:		yeah/ I think it'll be really nice/	
HANNAH:	and then just sort of-		yeah/

HANNAH:	like I mean you- it's- yeah/ we have the sort of relationship

---

BECKY:		yeah/
HANNAH:	where I can't really see . losing/	

On the other hand, most women acknowledge that in order to get onto this 'sure-footed basis', you need a period when interaction is fairly frequent. And all the women agreed that we apply different standards to friends who live close to us and those who live far away. If friends live close to us, then seeing each other frequently *is* significant. Mary said: 'we both make an effort to see each other at least once a week'. Meg said: 'I think if it was longer than two weeks I would think, "I wonder what Bea's up to?" you know'. Jo and Miranda were very clear that for them at this time in their lives, seeing each other regularly mattered. Miranda's words were: 'as we live so close to each other and I mean I suppose because Jo being my sort of closest friend in Oxford, I would feel very lost if I didn't you know [see her] . . . and I sometimes if I haven't seen her over a bit, and sort of millions of things are happening in my life, in between, that seems very odd'.

This idea – that you would get out of touch with significant events in each others' lives – is brought up in several interviews. Meg put it like this:

> There's a certain sort of degree of um shared experiences which you-you like to draw on, and if you don't see each other um you're forever having to kind of you know re-establish not your friendship as such

> but where [. . .] you're up to. Often you miss telling people about quite important events and say, 'Oh didn't you know that? I thought you knew that', um that kind of thing.

Helen, by contrast, stated her position as follows: 'it's not to do with how often you see somebody or even the kind of contact you have, somehow to do with what's happening in your own lives at the same time, which will come in parallel – the time in between doesn't matter'.

In support of this latter view, that frequency is unimportant compared with the quality of the relationship, Liz's distinction between friends and friend-friends is interesting: 'when the children were young and you've got all day, you sort of have a lot of friends, but they're not friend-friends, they're just friends because they've got young children'.

Liz's distinction between friends and friend-friends makes the point that frequent meetings may have no correlation with the strength of the friendship, but may just be the result of particular life circumstances. Real friendship – being a friend-friend rather than just a friend – depends on more solid interpersonal links than just having children the same age.

This debate raises key questions about the nature of women's friendship and its functions. On one hand, friendship is defined in terms of the intimacy that comes from knowing someone really well, 'knowing' here being defined as being in touch with key events in each other's lives. It's clear that women feel that, with friends who live close by, their everyday friends, we have a responsibility to make an effort to see each other regularly. (If we live close to each other and do *not* see each other regularly, then the friendship will fade.) On the other hand, what is implied by all those who said adamantly that meeting frequently was not a necessary component of friendship is the sense that, once a particular quality of link is established between two women, then 'the time in between doesn't matter'. Helen even goes so far as to argue that it's the quality of 'fit' between your life at a given moment and that of your friend which counts. (Helen is one of the women who talks later on in her interview about losing friends because their lives were no longer 'in parallel', as she puts it.)

The key components of friendship

When it came to listing the key components of friendship, many of the women mentioned basic things such as shared interests and a shared world view. The phrase *shared interests* occurred in many of the interviews, and Mirands asserted that 'people I choose to be friends with . . . have the same sort of fundamental values'. Mary clearly felt she was stating the obvious when she said:

MARY: well obviously you would feel that you- in the main you fit in with their world view
JEN: mhm
MARY: otherwise- and they must fit in with yours obviously.
JEN: mhm, so you share- pretty much share a world view?
MARY: yes, so you're going to have to share a world view.

Having fun together is another aspect of friendship that several women mentioned (an aspect of women's friendship that has been well illustrated in Gilda O'Neill's book about women having a good time together, *A Night out with the Girls*.) Becky sees a friend as 'someone to sort of take your mind off your worries and have a good time'. Helen considers this aspect of friendship essential: 'You have to enjoy friends' company, there must be fun about it'.

But the two components of female friendship which were brought up by everyone and which were very highly valued were mutual support and being able to 'be yourself'. Women's friendships were defined as 'total support' by Anna, and women who listed what female friendship meant to them put support first: 'support, shared interests, understanding' (Mary); 'support, empathy, trust, those kind of things' (Meg). Support was at the heart of why you liked another woman: 'you like them because . . . you bolster them and they bolster you' (Mary). Support is talked about as crucial when things aren't going well. Becky asserts the importance of friends 'being there when you know things aren't exactly hunky-dory and- and sort of supporting you'; Meg says of Bea, 'I look to you as someone when particular things go wrong that I can look to for support', and Anna says of Sue and Liz, 'I could come here and say, "My life's fallen apart" and that would be fine'. The reality of this was illustrated by the many anecdotes these women told to illustrate what they meant by friendship: they told me how invaluable their friends' support had been at particularly fraught moments in their lives – when a child or a parent or a grandparent died, when they were abandoned by a husband or a lover, when a child came out as gay. But they also mentioned support in more positive terms, as the way in which women validate each other and help to build each other's confidence: 'What friendship does is to support and to endorse [. . .] [so] friendships to me are about making me feel in the end a greater sense of confidence in what I'm doing' (Helen).

The other key component of friendship in the experience of these women was feeling they could 'be themselves'. The importance of being able to 'be yourself' was repeated time and time again in the interviews. Here are a few examples: '[with a friend] you can just be yourself I suppose, that's what it is' (Sue); '[a friend is] someone you can be totally yourself in front of' (Val); 'it's just having someone that you can just be yourself with [. . .] With Hannah and my older friends I feel comPLETEly I can be myself entirely' (Becky). Becky explicitly contrasts the feeling of being able to 'be herself' with real close friends like Hannah with the uncomfortable feeling she has with other, less close, friends (note the way Hannah joins in to support her in expressing this):

BECKY:	I mean I've got friends that- . . . sometimes I feel
BECKY:	like I have to put on a bit of a – you know say the-
BECKY: HANNAH:	you know [say the right words and things you know/ [say the right things/ . yeah/

The sense of being accepted, of not having to 'say the right things', was often expressed in terms of mutual understanding. Jo said, 'I think one very important element for me is I think in a lot of ways we're quite similar, and that means I experience a considerable degree of understanding'. Jill's view was that 'I've got to know how she feels and I'm sure that she knows how I feel, and often we don't have to um- to talk about it. That to me is a GOOD friend'.

Some women emphasized the fact the 'being yourself' meant not having to be 'nice' all the time. Miranda claimed that friends are 'people who actually like you even when you feel you're not being very nice and stuff', and Meg says she feels with her closest friends that she can 'display the rather nasty side of me'. Several people drew on the image of warts as representing not nice aspects of ourselves: Bea said to Meg: 'I think I value the fact that you're someone that I feel I can be open with and show my warts to', and Helen said to me: 'we all see each other's warts, that's the whole point, I know what your warts are and you know what mine are'. Warts are not necessarily terrible character failings: they may be aspects of our selves that we feel constrained to conceal from most people, because of the clash with our public persona, things like the fact that we enjoy 'grotty' films, or even that we're addicted to watching the soap opera *Neighbours* (both examples from the interviews). More seriously, being 'nice' is normatively imposed on women as an essential component of femininity. The imperative to be nice, to please others, is one we learn to obey from the day we are born female. Most of us learn to perform acceptably, but at a high price. As Margaret Atwood has argued (both in interviews and in her creative writing), women will only be liberated when they assert the right *not* to be nice.[12] It seems from the evidence of the interviews and from the warts-and-all character of the conversational data that close friendship with other women has a very significant function in providing a safe place where the imperative to 'be nice' does not prevail, and where we feel we can 'be ourselves entirely' (as Becky put it) – that is, whole people who are not fragmented into good and bad, nice and nasty bits.

Friendship and challenge

There's another theme – a theme of challenge – which came up in two of the interviews. Miranda said, 'I value friends who challenge me in some way'. This view – that is, the idea of challenge being a healthy component of human relationships – draws on psychotherapeutic discourses current today. But it's a view also strongly endorsed by many men, and is often articulated in order to expose the supposed shortcomings of women's friendship and its 'sympathetic circularity'. I'll quote a longer section of one interview here, in which the phrase 'sympathetic circularity' is used by Helen when describing her (male) partner's criticism of women's friendships.

> For some reason Nick's view is here, the problem with friendship with women is that it's always sympathetic circularity. He sees that as a problem. I think he sees that the important thing in relationships is to challenge and to expose. So what I feel good about in friendships is that it actually makes you fee- OK, we all see each other's warts, that's the whole point, I know what your warts are and you know what mine are, but we choose a time when to sort of be prepared to acknowledge it . . . we don't expose them at points when we think people can't deal with them.

In Helen's view, Nick sees the mutual support and acceptance that women give each other as problematic, because he thinks the task of a true friend is to help you to improve yourself by 'challenging' and 'exposing'. Helen contrasts this with her own view that acceptance is more fundamental, and that 'exposing' people's flaws will be counterproductive if done at the wrong moment. She gives an example from her own life: her friend tried to tell her (Helen) that her marriage to Tom was over, but Helen was not at that point ready to listen and resented her friend's comments. 'The other conflict was with my friend Gemma, the one who's gone to America, because she was the one- who was the one who was doing the Nick thing if you like, was saying to me when Tom and I were going through our- well Tom was sleeping with Kirstin and . . . I was still trying to pull myself together, she was saying to me, "You're flogging a dead horse . . . you've just got to accept that he doesn't want to go on with this relationship . . . ", so she was being that sort of person to me at a time when I didn't want to hear it [. . .] and I suppose I didn't like that cos it wasn't- wasn't- wasn't what I wanted to hear'. It's clear that Gemma's behaviour at this time did not endear her to Helen, because what she needed was support, not challenge. Other, more empathetic friends were the ones whose help Helen appreciated at that time in her life.

The evidence of this chapter is that Nick's view of the nature of women's friendships as mutually supportive is accurate. But the implication that there is something superficial or even saccharine about such friendships is certainly not supported by the data (either the interview data or the conversational data). In particular, the stress women place on 'being myself' demonstrates our desire for relationships which involve the whole person. 'Your real friends you can- you're gonna be more honest with' (Miranda). Exposing and challenging do have a place in women's relationships with each other, as Liz's answer to the question 'What do you talk about?' illustrates: 'I think if we were a little bit worried about something, well, which way to go or whatever, we'd talk about it, because you'd be confident that you'd be told if you were going to make an idiot of yourself'. However, women see acceptance of others, warts and all, as central to what being a friend means.

Sticky moments in women's friendships

The accusation of 'sympathetic circularity' was one I was sensitive to before I carried out the interviews, so I deliberately included a question on conflict and on how conflict was dealt with. This question triggered some very moving accounts of difficult moments in women's relationships with each other. This is a notoriously difficult area of women's friendships. When Margaret Atwood's novel *Cat's Eye* was published, exposing what could be called the 'dark side' of women's friendships, in particular the emotional cruelty involved in girls' subculture, many feminists were horrified at what they saw as a betrayal of women, in that it seemed dangerous to expose our 'nasty' side to the gaze of patriarchy. But like any intimate relationship, friendship between women has its sticky moments, which may or may not be successfully resolved. And we shouldn't feel that we have to conceal these aspects of our lives: this is another consequence of the pressure to be 'nice'.

Women find conflict scary, however, and my question, 'Can you give me an example of when you didn't get on [with your friend]'?, provoked denial in some women, while others became momentarily speechless, and had to have time to think. In the event, this question produced a rich fund of anecdotes. Conflict, or 'not getting on', was certainly seen as problematic. Several women gave me examples of conflict which had led to the end of a friendship. But there were many other stories about conflict which showed that women can work through disagreement and feel a sense of pride in being able to do so.

The issues which provoke conflict are very revealing of what is valued in women's friendships. For example, since women friends enjoy doing things together, disagreement about what to do can be problematic. Mary describes an episode in her friendship with Gianna when they'd decided to go to see a film. The problem was that 'I wanted to go and see *The Quince Tree Sun* and Gianna wanted to go and see *Un Coeur en Hiver* which I'd seen'. They ended up seeing *The Quince Tree Sun*. I asked Mary how they'd negotiated that decision. This was her account:

Mary's story[13]

Well basically because I- I'd already seen it. <LAUGHS>
I said, 'Well, I'm not going'.
I said, 'Oh well look, we can both go and you can go and sit in um- in one cinema and I'll go and sit in another',
cos I said, 'I don't want to see it again so soon'.
But she said, 'No, no, that's silly'.
[. . .]
Gianna said afterwards she couldn't get out of her seat,
and she said thank you very much for taking her to see it
because it was such a wonderful film.

In this brief anecdote, Mary makes the point that where good friends work through conflict successfully, there can be unexpected rewards. In this case, Mary was obviously pleased by the way Gianna responded to the film. This story reveals two friends negotiating a decision and then being happy with the way that decision works out.

The following story describes an incident which will be familiar to most women. Bea and Meg had a shared fiftieth birthday party and agreed to clean up the day after the party, but turned out to have very different views of what time the next morning this meant. (When Bea says 'we' in this story she is referring to herself and her husband, Geoffrey, except in the opening phrase, 'our great party', where 'our' refers to her and Meg.)

Bea and Meg's story

BEA: well there was our great party when we didn't turn up in the
MEG:

BEA: morning to- to clean up/ and again then
MEG: oh yeah/

BEA: you were angry and we- we made reparation by buying them
MEG: <LAUGH>

BEA: aromatherapy sessions <LAUGH>
MEG: [you certainly did/ it was lovely/
JEN: [< LAUGH--------->

BEA: <LAUGH>
MEG: . it was- it was a mi- that was a sort of misunderstanding

---

BEA: mhm/
MEG: as well wasn't it/ because you had different cleaning up party

---

BEA: yeah/ we cleaned up later in the day/ they got up at
MEG: habits/

BEA: eight to clean up and we were still sound asleep till ten/
JEN: right/

BEA: so it wasn't surprising that we weren't down there cleaning up/

BEA:
MEG: I I I mean that's one of the things about Bea/ I always
JEN: mhm

MEG: feel that if- that if I upset her/ or say something out of

---

MEG: turn/ she will TELL me/ if not then at some other point/ she'll

---

MEG: say slightly glassily and slightly . worrying/ you know
JEN: <LAUGHS>

MEG: anxiety-provoking/ she'll say- she'll say something like um .

MEG: 'I just thought that was rather a . si- silly thing to SAY or

---

MEG: .hh quite HURTful'/ um I I should feel- I feel quite

MEG: reprimanded about it/ but .hh the- the flip side is that .

MEG: you're- she's not HARbouring- I mean I- lot- lots of people
JEN: no/

MEG: that I know seem to harbour .hh TERRible things that I've said

---

MEG: and done over the years/
JEN: and yes- and then you can't move on can

MEG: no/ and it gives you a terrible bad feeling about
JEN: you?

MEG: yourself/ you think GOD these people fucking hate me/

Meg's comments here are very revealing: although not relishing conflict, she stresses that it is part of being a good friend that resentment or disagreement is dealt with, not suppressed. She experiences very unpleasant feelings where disagreement is not dealt with – 'it gives you a terrible bad feeling about yourself' – and she makes quite clear in this account that she values Bea's capacity to be honest with her when she is hurt or upset by something Meg has done. This extract is a strong refutation of the idea of 'sympathetic circularity': it demonstrates that when it comes to the crunch women friends do confront each other (however painful they find it).

Helen tells a story which also rests on the assumption of shared rights and responsibilities in friendship. At one time in her life she rented an allotment, which she agreed to share with her friend Judy.

Helen's story

oh we did have a huge row,
we did have a row, right. <LAUGHS>

We shared an allotment.
I got an allotment when I moved to my house in York.
5 After Tom and I split up I bought this little house
and I bought- I got an allotment
cos I realized I was entitled to an allotment.
Judy was very keen on this allotment
and I said, 'Well that's really a good idea',
10 cos it's really incredibly hard work,
and she was keen to grow vegetables cos they were vegetarians,
so we shared it.
And I went up there one Saturday a- a- about a year in,
and found all these strange plants on the allotment with little plastic bags over them and plastic tomatoes.
15 [. . .]
so I- I saw Steve at the school playground (that was it),
and I- I really went for him,
cos it was just- this is the Steve character and I'd never liked him.
He was a bit on the scene,
20 and I really went for him,
and he admitted he'd been growing cannabis on my allotment.
But he was so laid back and so phlegmatic.
That's all he did.
He just said 'yeah'.
25 That's all I got out of him was 'yes'.
So the next thing was that Judy came round,
she actually came round to see me,
and I was very very angry.
[. . .]
30 I mean to me that was a betrayal of friendship.

The seriousness of this conflict is brought out by Helen's use of the phrase *betrayal of friendship*. Where friends betray the ideal of friendship like this – by failing to respect what 'sharing' means, and by revealing a different world view – then they jeopardize the friendship. In this story, like many of the others telling of conflict, a male character is significant in disrupting women's friendship. Judy, in Helen's story, is described as torn between her loyalty to Helen and her absorption in her bloke, but ultimately, as the cannabis-growing incident revealed, the man's interests came first. Helen comments: 'I mean she was terribly sorry but she just hadn't seen- I mean she was just absorbed by that bloke in that culture'. The result was that Helen and Judy stopped being friends for many years (but have now renewed the friendship).

Men as sources of conflict

Some of the younger participants tell stories where a male is the actual focus of conflict. Becky described an incident which took place when she and Hannah were on holiday together.

Becky's story

Do you remember that French holiday?
And it was- I think that really good-looking boy fancied you,
and I think I was really really jealous,
and . . . we went to that really rubbish (well I remember it as being rubbish) dance.
[. . .]
We had a little shouting thing.
[. . .]
I remember you sort of stormed off,
or not stormed off but you went off,
because I was sitting there . . . feeling really grumpy,
and you said, 'Well why don't you come and dance and enjoy yourself?'.

While Hannah and Becky had dealt successsfully with this crisis, Becky found this incident very upsetting and says that she tries to avoid arguing with Hannah.

A man is also the focal point of difficulties in the relationship between Jo and Miranda which were going on at the time I interviewed them. Jo had recently started a serious relationship with a new man, a man who Miranda had trouble relating to. This was not intrinsically to do with the new man, Daniel, but with the fact that he is a social worker: 'part of it is that I work for Social Services and I really dislike most of the people I work with, which is social workers, and Daniel is a social worker'. Miranda struggles to make her position clear: 'cos I do hate Social Services, but I don't dislike Daniel <LAUGHING> cos I don't- you know, he's allowed to be a social worker and I have got good social worker friends, but they do get to me'. These two friends talked about how they'd been dealing with this crisis. It emerged that Jo had raised the subject with Miranda after becoming aware that something was wrong. This is how Jo described it (Miranda's contributions are in italics).

> I mean I'm very scared about doing that kind of thing and it's quite new to me you know. It's only because I've been reading all these

> books about that's what you do in relationships. <LAUGHS> So I thought, 'Well, friendships are relationships so I'm going to have a go (*yeah*) and see how it works'. (*yeah*) And it didn't work quite cos Miranda didn't answer like they're meant to. I still felt glad I'd raised it. I felt it was alright. (*yeah, yeah*) I hoped it had shifted something even if it didn't . . . resolve it entirely . . . cos I just think I felt easier after that. I hope you did. (*yes, I did.*)

Jo's opening comment, 'I'm very scared about doing that kind of thing', where 'that kind of thing' means talking about problems, reveals how difficult the negotiation of tension or disagreement can be for many women. She is very honest about the anxiety she felt about talking to Miranda, but feels the effort has been worthwhile even though 'Miranda didn't answer like they're meant to'. Jo uses humour skilfully here to deal with an area that is still very fraught for the two of them: when she says *Miranda didn't answer like they're meant to,* she speaks in a self-mocking voice that underlines the folly of trusting what is written in books and which acknowledges the unpredictability of real life. But Miranda is still sensitive to the fact that, even though the issue is now out in the open, she still has to work on her own prejudices. She is very aware of what she stands to lose if she doesn't do this:

> I mean the worrying bit is that you don't want to go and then have a whole area of somebody's life- I mean you don't want to resolve in a way that you can't share a large chunk of your life . . . I would really want to work out the kind of Daniel thing just because if he's going to be a kind of major part of Jo's life, as seems likely, then I really want to get that sorted out.

All three of the examples quoted above revolve around tension between women's relationships with other women and their relationships with men. Women friends have high expectations of each other, but they often have to accept second place in each other's affections, with first place belonging to a male sexual partner. Significantly, when asked about the term *best friend,* many women said it was a childish phrase which they associated with childhood, not with adult life, and two of the (married) women named their husband as their best friend.

Serious conflict

While some of these examples deal with relatively trivial issues, such as which film to go and see, or who's clearing up after a party, others, like Helen's story of the cannabis plants, become major tests of loyalty. Val's story, which I give in full below, is a good example of a more serious breakdown of friendship, arising from Val's failure to go to her friend Cathy at a time when Cathy needed her. Underpinning this story is an acknowledgement that women play a very significant part in each other's lives, and that failure to recognize this is potentially fatal to the friendship. Val, who lives in Liverpool, tells this story about her friend Cathy, who lives twenty miles away from her, in Southport. (It's not possible in the transcriptions to give any indication of the quality of the different women's voices. But in the case of Val, it's important to note that she has quite a strong Northern accent, so the humour in line 24 arises from the contrast between her everyday voice and the 'posh' one she puts on for the police officer.)

Val's story

This is difficult.
After she'd had another two children
[. . .]
and in between before she had Jack who's now five
she got pregnant
5 was thrilled.
They'd obviously been trying to have another child.
And this was before she had Jack.
When she had a miscarriage
at about three months.
10 And her father had died five months or so before
so it was a double double blow for her.
and returning from her house in Southport
I the previous week to her having the miscarriage
had been pulled by a traffic cop.
15 I was parked on a . a worn-out zig-zag line on the Dock Road.
I had the kids in the back, two of them
and I didn't have a licence.
I'd been driving for twenty years
I didn't have a bloody licence.
20 I didn't have insurance
I didn't have L-plates
and I was absolutely terrified out of my wits.
The kids were sobbing.
So I put on my best Oxford accent <MOCK POSH VOICE>
25 said, 'hush kids, don't say a word',
got myself out of it
but knew that I was gonna be severely penalized

if not removed from the road for life.
The only way I could get to Cathy was to drive along that same stretch of road
30 and I just couldn't force myself into doing it.
So I couldn't get to her when she had the miscarriage and she was so devastated.
Paul was away
and I just didn't dare go out again with no licence and no insurance.
And so I didn't go.
35 Oh Jen well that nearly ended the relationship at a stroke it was so awful.
[. . .]
but only last summer
six years later
when we had been at camp together for about five days
40 did I broach that subject
and say, 'I wanted to be there Cathy.
I just couldn't, I couldn't'.
'Oh', she said, 'that's water under the bridge now'.
She wouldn't even let me in to explain it as I've just done to you.
45 She just- but it was something that she'd taken in about me
that I c- I c- you know just that deeply upset me for a while.
But that didn't spoil our friendship,
we got back to being friends again
[. . .]
but it wasn't that deep trust friendship
50 I knew I'd really really hurt her.
and whe- it's still something when I remember it you know
I still wish to god I'd known how much she'd wanted me to- to BE there.
I didn't realize I was that important.
Something like I think- I mean if I'd known
55 if she'd been on the phone and said, 'You've got to come',
then I would have gone.
I'd have got a sodding taxi.
[. . .]
it was horrid
it WAS horrid
60 but she has forgiven me now
but she hasn't forgotten it.

Listening to this story was a powerful experience, and provoked me to tell a story of my own. What's interesting about the anecdote I tell is that I never reveal what the conflict was about, but focus instead on the way my friend and I have repaired the damage. My story was meant to comfort Val, to reassure her that even after severe conflict, close friendships can eventually be mended, and that this takes time. At the end of my story, Val comes in with another story which demonstrates what she had learnt from the first incident, and which underlines her commitment to this particular friendship. (Val's words are printed in italics.)

Jen's story

with my absolute absolute best friend
I had a thing like that which was terrifyingly scarily you know bad
and it took ages to recover the trust
but we have.
5 *by talking about it?*
and it's only recently, it's only last year that I brought it up
and we did manage, we did manage to talk about it.
I got a bit more insight into what it was like from HER position
which I hadn't appreciated
10 and I was really grateful to have her listening.
And then later on that same day she was talking a bit about her fears of being a lesbian
and I didn't realize what I was doing
but I laughed it off or changed the conversation
and she said, 'Listen to me! Listen to me!
15 You're not listening to me!'.
And she said, 'Think back – you said I wasn't listening when you tried to say about how painful it was for you'
and I- I- and she said 'And YOU'RE not listening now'.
and it was such – god, that was painful too.
But I was so proud of us
20 cos we struggled through this really difficult stuff
and I know we couldn't have done that years ago.
So although it was- it wasn't- I didn't enjoy it terribly
I knew it was real and good and we were not just hiding things (*yeah*)
putting them away.
25 *strengthening things really*
yes and it HAS, it did.
I mean subsequently (*yeah*) that bore fruit
but the- the actual moment it was very hard.
Because well having to see how I didn't listen to HER (*yeah*)
30 the c- and I thought, 'Why? What am I scared of'? (*yeah*)
and I said, 'But you said you LIKED it when we were young and I used to just laugh', (*yeah*)
and she said, 'Because it worked then.
That's what I needed then,
but I don't need it now.
35 I want you to listen.'
<u>Oh HELP!</u> <HIGH PITCH, LAUGHS>

Cos it is that thing about realizing how important you are to the other person, which is a bit scary,
but also then realizing you've got the capacity to let them down,
40 which is-
yeah, yeah, and how come –
what shocked ME about that was that I didn't read it right,
so I just didn't read it right,
I suppose I was [*obsessed with my* [*own little anxieties*
[yeah [your own, yes
45 *about producing documents.*
'Have you got your licence'? <IMITATING POLICE OFFICER>
'Not exactly, no'. (god)
but anyway no, it got resolved,
and in fact after Jack was born
[...]
50 *she then had another miscarriage, poor Cath,*
and this one was even more devastating,
because I think she thought she'd never be able to have a baby now.
And Pete came to tell us,
and we just got in the car and went,
55 *and she was so pleased to see us.*

All these stories of conflict illustrate in their various ways how strong the feelings associated with friendship are. They also illustrate the various strategies that women use to deal with conflict, ranging from negotiation through talk, compromise, change in attitudes, to outright anger and hostility. In the stories these women tell, only conflict which leads to anger and hostility results in the end of friendship; the other strategies all contribute to the successful resolution of conflict, and thus allow the relationship to continue and, in many cases, to grow. This is not to deny the painfulness of conflict: as these women's accounts show, working through problems is something many women find quite difficult. But when we have to do it, we are prepared to, for the sake of the friendship.

Men as friends

While all the women I interviewed talked at length about what friendship meant to them, it was when I asked them if they had male as well as female friends that the significance of female friendship in their lives really came into focus. To begin with, few of the women had any friends who were male (with the exception of male partners):

- 'Certainly for me, I don't have any relationships with any men at the moment that are anything like as close or as sort of honest and intimate . . . as with women . . . I think that's always been true.' (Bea)
- 'I don't think I'm actually friends with a man at the moment as- on a very close basis at all.' (Mary)
- 'I mean I- I think I have rather bad relationships with men on the whole.' (Meg)

Those that did have a male friend emphasized how rare it was to find a man that you could be friends with (in women's sense of 'being friends'):

- 'there are certain men that you can be like that with [i.e. friendly] . . . and the majority unfortunately you can't.' (Liz)
- 'I have very few friendships with men, and those that I do I try as much as possible to make the quality like my friendships with women . . . but um . . . I find that less common from men and- and I think that's the reason I have fewer friends who are men.' (Jo)

Anna and Liz said that gay men were an exception to the general rule. Both had men friends who were gay, and they claimed that one advantage of these friends was that they could say things to you which other (women) friends might not. They simulated the following dialogue:

ANNA: 'Why do you let your husband talk to you like that?'
LIZ: yeah
ANNA: 'Why do you put up with it?'
LIZ: yeah exactly you know, 'Darling, you must DO something about it'. <CAMP VOICE> <LAUGHTER>

This extract suggests that women may tolerate being 'challenged' and 'exposed' by men who are gay, perhaps because what is said can be heard as nonserious and therefore unthreatening. One reason for feeling comfortable with gay men was that, 'Of course they're no threat, are they' (Liz). The sense of 'threat', the sense that, in their relations with men, women can never just be friends because of the imposition of heterosexual meaning on such friendships, was expressed by many women:

- 'I think there's always an undercurrent, a sort of awareness that this is a man rather than a woman.' (Jo)

- 'I must admit . . . I have a hard time having a proper friendship with a man that doesn't have any sexual element in it.' (Bea)
- 'you're always more self-conscious when you're friends with a man . . . cos you wonder is it- is it only ever going to be this kind of relationship, or are they in it for something else?' (Mary)

Val, the only woman in my sample who has always had close male friends, explicitly divided men into those she found sexually attractive and those she didn't: her male friends always came from the latter group. In other words, even though she does have friends who are men, she is in agreement with the other women in not being able to tolerate ambiguity in friendship. This sense of ambiguity in male–female relationships is clearly a product of the heterosocial world view which is dominant in our culture. (By 'heterosocial world view' I mean that ideology which builds, on top of heterosexual relationships, a social structure which assumes the primacy of male–female relationships above all others, so that women are seen as being 'for men', and male–female relations are invariably sexualized.)

Some women particularly prize their friendships with women because of what they experience as a lack of ambiguity in such (homosocial) relationships. Bea says: 'It sort of came into my mind then that . . . it's only got one use which is the friendship, whereas the friendship with a man could have another use, it could become something sexual, but with a woman there is just the sort of two human beings together'. Mary says that while she doesn't actively 'go out and seek men friends', having women friends is an essential part of her life. Helen, in her efforts to distinguish between friends who are women and friends who are men, expresses disappointment about her relationships with men, and argues that there is a qualitative difference between relationships with women and those with men. This was quite a long stretch of talk: I've edited out repetitions and false starts to allow the key points Helen makes to stand out more clearly.

> In many ways I feel that I've much more in common with women than men . . . but at the heart of it it must be that relationships with women seem to be about growth. I mean they may not in themselves promote the growth, though I think that happens as well, but they mark it and it's that thing about mirror [i.e. women mirror each other], it's about role models, and it's about the sharing of experience in a common structure . . . And that's probably cos most of my friends have had similar

> experiences to me – that is, they've married, they've had children, they've had jobs, they've lost partners, they've had other partners, their children have had vicissitudes, and those are all markers in themselves. I mean, we've all kind of worked through those things, and come out of them. I mean, the people who we want to stay friends with have done that . . . [With men] what seems to happen is that it doesn't develop . . . you know you can bring up children with somebody that you are friends with or are married to, or whatever, you can do those things, but what you feel about it may not be the same thing, it may not in itself add to this growth or this confidence or this self-actualization. The point is . . . we don't have men- I don't think I have male friends in the sense that I have female friends.

What Helen seems to be saying is that women who are friends have gone through similar experiences, and have grown as people as a result of these experiences, and that this sense of shared experience and shared development is absent from even the most intimate relationships with men. This is a strong claim, and if it has any truth it begs the question: why do women continue to relegate friendships with women to being 'a backdrop to the real business of life', as Drusilla Modjeska puts it? The evidence of these interviews is that all the women except those who identify themselves as lesbian put a (sexual) relationship with a man at the centre of their lives. This is understandable in the case of those women who feel that they have established a good relationship with a man (to the extent that they would call their partner their best friend), but many women say things about the quality of their relationships with men which suggest that female friendship has as much – or more – to offer as a fulfilling human relationship. The key word to understanding this contradiction is probably 'sexual': given our heterosexual conditioning, most women split their intimate life in two, having an intimate sexual relationship with one man, while having an intimate emotional relationship with one or more women. It is arguably the case that, for women who call themselves 'heterosexual', female friendship provides a safe space, an oasis, away from the constraints of the heterosocial order. Current theorizing of heterosexuality has made far clearer the ways in which 'the gender scripts found in heterosexuality prescribe male dominance and female subordination'.[14] While this is speculation, one fact that emerges unambiguously from the interviews (and from others' research on female friendship)[15] is that friendships with women are a constant in women's lives. Sexual partners, whether heterosexual or lesbian, may come and go, but our friendships with women endure.

Female friendship: a homo-erotic subtext?

Maybe we need to look more closely at women's claim that their friendships with women are unambiguous; '[female] friendship exists for itself', as Mary puts it. It is clearly important to (most) women's construction of themselves as heterosexual that they assert this, though Bea does say, laughing, 'When I have friendships with women, it doesn't have a sexual element, or at least if it is, it's so unconscious that I'm not really aware of it'. When I listened to the interview tapes I was intrigued by the way words and phrases normally associated with the discourse of Romantic Love (and therefore with heterosexual relationships) appeared in women's descriptions of their friends. Women had a very strong sense that some of their female friendships were very special: 'to me that was SUCH a special friendship, and I don't- I don't think many people experience that' (Jill). When asked what they would do if their current women friends moved away, they say things like, 'I'd probably start thinking of people I knew, and decide . . . to make a play for getting to know them better and see what happened' (Mary). The younger women, who had more recent memories of 'sleeping over', said that they talked best just before falling asleep: 'I actually find the best place to talk is- is um when- when you're in bed and the night- the lights are off and like- . . . it's really nice because you can just lie there and we just- just chat away, and you don't really think about it' (Becky).

When they describe meeting a woman who has subsequently become a friends, they use phrases like 'I think we were attracted to each other . . . I think instinctively . . . we're attracted to each other' or, more explicitly, 'You know, it was almost like falling in love'. These utterances are even more powerful when read in context; for example, the second example here is embedded in this bit of story about a male friend, Pete, bringing his new girlfriend round to meet Val:

he brought her round to my house
[. . .]
and Pete said, 'You're putting weight on, Val Baker',
which was, well, how he'd known me,
and I said, 'It's because I'm having a baby, Pete',
and her face just lit up,
and she was just so w- warm,
and I saw her beauty was absolutely radiant.
She was so excited by this virtual stranger being pregnant

and I- you know, it was almost like falling in love.
She was just my very good friend from that instant.

Helen explicitly compared friendship with the early stages of a sexual or erotic relationship: 'it [female friendship] certainly feels like those relationships feel when you're first getting to know somebody – it's very exciting'.

So would it be reasonable to describe this aspect of the interview data as a 'homo-erotic subtext'? I don't want to insist on an erotic element in all friendships between women. But it would be equally wrong to deny any erotic element in close relationships between women friends. There is certainly evidence from other cultures and other times that the line between female friendship and lesbianism is a very fine one.[16] Adrienne Rich has redefined the concept of lesbianism to incorporate this fact. She writes: 'it is the lesbian in every woman who is compelled by female energy, who gravitates toward strong women, who seeks a literature that will express that energy and strength. It is the lesbian in us who drives us to feel imaginatively, render in language, grasp, the full connection between woman and woman'.[17] Janice Raymond has coined the word *gyn/affection* to refer to close female friendship. She defines it as follows: 'female friendship . . . a loving relationship between two or more women . . . a freely-chosen bond which, when chosen, involves certain reciprocal assurances based on honor, loyalty and affection'.[18] The word *gyn/affection* comes closest to expressing what is unique about the homosocial relationships between women normally called friendship.

Women's friendships: conservative or liberating?

In the final section of this chapter, I want to debate the issue of whether women's friendships are a conservative or a liberating force. Those that argue that female friendship is a conservative force acknowledge the strengths of women's friendships but claim that these friendships serve as an emotional outlet for women who are frustrated in their marriages or partnerships with men, and that they therefore help to support heteropatriarchy.[19] In other words, by taking up the slack in male–female relationships, female friendship helps to prop up the institution of marriage, and thus helps to perpetuate male domination of women.

But some argue that, far from being a relationship that perpetuates the status quo, friendships between women are potentially liberating, and many twentieth-century women writers argue that female friendship can be a form of resistance.[20] Certainly women's friendships continue to flourish and are at last being overtly recognized as a key relationship in women's lives. The evidence of the *The Hite Report*[21] is that 87 per cent of married women and 95 per cent of single women reported that they had their deepest emotional relationship with another woman. Current statistics on marital breakdown throughout the Western world suggest that traditional structures of marriage and the nuclear family are in trouble.

Some commentators see friendship as the relationship of the future: 'Friendship may be making a bid for first place or rivalling first place as a provider of the intimacy and support needed by every woman at some period of her life'.[22] Friendship is unlike other close relationships we have in our lives: there are no formal contracts, no socially accepted rituals, no rites of passage associated with friendship. It is also unusual in that the relationship is based on equality. Even when there are differences of age or social class or ethnic background, friendship can only be sustained – will only deserve the name – if participants treat each other as equals, and adhere to an ethic of reciprocity.[23] In other words, friendship is a symmetrical relationship. Most of our kinship relations are asymmetrical (parent–child, aunt–niece, even sister–sister, since one is older and therefore has different status in the family). And it can be argued that, as long as societies construct women and men as unequal, then marriage is also an asymmetrical relationship.

Both these aspects of friendship – its fluidity as a cultural form, and the fact that it is a relationship of equals – make it a significant model for relationships in the twenty-first century: 'Friendship arguably represents the relational genre of the future'.[24] Helen and I got into a long discussion, near the end of my interview with her, where we grapple with these issues, and Helen struggled to express what it is in female friendship that makes it unique as a form of human relationship. (Key points are printed in bold, to make them stand out. I have omitted minor contributions from me.)

> I think the difference is that you choo- you choose female friends and you choose to keep it going, cos we said before, you can choose NOT to. You don't- you don't choose family [. . .] and in a sense you don't choose partners. Look at what we said before – you choose them on one level, but there's another level at which you don't choose them <LAUGHTER> [. . .] What I've just thought is that I think it's like this – I think the closeness [of women's friendships] is the closeness that you get when you enter a relationship with a man, when you- at the beginning of that relationship, you know, when all that sort of self-disclosure

> happens and it suddenly feels- this- this wonderful promise of, you know, two people drawn together because they have all these hidden depths which will somehow be- What- What will it be? What does it promise? It promises all sort of things, but what it- **what friendship has is all that without any responsibility for it.** Oh, you have responsibility to the person, cos obviously that's part of the friendship, but **you don't have responsibility to- to commit yourself to it forever and ever and ever in any other way than the way you both choose so it's- it's defined by both- both parties on fairly equal terms, and there aren't any rules for it either**, whereas there are rules for partners. [. . .] **The rules of friendships are very- very much looser** than that – you can do anything you like, it doesn't matter, and therefore there's much less tension about it. I mean I think it's to do with- it's somewhere- somewhere around all that – it promises something, yes [. . .] It certainly feels like those relationships feel when you're first getting to know somebody – it's very exciting, but I think **women can sustain that level of closeness through friendship ((without the hassle))** <LAUGHS>

In this discussion, Helen picks out the following aspects of women's friendship as making it unique: it is freely chosen, there are no rigid rules constraining what form the relationship can take, both parties contribute equally to defining it, and the closeness of a good intimate relationship is sustained without 'the hassle' of other intimate relationships. Moreover, Helen asserts that female friendship is unique in offering us an experience of a relationship of equals: 'it's the only one [i.e. relationship] where you're not playing out parent-and-child'. According to Drusilla Modjeska, who I quoted at the beginning of this chapter, 'Equality, acceptance and free play are required for friendship to flourish'. In the case of the women I interviewed, equality, acceptance and free play were all in evidence. Friendships like these provide us with an arena where 'we best learn to be ourselves'.[25]

3

'We never stop talking': Talk and women's friendships

If friendship provides the arena in which we 'learn to be ourselves', then talk is the means by which this learning takes place. The centrality of talk in women's friendships has been widely documented by researchers, but I was still taken aback by the response I got to my question: 'What do you do with your women friends'? Jo said, simply, 'Talk'; Bea said, 'We talk'; and Val said, more emphatically, 'We talk, primarily we talk, we never stop'. Hannah thought for a while, and eventually said: 'For me just what I remember about the relationship is . . . just you know the amount of time we just spent sitting around and talking'.[1] What surprised me was the completely unequivocal way in which women acknowledged the primacy of talk in their relationships with their women friends. Even when women mentioned other activities, they were clear that talk was the main thing they did once they were asked to rank their activities (I asked them to do this in terms of a pie chart, where different activities are represented as larger or smaller slices of a pie). Liz and Sue's response is given below:

JEN: what would be the fattest slice of the pie?

LIZ: the fattest bit would be- would be talking=

SUE: =yeah meeting [and talking
LIZ: [meeting and talking

This finding – that talk is central to these women's friendships – is strongly supported by other research on female friendship. The following are six brief extracts from social scientific research in this area, all published in the last fifteen years.

- 'the people I call my real friends are the ones I can talk to'[2]
- 'the principal activity of friendship was talking'[3]
- 'talk is the main leisure pursuit of adolescent female friends'[4]
- 'they [adolescent girls] *did* their friendship through the practices of day to day talk'[5]
- 'talk is central to female friendship'[6]
- 'our research demonstrates that talk is the substance of women's friendship'[7]

The unanimity of these findings is striking. But how much do we know about the talk of women friends? What do women talk about? *Where* do women talk with their friends? What is women's friendly talk like? Does it differ from other kinds of talk? If talk is central to female friendship, what are its functions? Although researchers have pinpointed the significance of talk for women friends, no one, as far as I know, has carried out linguistic analysis of such talk, though some linguistic research has been done on the language of girls with their friends.[8] In this chapter I'll summarize what women told me about their talk with their friends and will refer briefly to the conversational data to demonstrate the accuracy (or inaccuracy) of their claims. It's not necessarily the case that our accounts of what we do are consistent with what we actually do (particularly since, as I've argued, our accounts are inevitably affected by the discourses available to us). However, in the case of women friends, our descriptions of how we talk and what we talk about accord very well with the empirical evidence. (A fuller account of selected features of the talk of women friends will be the subject of the next six chapters.)

Other shared activities

Of course, we do other things with our friends besides talk. The women I interviewed mentioned walking, going out for coffee or for a meal, going to the theatre or cinema or to an exhibition together. But often these activities are an excuse for talk, or can stimulate further talk. Mary said that she and Gianna would sometimes go to the Tate Gallery on Merseyside to see an exhibition, and would then sit and have a coffee, looking out over the Albert Docks, with the implication that this aspect of the outing – sitting and talking over a coffee – was a core component. In Miranda's view, 'It's particularly nice to have a sort of shared experience . . . to have gone to a play or to a poetry reading or a- you know or a film . . . so that you've got . . .

mutual themes to sort of talk about'. In contrast with this, Helen told a rueful story to illustrate how talk can sometimes make you oblivious to what you're doing or where you are, so that far from another activity promoting talk, talk can, as it were, drown out the other activity.

Helen's story

I mean in fact the worst walk I ever had in my life is I took- <LAUGHING>
Annabel and I met in Brecon
cos we- I- cos we were going to go to Cwm Bach [an old farmhouse] for the weekend.
[...]
And so we met
and then we took- we drove up to the house.
You haven't been there either but it's- it has this absolutely stunning view.
But we talked non-stop from the time we met in the cafe in town to the time we got to the house,
and it was a beautiful day. <J LAUGHS>
I said, 'Let's go for a walk'
and there's this classic walk we always do when we arrive at the house
which is through- down to the orchard, over the woods, down over the river and up over the- over various sort of fields
and you come then to the foot of Mynydd Llangattock
and you go round
and it's an amazing walk.
It's the first time she would have done it.
We talked absolutely solidly from the moment we got out of the car to . . . until we got back to the house
which is an hour and three quarters later
and she hadn't at one point said, 'God this- this is amazing, this is amazing' <J LAUGHS>
which- that- it was SO inTENSE.

We could infer from these three examples – Mary's, Miranda's and Helen's – that context is, in some sense, irrelevant: when women friends are together, wherever we are and whatever we are doing, we will talk. Most of us have probably had the experience of going to stay with a close friend after a longish break, and following our friend around the house while she got on with mundane chores like putting the kettle on or preparing vegetables for a meal or hanging out clothes (which we joined in). But all of us have particular places where we prefer to talk. Jo and Miranda both said initially that they would talk 'anywhere', but later qualified this: 'you have to kind of be able to make a kind of oasis' (Miranda). The places women prefer to talk are places which satisfy our need for an intimate space away from noise and disturbance.

Places to talk

Most women I talked to interpreted my question 'Where do you talk'? to mean, 'Where are the best places to talk'? or 'Where do you like to talk'?; in other words, they took into consideration the need for 'an oasis'. A wide range of contexts was mentioned, both outside the home – in cafes or pubs, or while walking in the countryside – and inside the home – in the living room or the kitchen. There were occasional contradictions: Mary mentioned going to a pub with Gianna, but Bea said (of herself and Meg), 'We don't go out and meet in the pub'. And of these various contexts, some were definitely favoured. Outside the home, the only context repeatedly mentioned was while walking. This included urban walking – Becky and Hannah used to walk to school together in North London: 'we walked to and from school and it was an hour a day, like half an hour there, half an hour back, and THAT was a good time to talk' (Becky). Walking in the country was brought up by several women – Helen's story above is an illustration of this, and at the end of a story Miranda told about a walk she and Jo had done together on the Oxfordshire Way, Jo said, 'Well, that's my symbol of companionship, you know, walking and talking'.

But the home was definitely the favoured context, and was so taken for granted by many women as the place to talk with friends that they reacted with puzzlement to my question, repeating the question to check they'd heard correctly. (Meg even commented, slightly reprovingly, 'What a funny question, Jennifer!'.) Liz and Sue justified their preference for the home as follows:

- -

SUE: I mean in someone's house it's easier to talk than= =out
LIZ: =out=

- -

Within the home there are one or two favoured spots, notably the living room and the kitchen. Which is favoured will depend on a number of circumstances. Echoing Miranda's strictures about finding 'an oasis', Meg said, 'Well, you go where you're- you're relatively private, I think that's the key'. In Bea's view, the kitchen was favoured when we had small children, but is less significant as a place to talk now the children have grown up:

BEA: I think one of the reasons it used to be the kitchen was- didn't we

---

BEA: use to try and keep the children in the sitting room where the toys

---

BEA: were and then we would be . [away from them and hide in the kitchen=]
JEN: [we escaped!]

BEA: ((xx)) =yes where the kettle was=
JEN: <LAUGHS> =where the kettle was= =not to
MEG: =yeah exactly=

BEA: =yeah but now we've- we've recovered
JEN: mention the gin bottle= we've-

BEA: the sitting room=
JEN: =that's right/ it's our territory again=
MEG: =yes/

Val claimed that the reason she and Cathy like to talk in the kitchen is 'because the men don't come and follow us in there'. Both Bea and Val, in their accounts of where they like to talk, draw on a sense of the kitchen as a woman's space, a refuge both from children and from men. And while some women have 'reclaimed' the sitting room, many still favour the kitchen, particularly sitting 'at the kitchen table' or 'round the dinner table' or more generally 'round the table'. Sitting round a table, with a cup of tea or over a meal of some kind, was seen as a classic locus of good talk, and was explicitly contrasted with sitting round a table in a more public space such as a restaurant:

SUE: we have [gone out for a meal] but I don't know that it's the same=
ANNA: =no=

SUE: =I mean you can't shriek with laughter can you
LIZ: =no it isn't as relaxing=

SUE: when you're out= =you [have to be very controlled= =yeah you
LIZ: =no= [well you CAN/ =you CAN=

SUE: can but you get chucked out/
JEN: <LAUGHS>

This extract hints at other aspects of women's talk, and suggests that the kitchen is preferred not just because it's a refuge from other domestic demands, but also because it's a place where women feel uninhibited about expressing themselves. This claim is supported by the way women describe the quality of talk which takes place in the evening or late at night, a time when women feel free to express themselves. I've already quoted Becky's statement that bed is the best place to talk: 'I actually find the best place to talk is- is um when- when you're in bed and the night- the lights are off . . . but it's really nice because you can just lie there and we just- just chat away, and you don't really think about it'. Val also emphasizes the special quality of the night-time talks she and Cathy enjoy when they take their children camping: '[We like to talk when] the kids are drowsing off with their torches and their books, five little heads, five little torches . . . we zip them in and we sit in the outer area of the tent on the ground sheet, then we get up and stagger off for a pee and look at the stars, and we love that too, you know, we love that, we- we giggle like teenagers'.

The conversations I've recorded, or that women friends have recorded for me, all take place in the home, apart from one which was recorded by a group of teenage friends in a room at the local youth centre. In the home, the kitchen and living room predominate as the sites of talk. For younger participants, bedrooms are another site of talk, which is not surprising, since the only private space that a teenage girl can really call her own is her bedroom (that is, if she is lucky enough to have a bedroom to herself). It's also worth noting, given the frequency with which women mentioned food in conjunction with talk in the interviews, that many of the taped conversations are accompanied by noises of eating and drinking (making transcription a nightmare in places!).

Topics of conversation

The rest of the book will illustrate the range of topics talked about by women friends in spontaneous conversation. This seems very much in accord with what women say they talk about when questioned. Some women responded with a simple, summative type of answer:

- 'people mostly' (Jo)
- 'our experiences in our lives' (Hannah)
- 'everything and anything' (Val)

While Jo and Hannah narrow their answers down to what they see as the most common themes of their talk with their women friends, Val's answer challenges the notion that there is any set agenda. What she wants to emphasize is the possibility offered by friendship that you can say anything at all, even though what she says at other points in the interview makes it clear that people and personal experience are the chief topics of converation for her too.

Other women chose to answer in a more comprehensive way, giving me a list of topics which they implied were the most important ones. Here are three examples of these more comprehensive responses (the underlined portions mark where the speaker is laughing).

> We probably talk quite a bit about work . . . and we also talk about the children, we catch up on all the kids and what they're all doing, and . . . she [Annabel] will talk- talk to me about these- these- these adventures she's been having <LAUGHS> in attempting to lead this positive life, and I will bring her up to date in terms of where Nick and I are . . . those will be the themes. (Helen)

> We'll talk about our relationships with our children, our relationships with our partners, books, films, work, um how we feel, um repairs to the house <LAUGHS>, if you like future plans, where we'd like to be, what we'd like to do, . . . um talk about friends we know, friends we've got in common. (Mary)

> We talk about our current lives, and then we talk about our feelings about that, and we talk about our relationships with our partners and our relationships with our children, and we complain to each other. <LAUGHS> (Bea)

It's noticeable how closely these accounts match each other. Central to women's accounts of what they talk about are people (as Jo's terse answer above suggested) – partners, children, friends, and of course themselves and what's happening in their own lives. In Helen's words, 'they're pretty fundamental themes really, I mean they don't change much'.

Although only Helen (of these three women) actually uses the phrase 'catching up', this is clearly what a lot of the talk is about. A fuller version of Helen's answer begins: 'We probably talk quite a bit about work in a sense, because we've got some people in common anyway, so we do a bit of *catching up* . . . and we also talk about the children, we *catch up* on all the kids and what they're all doing' (italics added). As the last chapter revealed, keeping up with each other, keeping in touch with each other's lives, is a very important aspect of the work needed to keep a friendship going. So it is not surprising that we find this emerging as a significant topic of conversation. Miranda's answer to 'What do you talk about?' focused on this aspect of talk: 'I think that with a lot of women friends it's sort of catching up with each other you know, it's like kind of reporting back . . . your sort of habitual discourse with women friends is a sort of catching-up one, cos that's the nature of one's life, that you're sort of catching up with people'. Liz and Sue and Anna help each other to make the link between talk 'about ourselves' and 'catching up':

LIZ: we talk about ourselves
SUE: mhm
ANNA: and we catch up on what each other's been doing

While Sue and Liz's account implies that talking about ourselves and catching up can be done simultaneously, Helen argues that catching up has to come first, because in her view the 'habitual discourse of catching up' functions to check that the shared world, the shared values, are still in place. She says, 'It's very important that, isn't it, cos it's- I'm- I think we aways do that first before we get to ourselves, so it's like making sure everything is all right, everything is in place and then it's safe to- to assume it's OK'.

If we return to the three more comprehensive responses quoted earlier (on page 50), another aspect of these responses that is worth commenting on is that, in each one, part of what is said is marked off from the surrounding text by laughter. Helen's laughter about her friend's escapades (these adventures she's been having <LAUGHS>) reflects both amusement and also perhaps envy of a woman who is leading a more zany independent life. The laughter highlights the contrast between Annabel's 'adventures' and Helen's current life – 'where Nick and I are'. The laughter in Mary's and Bea's answers arises, I think, from their perception of me and my feminist position, and signals that they don't wish this part of their answer to be treated in the same way as the rest. Mary laughs as she says, 'repairs to the house', to tell me that she sees this as an incongruous member of her list of topics, a topic that is less typically woman-oriented. The laughter in Bea's answer functions to deal with a different kind of problem. 'We complain to each other' is probably one of the things we all do with friends. But Bea's laughter reveals an awareness that this is a fraught area: women's talk is often denigrated as 'bitching'; there is a negative stereotype of women that portrays us as indulging in character-assassination behind people's backs. Bea may also be sensitive to the fact that friends complaining to each other may not be viewed as 'politically correct'. Janice Raymond, for example, in her book on friendship, *A Passion for Friends*, is scathing about this aspect of friendship. She argues that good friendship between women cannot be based on what she calls 'victimism' – that is, relationships where women 'emphasize their heritage of shared pain'.[9] This is a highly controversial point of view: the evidence of both the ethnographic and the conversational material that I've collected is that women don't spend all their time complaining to each other or dwelling on painful experiences. Moreover, the mutual self-disclosure that is typical of women friends' talk allows us to talk about difficult subjects, to check our perceptions against those of our friends, and to seek support.

More 'feminine' topics

There was a great deal of laughter and irony and self-mockery around topics which were seen as incongruous with our identity as well-educated, white middle-class women who would describe ourselves as sympathetic to feminist ideals. These were topics belonging to that set of domestic or 'feminine' topics which we may not normally admit to talking about. These topics were mentioned in a kind of follow-up answer. Answers tended to come in two bursts: there would be an initial answer, then a secondary one where women would either qualify what they had just told me or would add something. For example, Mary added this to her initial response: 'I mean we might even talk about things like recipes and things like that'. The words *might* and *even* do the work of telling me that talking about recipes 'and things like that' is not a central part of her conversations with Gianna, but that she is mentioning such topics in the interest of completeness. Meg's reply (which she added to what Bea said above) was: 'We talk a bit about domesticky sort of things – recipes, um clothes, um things for the house you know like curtains and stuff', the underlined part said in a self-mocking voice inviting laughter. This 'domesticky' agenda is clearly highly charged, and some women explicitly deny discussing these topics:

LIZ: um don't talk about fashion much do we/ clothes/

ANNA: no actually we don't [we're not- we're not concerned with trivia like
LIZ: [or make up/ not GIRLY things/

ANNA: that, are we?
LIZ: no far too- [far too upmarket for that/
SUE: <LAUGHS> [no that's true/

Fashion and clothes and make-up, as topics of conversation for women, are dismissed here as being 'trivial' or 'girly things'. But there was again a humorous, self-mocking tone tone to this discussion, which means it shouldn't be taken at face value. I was aware that many women participating in these interviews struggled in their answers to tell me what seemed to them to be 'true', but at the same time were slightly uncomfortable about what this revealed and how this might expose them to censure. I have no intention of judging these women's responses as 'good' or 'bad', and I recognize and sympathize with the problems of self-presentation that interviews present to participants. All these extracts show us women struggling to give a thorough answer to my question and, at the same time, trying to deal with the contradictions they felt were exposed by their answers in terms of different – and conflicting – versions of femininity.

The discussion of ideas

Another set of topics which was mentioned was that focusing on the discussion of ideas. Although nobody raised this kind of 'serious' topic in their initial response to the question, several women added these more intellectual, less personal topics in their follow-up response. For example, Bea said, 'Sometimes we talk about more erudite things, though less often I would say', and Anna said, 'Sometimes we talk about sort of moral issues'. The inclusion of the word *sometimes* in both these responses indicates that these topics are not of central importance for these speakers. Val shows an awareness that the discussion of ideas is part of her talk with Cathy, but through making a joke about it: 'There's nothing we don't talk about, nothing. <PAUSE> I mean, I don't think we've ever discussed nuclear physics. <JOKEY>'. Rachel explicitly claimed to have moved away from 'trying to compete in a sort of intellectual interesting way', a way that her parents had encouraged through overtly discouraging talk that was not serious or intellectual: 'My mother would say "They [non-intellectual topics] are really not important"'. In her early 30s, away from her parents in America, Rachel discovered women's talk with a new set of friends, and is quite clear that she prefers this kind of talk to the more intellectual discussions valued by her family. By contrast, in an answer which suggests some ambivalence about the relative value of different topics, Jo wonders if women friends 'sell each other short' because of their concentration on personal topics. I will quote what she said in full, as I think she raises some interesting questions about the talk of women friends.

> I have a feeling sometimes of unsatisfactoriness, and I think, 'Why didn't I sort of not exactly set more of an agenda, but why didn't sort of you know some more productive sort of talk come out of that, cos you know we kind of need it and- and um it ought to be possible, and in some way the very easiness and the comfortableness of it and the sort of fact that you can- you know if you're feeling bad you CAN just be grotty and have a moan, and you don't need to sort of say anything very intelligent, because that's alright, it sort of becomes a- a habit, a kind of almost a laziness of mind, and I realize that when I'm talking to men friends I'm much more on my mettle to sort of think, you know, 'This has got to be an interesting conversation and I'm going to really sort of make some good input here and get some back', you know, and I'm not sure what that's about, I mean it sort of cuts both ways: it's nice to have the su- supportive feeling that you don't have to be on your mettle, but on the other hand you feel it's perhaps selling your women friends short if you don't- if you aren't giving of your- you know, your most exciting, the best and most interesting self.

This immediately raises the question of who gets to define what is our 'best and most interesting self', and who gets to define what constitutes 'an interesting conversation'? This sense of doubt about ourselves and our everyday practices is probably familiar to us all. And we certainly don't want to sell each other short, by restricting what we talk about unnecessarily. Bea's mocking reference to complaining to each other has already raised the question of the (un)desirability of nonstop mutual 'having a moan'. But it may be that Jo's sense of the 'unsatisfactoriness' of some talk with women friends arises from or reproduces scripts we have been given by a male-dominated society, in which masculine culture is valued over feminine culture, and where masculinity and rationality are closely linked.[10] Underpinning dominant notions of masculinity and femininity is the idea that the world of ideas is masculine while the world of feelings is feminine. There is also an equation made in what Jo says between what is good or 'productive' or 'exciting' and what is intelligent.

Talk with women friends is characterized as easy and comfortable, where 'you don't need to say anything very intelligent'. Saying something 'intelligent' seems to mean talking in a clever way to impress other participants in talk, a way that is explicitly contrasted with the 'comfortableness' of all-female talk. This fits what other women say about the difference between talk in mixed company and talk with women, though most women are adamant that they prefer all-female talk; I'll return to this point later in the chapter. But it is courageous of Jo to raise these questions, since complacency about what we do is as bad as self-denigration.

Jo and Miranda are the only two women I interviewed who feel any sense of dissatisfaction with the talk they do with women friends. (This does not mean they are untypical of women in general, but just that they were not typical of the women in my small sample.) The evidence from the ethnographic data, as the next two sections will demonstrate, is that some women felt very strongly that the kind of talk done with women friends was an ideal never fully realized in interaction with male friends. Moreover, the evidence from both the ethnographic and from the conversational data is that women friends do discuss serious issues. However, as the conversational data reveals, such talk nearly always makes links between the general and the personal, and very often discussion of serious issues, such as the origins of child abuse, or appropriate behaviour when a parent dies, or the role of obedience in marriage, will arise from the telling of a personal anecdote (see the extracts 'Child abuse', chapter 8, pages 198–9; 'Funerals', chapter 7, pages 169–70; 'Obedient husband', chapter 6, pages 147–51).

The patterns of women's talk

I asked the women I interviewed to describe the way they talked with their women friends, to try to characterize it. I thought this would prove a difficult question, but women seemed happy to reflect on their conversational practice, and to search for the best way to describe it. Maybe this was because this was the kind of question they expected me to ask, whereas when I asked them what seemed to me simple questions like where they liked to talk, they were taken aback. I find the responses to this part of the interview moving: these women seem to me to express themselves very eloquently on this subject, and many of them also communicate a strong sense of pride in what they regard as a very special form of talk. The accuracy of their accounts will be tested in subsequent chapters, when I analyse the conversational data. (Chapters 4 and 6 in particular will focus on the ways women's talk is structured.)

Rachel characterized women's talk in terms of 'warmth and nurturing and closeness'; Jo gave a list of adjectives: 'intimate, exploratory, provisional – I mean, open-ended'. These two responses hint at two sides of women's talk: its intimacy, the sense of connection between women that it engenders, and also its potential as a collaborative tool for exploring our world. Helen focused more closely on the shape of the talk: 'it's all done in a very kind of slightly chaotic way I suppose, I mean in that one- you know, it'll kind of flow in and out, there's no particular structure'. Helen sees this as a strength of women's talk: she says with evident approval 'it goes all over the place'. This perception of women's talk fits with Val's claim to talk about 'everything and anything'. Val elaborates on this as follows: 'we talk, we just swap everything, we jump from one topic to another, from the most serious- we cry a lot . . . then we laugh and blow our noses and move on or- or go back'.

Val's description makes explicit how 'everything and anything' covers a range of topics, serious and sad and funny. She also says that she and Cathy 'jump from one topic to another', which fits Helen's notion of women's talk going all over the place. But Val's use of the phrase *we swap everything* ties in with another set of descriptions. The answers of several women suggest that there is a certain pattern to our talk with our friends, associated with ideas of balance and of sharing. Here's Mary's answer to the question 'What's the talk you do with friends like'?:

> We probably laugh a lot and find things that are in common . . . so that you would- you would pick up on one thing and then the person reinforced that by saying well the same thing happened to them, or it happened in a different way, then you'd have a laugh because it's a shared thing.

She is saying that we establish common themes and take it in turns to tell stories arising from these themes, stories which complement each other or which are in contrast, but which result in a sense of shared understanding. Laughter (a very important component of women's talk, as the taped conversations testify) results from this sense of shared experience.

Mary's view is very closely shared by Meg and Bea, who describe the talk of women friends in the following way. (This extract comes from a very rich section of my interview with these two friends; it is edited here to allow the main ideas to stand out – in particular, I have cut out the frequent *mhms* which Meg and Bea use to support each other as they talk.) This extract begins after Meg has introduced the word *shape* to their description of friendly talk, when I ask them to clarify what they mean.

JEN: can we pin down this 'shape' at all?
BEA: sort of one person talking about themself or their idea or their feeling or whatever, and the other person listening to it and responding to IT but then maybe coming back with something of their own so that it isn't all one-sided although it COULD be if- if- if one or the other of us were say very very distressed about something then that person would probably get most of the time, it wouldn't be equal.
MEG: but if Bea's for instance to tell me about her- ((well but)) Bea told me this business about her Mum not wanting to travel east, right? now she would- she'd- she'd outline that and I'd listen and then I would want to tell Bea about the current problems I'm having with MY Mum [. . .] so you expect to be- to give, you expect sort of- it's a sort of sharing of the time [. . .] how I would look at the pattern would be: Bea would say something, I would listen, I would say something, this would go on for a bit, and then we would both- we'd draw some general conclusions from it and- and some sort of philosophical sort of- and it could be in the form of something profound or it could be just a joke like 'Oh God we'll be like that one day ourselves'.

In this passage, Bea first proposes a 'shape' for women's talk which consists of one person saying something about themself and then the other person responding with something from their own experience. Meg elaborates on this with an example of how they might exchange stories about their mothers. Both she and Bea assume that normally time will be shared equally between them, except when one of them is having a crisis, when the normal rules are suspended. Meg ends by restating the pattern Bea began with, only emphasizing the way the pattern can be repeated, and adding the detail that after a few cycles a concluding section is added, which may consist of them saying 'something profound' or which may be more of a joke. This latter option means that a series of turns on a particular theme will end in laughter, a pattern which matches Mary's account – 'then you'd have a laugh'.

If we use these two accounts (Mary's plus Meg and Bea's), we can represent the basic pattern of women friends' conversation as follows:

$$(X_1 + X_2 + X_3 \ldots X_n + C_X) + (Y_1 + Y_2 + Y_3 \ldots Y_n + C_Y) + (Z_1 + Z_2 \text{ etc.})$$

where X, Y, Z represent topics and themes which provide the basis for any number of turns, followed by C, which represents a concluding section which rounds off that particular topic or theme. Hannah gives an instance of this kind of talk when describing what she and Becky talk about: 'I remember saying the most STUpid thing once, I remember saying to her, "When I get into a bath I always get my knees wet last", and SHE said to me, "So do I" [. . .] it was so nice to know that someone else felt the same way as me <LAUGHING>'.

Here we have the basic 'shape': Hannah tells Becky something about herself, and Becky responds by mirroring this – that is, by saying she does the same thing. (Hannah's account gives us X_1 and X_2 but doesn't say if there was a C component.) This basic shape is also assumed by Jo, when raising the question of who you can talk to about your relationship with your partner: 'With women friends it's alright to talk about your relationship because . . . it can be actually helpful to share, you know, if they're prepared to also sort of say, "Yes I've kind of experienced that kind of thing, this is what I felt about it", you know, there's a sort of mutuality about that'. In this case, the *mutuality*, as Jo calls it, the possibility that sharing such experiences might improve understanding and therefore improve the quality of relationships, is what makes it 'alright' to talk about such relationships.

Val uses the image of ping-pong to describe this pattern when she talks about the shape of the talk she does with her friend Cathy. The notion of 'balance' is an integral part of this description. 'There seems to be more of a point in talking to her than lots of people. There's more of an interchange and a real balanced- kind of balanced game of ping-pong'. Rachel's description of talk and friendship draws on these same images of sharing and of balance, while introducing the notion of vulnerability: 'I think the friendships I've made have always- always been around you know sort of STRAIGHT talking, VULnerable talking, and it's exCHANGEd vulnerable talking. It's just like you can say whatever you think or whatever you feel, and you do to some extent expect it back, I mean, and it COMES back'.

This emphasis on the importance of being able to say anything at all links back to what women said about feeling safe with each other and being able to be themselves (see last chapter, page 0). Given the topics women choose to talk about – ourselves, other people, and our feelings about them – then *vulnerable* seems an important word to add to the description of women's talk. But what Rachel emphasizes is the symmetry in the talk: vulnerable talk is 'exchanged' – that is, it is not one-sided: you say whatever you think and feel and 'it comes back'. (In other words, for every X_1 there is an X_2.)

Similar or different?

Initial reactions to the question, 'Is the kind of talk you do with women friends different from the kind of talk you do with other people such as members of your family, your partner, women who are not close friends, etc?', ranged from the more thoughtful, such as 'I suppose it is' (Jo) or 'it doesn't seem to me to be a completely different type of talk' (Meg) to very clear direct responses such as 'definitely different' (Anna). Certainly, difference rather than similarity is what emerged as salient.

In terms of the family, the only categories of people who were described as similar in terms of talk were sisters and daughters. For example, Bea said to Meg, 'I think I talk with my sister and probably my daughter in a similar way to the way I talk with you', and Meg echoed this. Some people, on the other hand, expressed disappointment that sisters were *not* like friends, and Rachel said explicitly that she was deprived of 'female warm language' as a child because her father and brothers were so dominant, and because 'I haven't got a sister and I haven't got a mother who talks warm female language'. Jo and Helen both said they talked to daughters in a way that was comparable to talking to women friends, but Jo thought she could do that with her son, too. Meg insisted that the similarity between talk with daughters and talk with women friends needed to be qualified:

> But I think you get that [i.e. a style of talk typical of women friends] with, say, with your daughter although it would be for briefer periods of time, and other types of conversation would come in, like directives like, 'Isn't it time you washed your hair'? or something. <LAUGHS> You- you move into maternal mode so you- so you- the whole conversation wouldn't have the same shape, although the elements that we've described would be part of it.

Meg also said initially that she might occasionally talk in a similar way with the man she lives with, but she later contradicted this. Mary said explicitly that she talked with her (male) partner in the same way that she talked with close women friends, though she qualified this claim by saying that her talk with her partner involved a lot of routine talk about the organization of the house and children which was obviously not part of her talk with friends. Val also emphasized in her description of talk with her partner, 'We talk about practicalities'. Helen makes the more general claim that men don't enjoy the kind of talk she values, and that her partner, Nick, is a typical man in this respect:

> Let's take Nick as the example, and I think this is to do with maleness not just to do with Nick but . . . I think Nick doesn't enjoy talking in the way that I really like talking and so a lot of the- I can find myself talking in this house and there- and there's no response. It's not because

I'm particularly saying anything profound or- or anything, but it's because the process of sharing – sharing discussion or sharing- just sharing any kind of trigger is just enjoyable in itself.

Sharing is a key word here, and Helen implies that Nick does not enjoy this sharing type of talk (the type of talk that was described as typical of women friends in the last section). She also seems to be saying that it's not just *what* is talked about that matters, but *how* talk is done. This theme of sharing is one we'll return to.

Like Helen, the majority of the women who were interviewed singled out men as examples of people who you could *not* talk to in the same way as you talked to women friends. They complained that with other people, and in particular with men, talk did not 'come back' in the way we are used to in talk with women friends. Val described talk in her family, particularly with her brother, as follows: 'Val does HER thing, kerboom, Don does HIS thing, kerboom', and contrasts this with the interchange and balance of the talk she experiences with Cathy. At the heart of her complaint is the notion that what she says is not taken account of by the other speaker. This is an idea which is brought up by other women in the interviews. Maxine said, 'They just brush you off, they say, "Yeah, yeah that's what you said, but this is what *I* want to say"'. These two women imply that talk with men is structured (X + Y + Z) rather than ($X_1 + X_2 + X_3$); what women want is acknowledgement of their X_1 in what the next speaker says.

Sue, Liz and Anna were adamant that their talk would be profoundly altered if a man was present, even Sue's husband John, who they all like a lot. Liz said: 'If John was there, say, sitting at the table, it just wouldn't be the same'. Later, Sue contrasts the satisfied feeling she has after an evening of conversation with her women friends with the dissatisfied feeling she has after an evening in mixed company: 'At the end of the evening you feel, yes, dissatisfied. You can come home and you think- you think you didn't have a good talk, do you know what I mean? . . . you couldn't put your finger on it but you just- something was missing'.

Meg and Bea talked to me very openly and honestly about the difference between their talk with their partners and their talk with women friends such as each other. (This extract from their interview is again slightly edited.) This extract starts at the point where Meg is trying to explain how conversation with Mike (her partner) is different from conversation with Bea (significant words are given in italics):

MEG: it [talk with Mike] never kind of develops in the way that say it does wi- wi- with say Bea . . . and nevertheless we say the same sort of thing, the same type of way, but somehow it doesn't have- I don't know how you're gonna work this one out, Jennifer, cos I'm sure this is quite an important and subtle difference, but I wouldn't know how to describe it. Would you Bea?

BEA: No. I think I know what you mean that- it- that the men don't get into it to such an extent and carry it on. They kind of listen to what you have to say and sort of say, 'Yes that does sound bad' or something, and it doesn't go- it doesn't go much further . . .

MEG: Yeah. One of the differences is- is that they don't *mirror* it. I think that's really an important difference because I mean Mike will listen patiently and interestedly and concernedly to- to various things that I have to talk about, but he doesn't make those kind of- I mean like you and I have- I mean I- I'm- I'm always aware of the kind of *balanced* um- the *balance* that come into conversation between two women, between two friends,

BEA: mhm

MEG: and um you just don't get that in my experience with a man.

These two women provide here an example of what they are struggling to describe: they work together, rephrasing what each other says and adding new material to it, to arrive at an account that satisfies them both. The words *mirror* and *balance* are key terms here. While men may have the conversational skill to listen in a sensitive and concerned way, what they fail to do, according to this account, is to respond with parallel disclosure of their own. (I am interpreting mirror, balance, sharing, exchange and mutuality in the various accounts of women's talk that I've quoted as meaning, among other things, reciprocal self-disclosure. As we'll see in later chapters, reciprocal self-disclosure plays a key role in structuring the talk of women friends.) What the women I interviewed all seem to appreciate in their talk with friends is this mirroring exchange of personal experience.

Later on, Meg tries to pin down further the way men talk (italics added).

MEG: I always find that men will say, 'Oh it's different'. They're- they *look for the differences* between your experiences rather than the similarities. Like my brother, and he's in the army, and say if we're talking about interviewing, um I say, 'Well I had to interview all these people', and he'll say, 'Oh well we interview in the army', and I'll say, 'Well, isn't it amazing how so and so', and he'll say, something like, 'Oh well it's different', you know, 'We have a set interview room'- um but there ARE elements that are the same but he- he *always looks for the difference* and so does Mike.

JEN: and what do you feel like?

MEG: well it- it- it- it HAS that- you know you feel that you're different, that you're slightly inferior, that their- their method is better, although I suppose you could feel
MEG: [the other way around
BEA: [the other way- mhm
BEA: Yes, I'm trying to remember now sort of talking with Geoffrey. I'll- I'll tell him something, then he'll often come back with something of his own, but it's- it's not quite- it's not quite the same. It's more *separate* somehow.
MEG: mhm
BEA: I can't really describe what it is but the- the things don't sort of *blesh in together*, it's sort of one *separate* thing and another *separate* thing.
JEN: Did you say 'blesh'?
BEA: 'Blesh', yes, blend and mesh. <LAUGHTER>
MEG: Is that- is that like 'brunch'?
BEA: Yes, it's like 'brunch'
JEN: Well that's real- really interesting. And do you feel more or less satisfied with any of these shapes?
BEA: I think I prefer *the feminine shape* which- which IS more
MEG: mhm
BEA: *melding in together.*

Meg's sense that men 'look for the difference' rather than looking for what is similar underlies Maxine's claim that 'men quite often take up an opposing argument even if they don't believe it, just to- to have a debate, cos they like argument'. Notice how Meg's imaginary conversation with her brother demonstrates how, even when her brother has the possibility of adding I_2 to I_1 (a mirroring story about I, interviewing), he doesn't choose this option but instead 'looks for the difference'. This pattern is more (I + notI).[11] By contrast, Bea emphasizes the *separateness* of men's contributions to mixed talk – that is, she draws on the idea of men's talk following the (X + Y) pattern I described earlier as typical of male talk. She compares the 'separateness' of men's talk with what she calls 'bleshing in together' or 'melding in together' which goes on in the talk of women friends.

The idea that women's relationships are characterized by connection rather than separateness has been explored by the feminist theorist Nancy Chodorow, notably in her book *The Reproduction of Mothering*. Chodorow argues that gender identity is profoundly different for girls and boys, as a result of women's role as the primary caretaker of children in all known societies. Boys' development is marked by discontinuity, because they have to define themselves against the mother, as not feminine, while girls develop in connection with the mother. In Chodorow's words: 'the basic feminine sense of self is connected to the world, the basic masculine sense of self is separate'.[12]

It's important to note that, while they recognize a 'separate' style of talking as being more typical of men, and while they are unanimous in their sense of the pleasure they get from talk with women friends, some women may enjoy adopting a more separate discourse style from time to time. Meg said: 'You can have a kind of sparring chat [with a man], you know, a sort of match, and I find that quite fun, quite stimulating'. It is this kind of talk that Jo may be referring to when she says that with men she is 'on her mettle' in conversation.

What is special about talk with women friends?

Some of the women I interviewed were tired by the end of the interview, but others became eloquent at this point, as the connections between the things they had said began to impinge on them. Many tried to sum up why talk with women friends is so special, why it means so much to us. Sue, Liz and Anna, for example, summed up what they got out of talk with each other as follows:

ANNA: yeah/ and that's as/ Liz [said at the beginning/
SUE: satisfaction/ [a satisfied feeling/

ANNA: support=
LIZ: = support/ it's just the- it's just the feeling I think that

---

LIZ: it's ongoing/ but it is for me anyway/ that it's- it's something

---

ANNA: and light relief as well from-
LIZ: that's- never changes really/

ANNA: from whatever we've else we've been
LIZ: yes/

ANNA: [doing/ mhm/
LIZ: [doing/ yeah cos it's totally different/
SUE: and you can say all you

SUE: want to say/

This idea of being able to 'say all you want to say' gets expanded after Sue makes the comparison with having friends over for a meal, or going out for a meal:

SUE: sometimes you have a dinner party and there's four of you or

ANNA: [yes but it becomes chit-chat/
LIZ: =couples/ yeah/
SUE: whatever= and [it's pleasant and it's very nice/

ANNA: and you stick to safe sub[jects/
LIZ: [yes you stick to [safe subjects/
SUE: yeah ((xx)) [yeah I suppose so/

LIZ: whereas I don't think we have any ta[boo about what we talk about/
SUE: [no/

This idea of the potential for talking about anything at all is brought up as one of the strengths of women friends' talk in several interviews. While other groups of people are associated with particular rules of talk, women friends construe the talk they do as not being constricted by rules or taboos, but free to go anywhere. Their assertion that with other people 'you stick to safe subjects' implies that with women friends we are free to broach dangerous or unsafe subjects (which is why women's talk can be characterized as 'vulnerable'). I've already quoted Helen's comment 'it goes all over the place', and Val's claim that talk with her closest friend is about 'everything and anything'. Coming at this same point from a different angle, Liz says that what she values especially about talking with Anna and Sue is that 'there's no expectation at all of the evening'. This theme of 'no expectation' proves fruitful: the three friends start to identify what it is that they are doing when they meet:

LIZ: I know that these two don't expect anything from me/ same as I don't

ANNA: [yeah/ [we're accepted
LIZ: ex[pect anything from them/ they're just them and [that's it=

ANNA: for what we are/ each of us/
LIZ: and we're OK/ and you're accepted
JEN: =and you're OK?

ANNA: yeah/
LIZ: as being OK just by being you= =yes/ yes/ <LAUGHS>
SUE: =just by turning up=

The theme of acceptance here makes a clear link between what is said – anything at all – and what friendship is all about – being supportive and allowing us to 'be ourselves'. In Val's words, 'The difference [between talking with her closest woman friend and talking with others] is that I don't have to think about what I'm going to say'.

Rachel claims that this feeling of acceptance, this confidence that you can say anything and not be judged, allows women to express themselves with more care and even with more creativity. This is an important claim, especially as she explicitly contrasts this aspect of women's talk with talk with men:

> Talking with women I'm- I'm much happier about struggling around how to say things cos I know enough to know that sometimes we don't have the words so- and also women give you time to struggle with it cos I haven't found with men- if you're having a conversation with men . . . they tend to sort of come crashing in.

The struggle for words, the search for the right words, is so important that, if Rachel's observation is correct, then it seems that we are right to value so highly the talk we do with women friends. But her comment begs the question: do men 'come crashing in' as a regular thing, in all contexts? The following extract from a dialogue between two men on the subject of being in a men's group is suggestive:[13]

GEOFF: I think men in general seem to have some sort of difficulty in talking to each other personally . . . Men's groups in a way have provided me in the past with a situation . . . where we're talking to each other and *listening* to each other, which I think is one of the things men have to learn to do.

TONY: One of the most striking things about the first few sessions of the men's group was the sense of 'you had enough time'. You could have difficulty with your words, you could try a sentence seventeen different ways round, and nobody minded or jumped down your throat or told you how to say it.

Tony's 'try a sentence seventeen different ways round' matches Rachel's point about struggling for words, while his 'jump down your throat' sounds as if it refers to the same phenomenon as Rachel's 'come crashing in'. They are both claiming that men typically jump in, and contrast this with a situation where people give each other time. There are hints here that the talk of women friends offers something quite unique. While talk among men and between men and women does not characteristically allow people time to express themselves, talk among women friends *does* typically allow the time for that struggle.

One problem for us in re-evaluating the talk we do with our women friends is that we have to contest men's evaluation of such talk. Thinking about women's friendship and women's talk as she answered my questions had the effect of making Helen indignant about (some) men's failure to appreciate what was so important about women's talk, or to understand what conversation was fundamentally about (my contributions are given in italics):

> but you know there's this feeling that life's full of things to be said, and it's- it's the source of women's writing and oral history and all that, isn't it. It's the richness of it . . . (*it's the pleasure of the minutiae- the minutiae of life*) yeah, absolutely, you see and that's what Nick would call trivia, I mean he actually said to me the other day something like, 'I'd always assumed that you wanted more than just basic conversation'. (*oh oh oh!* <LAUGHING>) I really freaked out at that because I thought this is- I thought- I said, 'This is the most significant thing you've ever said to me because this is so loaded (*yes*) if you unpick every bit of that (*yes, oh my god*) you know it's- it's absolutely fascinating . . . I mean what is basic conversation? yes if- I mean basic conversation is absolutely like the blood of life – it's out of that everything serious comes (*yes*) you can't separate it out, it's got to come out of the minutiae of experience, and our own experiences, not somebody else's.

While it was me who introduced the phrase *the minutiae of life*, it's Helen who develops this into a passionate argument in defence of 'basic conversation'. Far from being trivial, Helen defines such conversation – that is, conversation which deals with our everyday experiences – as 'the blood of life'. (Helen's position can be contrasted with Jo's anxiety that talk with women friends is not always 'productive' or 'intelligent', see page 54.) At the heart of Helen's defence is her commitment to a politics of experience, and her conviction of the futility of thinking you can ignore personal experience.

Talk as action

I opened this chapter by summarizing what women said to the question, 'What do you do with your women friends?'. In fact, while it emerged that talk was the central activity of women's friendships, many women balked at the word *do*. For example, here is how Meg and Bea responded to the question:

JEN: What do you do together?
BEA: We don't 'DO' much of anything, we- we tend to TALK, I mean we- we- we talk.

MEG: mhm
BEA: We- I mean you play golf – if I played golf I could go play golf with you but I don't.
MEG: I know, we don't do anything.
BEA: We don't do anything.
MEG: We don't make jam together or-
JEN: <LAUGHS>

Meg's incomplete utterance 'we don't make jam together or-' calls up an imaginary list of 'things women might do together'. Her statement that she and Bea *don't* make jam together challenges the premise of my question (she is saying, in effect, 'the sorts of things women have traditionally done together are make jam, weave quilts, wash clothes at the stream, but surely these aren't the answers you expect?'). At the same time, she seeks refuge in humour because she is unsure how to answer the question. Hannah qualified her answer in exactly the same way. She said: 'But for me just what I remember about the relationship is NOT like what we DID together, but just you know the amount of time we just spent sitting around and talking'.

These three speakers all conceptualize talk as outside the realm of 'doing'. But talk *is* doing. In fact, talk is a very powerful form of social action. It is through talk that we maintain or subvert existing social sturctures, and through talk that we establish and maintain social relationships.[14] Talk is intrinsic to friendship: without talk, we could not form close relationships, and forming close relationships is essential to our development as human beings. It is one of the goals of this book to demonstrate that women friends talking are women who are *doing*; what they are doing is friendship.

4

'We talk about everything and anything': An overview of the conversations

This chapter will be the first of six which will focus on the spontaneous conversation of women friends. Women's social practices typically involve shared projects, collaboration rather than competition. Conversation is a form of social practice, and in these central chapters I shall try to characterize the conversational practices of women friends. What linguistic strategies are characteristic of friendly talk between women? How are sharing and collaboration realized in talk? My findings will be compared with what was said in the interviews, in women's own descriptions of how we talk.

In this chapter I will focus broadly on the structure of women's conversations, and will test the claims made in the interviews about balance and mirroring. I will also illustrate the range of topics covered in the talk of women friends, and will show that these women's claims about what they talk about are substantially accurate.

Topics in conversation

To give some idea of what women friends talk about, and to begin to probe what an average conversation between women friends looks like, I present here skeleton accounts of four extracts from the recorded conversation, listing the main topics occurring in a forty-five-minute period. (I'm using the word *topic* to refer to any chunk of talk that hangs together because it's about the 'same thing'.)[1] I've chosen these four extracts in order to represent both girls and women, and to include conversations between two, three, four and five speakers.

Hannah, Becky, Jessica and Claire (age: 14)

Periods
Gymnastics
Holiday
Mums and dads and their moods
Reminiscing about Brownies
Brothers and boys and the male body
Embarrassment at parent–teacher meetings
Dreams and sleepwalking

Sue, Liz and Anna (age: early 30s)

Antiques
Fantasies about weekend trip
Gulf War
Holidays
Skiing
Rabbits
Piano lessons
Musical instruments
Relationships and equality

Pat and Karen (age: late 30s)

Christmas cards
Karen's recent operation
Christmas trees
Christmas lights in London
Illness
School plays

Meg, Bea, Mary, Sally and Jen (the Oxton group) (age: 40s)

Removals
Pleasure in others' failures
Competition about children

Taboo and funerals
Child abuse
Loyalty to men
Fear of men
Meg's visit to London
Trains and ships in the docks

Just giving the bare bones of these four extracts from conversation between female friends shows how varied the topics of conversation are. Some of these topics are doing the work of 'catching up' which women considered so important in the interviews. For example, in 'Karen's recent operation', Karen tells Pat about her check-up, and in 'Removals' my friends ask me how my plans for moving to London are developing. The topic 'Skiing' begins with Sue telling Anna and Liz about John's (her husband's) recent holiday.

Much of the talk is about significant people in our lives. Parents are the subject of the topic 'Mums and dads and their moods', in which the girls talk in particular about their anxiety about upsetting their mothers. Parents are also the subject of the topic 'Illness', in which Karen tells Pat she's worried about her father's complaints of chest pain; and of 'Taboo and funerals', where Bea talks about her father's death and the rest of us contemplate our parents' mortality. Our children are another frequent topic: they are the subject of the topic 'Piano lessons', when Liz talks about her daughter's progress on the piano, and of the topic 'School plays', when Pat and Karen exchange stories about their children's participation in end-of-term productions at their schools. Friends, partners and brothers and sisters also get talked about. In 'Brothers and boys and the male body', for example, Jessica tells her friends how she saw her brother with an erection; in 'Skiing' Anna tells the story of a disastrous holiday with her sister, who had just split up from her boyfriend; in 'Illness', Pat and Karen talk about their friend Lynn and her impossible mother; and in 'Trains and ships in the docks', Mary, Sally and Bea talk about their husbands and children going to see the *Golden Hind* when it was in the Albert Dock as part of the Tall Ships visit to Liverpool. As these examples illustrate, most of the topics arise directly from women's personal experience.

Examples involving self-disclosure are: Hannah and her friends sharing their experiences of backache and mood swings associated with periods ('Periods'); Karen confiding in Pat about her physical state following an operation ('Karen's recent operation'); Sally and Meg talking about being afraid to go home in the dark at the time of the Yorkshire Ripper case ('Fear of men').

What Meg called 'domesticky sort of things' also appear as topics. In 'Christmas trees', Pat and Karen exchange stories about buying their christmas trees, in 'Rabbits', Sue tells Liz and Anna about the school rabbit which she is looking after for the weekend, and in 'Removals', I tell my friends about getting my furniture packed up for the move to London.

Topics involving the discussion of serious ideas are also quite common, despite the lack of prominence such topics were given in the interviews. Certainly Jo's anxiety that women friends sell each other short by indulging in 'having a moan' rather than talking about more challenging subjects appears to be misplaced. In the conversations outlined above, for example, Sue, Liz and Anna talk at length about issues related to relationships and equality ('Relationships and equality'), and the Oxton group discuss the subject of child abuse ('Child abuse').

Work as a topic of conversation, by contrast, was mentioned by several women in the interviews, but is not a prominent topic in the recorded conversations. There are no examples in these four extracts (though the topic 'Taboo and funerals' begins with Meg telling an anecdote about someone she met at work, a postgraduate student working on taboo).[2] Nor do intimate details of sexual relationships appear here – or anywhere else in the conversations, for that matter. This confirms what women said in the interviews, though some women claim that this is what men think we talk about. Anna, for example, said: 'He [i.e. John, Sue's husband] finds it fascinating that we sit and talk, and I think he thinks that we talk about men and sex, compare sexual experiences and things like that, but then I think that's perhaps a fantasy that men have about women when they're together talking, and we never do'.[3]

This analysis of four conversations demonstrates the wide range of topics arising in friends' conversations, and also confirms the claim that women talk predominantly about people and draw heavily on personal experience. Does it support the claim that women's talk is about 'everything and anything'? The answer has to be a qualified 'yes'. On the one hand, virtually any topic can turn up in any conversation – women friends enjoy the sense that there is no set agenda. On the other hand, it is clear that some topics arise because of particular local circumstances. For example, the 'Holiday' topic in the first of these four conversations arose from a recent holiday that three of the girls had been on. Talk about the Gulf War (from the second conversational extract) occurs in a conversation recorded in January 1991 when the Gulf War was in progress. The christmas topics in Pat and Karen's conversation are the nonrandom result of this conversation being recorded just before christmas.

Are topic shifts in these conversations gradual or abrupt? Helen's comment, 'it [talk] goes all over the place', implies both that talk can be about anything, and also that it progresses in a random way from topic to topic. But this is not true in many instances: besides the contemporary significance of many of the topics, the links between these topics are often quite coherent. In the second of these extracts, for example, conversation moves from talk about piano lessons to talk about the playing of other musical instruments, which includes an anecdote about a wife who forbids her husband to play his guitar, to talk about whether couples are ever really equal. Some topic changes, however, are abrupt. For example, in the same conversation there is no link between the topic 'Skiing' and the topic 'Rabbits': the 'Skiing' topic comes to an end, Liz comments on how nice the salad is that they're eating, and Sue announces that she's brought the school rabbit home for the weekend, which launches general talk about rabbits. Similarly, in the last conversation outlined above, Meg tells an anecdote which introduces the topic of 'Taboo and funerals', and makes no attempt to link this new topic with the previous one, 'Competition about children' (which ended with me telling a story against myself about cheering my 5-year-old son on to win an egg-and-spoon race).

Topics: internal structure

An analysis in terms of topic gives us only a superficial idea of the way women's conversations are constructed. I shall now look in more detail at a few of the topics listed above. Conversations between women friends can be analysed in terms of two main components: narrative and discussion.[4] In other words, most sections of talk between women friends can be described as a story or as a discussion, and in friendly conversation there is a constant fluctuation between the two. By *story*, I mean both autobiographical accounts of things that have happened to us, and anecdotes about other people and events. To count as a story, these accounts must be structured in a particular way, which in our culture basically entails having a beginning, a middle and an end. By *discussion*, I mean those parts of conversation where everyone joins in to mull over particular issues (usually issues which have been raised in a story). Stories typically involve just one speaker, the narrator, while discussions typically involve all participants. The next chapter (chapter 5) will examine women's story-telling practices in detail, while chapter 6 will look at the way the complex multi-participant talk found in discussion sections is organized. But in this chapter, I want to keep a broader perspective, looking more generally at the way individual topics are developed, and at how stories and discussion fit together in women's talk.

Let's look at some of these topics in more detail. I'll begin with a relatively straightforward one, in which a sequence of three stories is followed by a discussion.[5] (I'll give the duration of each of these topics in minutes and seconds.)

Example 1: 'Taboo and funerals' (Meg, Bea, Mary, Sally, Jen) [4 minutes 32 seconds]

Story about postgraduate student doing research on taboo and whether there are circumstances when you could miss your mother's funeral (Meg)
Story about neighbour whose mother has just died and who is going to Australia for funeral (Sally)
Story about not going to her father's funeral in the USA (Bea)
Discussion about issues arising from these stories

This is a very coherent example of what I am calling a topic. In this example, Meg's opening anecdote flags up an interesting question: is it taboo to miss your mother's funeral? This story, then, functions to establish a new topic. Sally then tells a story which gives a concrete example: her nextdoor neighbour's mother has just died, so he is about to fly to Brisbane to attend the funeral. Sally makes it clear that she thinks this is absurd (in other words, she thinks there are circumstances when it *is* possible to miss your mother's funeral). Sally's angle is explicitly followed up in Bea's story, which is a personal anecdote recounting how Bea missed her father's funeral because of the problems involved in leaving a very young child and flying to the USA, and because her mother told her not to come. The discussion which follows this story is complex: at the general level, the five friends debate whether funerals are primarily to comfort the surviving relatives or to make a public statement about your dead mother or father, and whether distance can affect the decision about whether or not to attend a funeral. At the personal level, each of the five women has their own views about funerals and about the death of parents which they need to explore and share. So the discussion section combines the general and the personal: general points are teased out at the same time as individual speakers gain each other's support as they work through their feelings on the subject.

The 'Taboo and funerals' topic demonstrates a very simple pattern: a story or stories leading into discussion. I used to argue that this pattern was the normal way that topics developed in friendly conversation.[6] I now think that this oversimplifies what happens in women's friendly talk. To demonstrate the range of possibilities, let's look at two more detailed examples.

The first comes from the conversation between Pat and Karen outlined at the beginning of the chapter. The topic 'Illness' is developed in a sequence of seven sections, as outlined below.

Example 2: 'Illness' (Pat and Karen) [6 minutes 13 seconds]

Story about her father's chest pains (Karen)
Story about neighbour's indigestion diagnosed as heart attack (Pat)
Discussion – they mull over these two stories
Story about friend's mother's blood-pressure problems (Pat)
Discussion about blood pressure and importance of going to doctor
Story about friend's mother fainting in the street (Pat)
Discussion about how difficult friend's mother is – a 'dragon' – who won't accept medical help

While this example resembles 'Taboo and funerals' in that the topic is initiated by a story and ends with a discussion section, what is different is that the topic develops through a *sequence* of story (or stories) followed by discussion. By comparison with the 'Taboo and funerals' topic, which is a very coherent example, as the subject raised by Meg in her opening anecdote is maintained as the focus of attention throughout, the topic 'Illness' is less coherent: while all sections of the topic are about the same subject, each discussion section is oriented specifically to the preceding story or stories. There is no general discussion section which deals with everything that has gone before. This kind of topic development may be more what Helen meant when she said that women's talk 'goes all over the place'. A topic such as 'Illness' is established, but talk arising from that topic wanders around in a serendipitous way and ends, in this case, not because the friends have come to any philosophical conclusions about illness, but because they've said what they want to say on the topic and move on to another.

These two examples illustrate two different patterns. First, there is the simple pattern, exemplified by the topic 'Taboo and funerals':

Story ----> Discussion

Secondly, there is the more complex, chaining pattern, exemplified by the topic 'Illness':

[Story ---> Discussion] + [Story ---> Discussion] + [Story ---> Discussion]

In both these patterns, the story slot may be filled by one or more stories. Let's look at a final example, to see whether it's possible to apply these two patterns to all topics. I shall look at two consecutive topics from the extract from a conversation between Sue, Liz and Anna; the topics are 'Musical instruments' and 'Relationships and equality'.

Example 3 (Analysis 1)

'Musical instruments' [10 minutes 18 seconds]

Story about piano teacher's son playing trumpet in band at Christmas concert (Liz)
Story about piano teacher practising for a recital (Liz)
Discussion of Sue's husband John and his saxophone playing
Story about friend whose wife won't let him play his guitar (Sue)
Discussion about marriage and ideas of obedience and rebellion focusing on the 'obedient' husband

'Relationships and equality' [4 minutes 47 seconds]

Discussion of whether partners in a couple are ever equal, and whether living on your own is preferable to being part of a couple

I've chosen this example to show how arbitrary decisions can be about topic boundaries. Where topic shift is gradual rather than abrupt,[7] it can be difficult to decide whether a particular stretch of talk should be counted as a new topic or a further section of an existing topic. This is the problem with the example above. The first four components of the topic I've called 'Musical instruments' are all explicitly about people playing musical instruments. The discussion section which follows is oriented explicitly to Sue's story about the man who is not allowed to play his guitar, and so seems to me to be part of this topic. But this discussion section shifts the focus of talk away from musical instruments and towards relationships between husbands and wives. It could thus be seen as transitional in some way, between the topic 'Musical instruments', and the new topic 'Relationships and equality'. In other words, these two topics overlap, and it isn't absolutely clear where the new topic starts.

As I've divided them at present, the topic 'Relationships and equality' appears anomalous because it consists simply of a discussion section. The previous discussion section, which focused on the 'obedient husband', ended with Liz saying, 'it's strange isn't it the life some people lead', at which point Sue laughs and Anna says: 'I wonder if anybody's ever done a study of sort of coupledom'. This launches a long discussion about power balances in relationships, and of the pleasures of independence compared with being in a couple.

If I wanted to preserve a model of topics consisting of a story or stories followed by discussion, I could argue that the story about the guitar-playing husband should more accurately be seen as the opening of a new topic. The two topics would then be organized as follows.

Example 3 (Analysis 2)

'Musical instruments' [2 minutes 5 seconds]

Story about piano teacher's son playing trumpet in band at Christmas concert (Liz)
Story about piano teacher practising for a recital (Liz)
Discussion of Sue's husband John and his saxophone playing

'Relationships and equality' [13 minutes]

Story about friend whose wife won't let him play his guitar (Sue)
Discussion about marriage and ideas of obedience and rebellion, focusing on the 'obedient' husband
Discussion of whether partners in a couple are ever equal, and whether living on your own is preferable to being part of a couple

From an analyst's point of view, looking at the transcript of the conversation with hindsight, this way of organizing the topics makes a lot of sense. But the evidence of the audiotape is that Sue tells her story about the banned-from-playing-the-guitar husband in response to the preceding discussion about John and his saxophone playing (which she finds noisy). In terms of textual coherence, the story of the obedient husband is carefully oriented to pick up many points made in the previous discussion: both sections focus on a husband who plays an instrument and a wife who finds his playing annoying. The big difference is that where Sue tolerates John's playing, the wife in her story does not. The potential of this story to trigger wide-ranging discussion on the norms of behaviour in marriage and on relationships between couples in general only emerges as Liz and Anna begin to elaborate on Sue's story.

The problem with the second analysis of these two topics is that I am left with two consecutive discussion sections, which is a new pattern. I could call these two sections *sub*-sections of a long discussion on the subject of relationships, which would avoid the need to invoke a new pattern. It is tempting to use such sleight-of-hand, but I think it's more important to remain as faithful as possible to the conversations themselves. Clearly, the relationship between topic and the two conversational components, story and discussion, is not straightforward, and many different combinations are possible.

The range of possibilities

To demonstrate briefly how wide the possibilities are, I'll consider each of the various possibilities in turn, drawing on all twenty conversations. First, is it possible for a topic to consist just of a story or stories? The answer seems to be yes: the topic 'Cystitis' consists of one very long story told by Anna to Sue and Liz. An episode from this story will be discussed in the next chapter (see page 104; the whole 208-line story is reproduced in appendix A). This topic arises as part of a long chunk of 'catching up' conversation in which Anna tells her two friends what she's been doing, the two main topics being her trip to Philadelphia to be matron of honour at a friend's wedding, and her holiday in Rome. She starts to tell Liz and Anna about Rome, then interrupts herself to say: 'Oh and the worst thing was- I haven't told you this'. 'This' turns out to be the story of how she developed cystitis on the plane flight to Rome. The story, and thus the topic, ends with the words 'So anyway that was that'. The next topic (which had in a sense been deferred by Anna's self-interruption) is 'Holiday in Rome', which opens with the words 'And we had a fairly nice time in Rome but Rome wasn't at all what I was thinking it would be'. These utterances at the beginning and end of the topic 'Cystitis' clearly mark it off as a separate topic.

So a topic can consist of a story component on its own. A topic may also consist of a discussion section on its own. The only example I've discussed is the controversial one, 'Relationships and equality' (controversial in that if analysed in a different way, this discussion section will not stand alone). But discussion sections do appear as free-standing components, initiated not by a story but by a simple question or statement. For example, the Oxton group's discussion 'Apes and language' is triggered by my question to my friends 'Did you see *Horizon* last night?' (*Horizon* is a relatively highbrow BBC TV series which looks at developments in the sciences.) Bea responds: 'Mhm, about the language of the apes', and the topic is launched. Most commonly, though, as the three examples discussed earlier showed, topics consist of a combination of story and discussion (in that order).

These components themselves vary from the epic story 'Cystitis' which is 208 lines long and lasts eight minutes thirty-nine seconds, to the ultra-brief two-line story which introduces the topic 'Quizzes': 'You know the quiz Vicky goes to on Wednesday? She drew with Robin Lee last night'. ('Quizzes' will be analysed in some detail in chapter 6, page 0.) Discussion sections also vary from long (for example, discussion arising from the 'Obedient husband' story lasted seven minutes forty-eight seconds) to short (for example, Pat and Karen's discussion of their friend's mother, which ends the topic 'Illness', lasts only forty-six seconds). Moreover, in many conversations women subvert the norms of the story and of discussion to produce more complex forms of talk. For example, stories are sometimes told by two or more friends, as we'll see in the next chapter: the story which introduces the topic 'Trains and ships in the docks' (from the fourth conversation analysed at the beginning of this chapter) is a good example of this. A different kind of example is provided by Sue's story about an obedient husband: this story is hi-jacked by Liz and Anna, who join in so that the story mutates into a discussion about relationships (see chapter 6, page 00ff. for further discussion of 'Obedient husband').

In conclusion, this analysis of the internal structure of topics in the conversation of women friends demonstrates that the structure varies considerably from topic to topic, both within and between conversations. Topics are composed of story and discussion sections, and these components are extremely flexible, varying in length depending on speakers' needs. Women friends explore a wide range of topics through telling stories and through discussion, and also through forms of talk which blend these modes.

'A real kind of balanced game of ping-pong': balance and sharing

Now that we've begun to pin down a bit more firmly the way women's talk works, let's examine the claim which emerged in the interviews that there is a pattern of balance and of sharing to be found in the talk we do with our friends. As we saw in the last chapter, both

Mary and Meg (with Bea), in separate interviews, proposed a 'shape' for women's talk which consisted of one person saying something and then the other person responding with something from their own experience. What this means is that turns – and time – are shared more or less evenly between speakers. The only exception is when someone is perceived as being in great need: as Bea put it, 'if one or the other of us were say very very distressed about something then that person would probably get most of the time, it wouldn't be equal'. In the extract from Pat and Karen's conversation outlined above, Karen's story of her visit to the hospital for a check-up after her operation does not elicit a balancing story from Pat, and during this topic Karen gets an unequal amount of talking time. This seems to me to be a good example of what Bea is describing.

In the last chapter, I suggested that this pattern of shared turns could be represented symbolically as $X_1 + X_2 + X_3$ (and I contrasted this pattern with other possible patterns such as the X + Y + Z pattern, or the X + notX pattern). What is unique about the $X_1 + X_2 + X_3$ pattern is that participants in talk *mirror* each other's contributions in matching contributions of their own. That is, through very sensitive monitoring of what each other says, we tailor our contributions to match what has gone before.

'It comes back': balance involving mirroring turns

This pattern of mirroring occurs at all levels of talk. I'll start at the most basic level, the turn. The topic 'Periods' (in the conversation between Hannah, Becky, Jessica and Claire outlined earlier) starts with a mirroring sequence of turns about back ache. I'll list these turns, with false starts, repetitions, etc. edited out for clarity of presentation.

Sequence 1 'Backache'

Turn 1: my back is connected with my periods/ (Becky)
Turn 2: so's mine/ I get really bad backache down there/ (Jessica)
Turn 3: so do I get backaches/ I can't go like that and I can't go like that and I just ((xx)) a back rest/ (Claire)

We could represent this sequence of turns as $BA_1 + BA_2 + BA_3$ (where BA stands for backache). First, we can see how these three turns involve *sharing*: the talking time available for participants to involve themselves in this subtopic is shared between the three speakers (Hannah does not join in this cycle). Secondly, in terms of the claim that female speakers *mirror* each other's utterances, note how closely these three turns match each other. Becky introduces the subject of backache, and links it with her periods; Jessica says that her experience is the same: her concise utterance *so's mine* is equivalent to her repeating what Becky said: *my back is connected with my periods*. She then explains where her back aches. Claire also claims the same experience – *so do I get backaches* – and develops this in relation to how it incapacitates her. So turns 2 and 3 both involve direct repetition of Becky's opening theme – that is, both turns overtly mirror what she says.

This sequence of turns is immediately followed by another sequence involving all four friends, in which the mirroring is so carefully done that three of the four turns start with the phrase *hot water bottles*, and all four turns use the verb *help*.

Sequence 2 'Hot water bottles'

Turn 1: but hot water bottles help (Jessica)
Turn 2: hot water bottles help (Becky)
Turn 3: hot water bottles help me as well (Hannah)
Turn 4: help so much (Claire)

We can represent this sequence of turns as $HWB_1 + HWB_2 + HWB_3 + HWB_4$ (where HWB = hot water bottles). The careful linguistic parallelism in these two sequences is designed to maximize solidarity between the four friends: they share very personal experiences and validate each other's experiences through confirmation that their experience is identical. These examples demonstrate very clearly what one of the women meant in the interviews when she said 'Women like to sing the same tune'.

Let's look now at the unedited version of the conversational extract from the topic 'Periods' which these sequences come from. Note how the four friends don't just affirm each other by framing parallel utterances; mirroring and balancing is also carried out through the way the talk is structured, so that some turns are perfectly timed to follow another turn, while others are spoken simultaneously.

- -

BECKY: my back- my back is connected with my periods/ cos I ((xx))

- -

BECKY: yeah/
JESS: so's mine/ I get really bad back a- back ache down there/

CLAIRE: so do I/ back aches/ I can't go like that/ and I can't go like

---

BECKY: yeah/
CLAIRE: that/ and I just ((xx)) a back rest/
JESS: but . ho- hot water bottles

HANNAH: [hot water bottles help me [as well/
BECKY: [hot water bottles help/
CLAIRE: [help so much/
JESS: help/

Note how Becky, who introduced the subtopic 'Backache', responds to both Jessica's and Claire's contributions with *yeah*. Her second *yeah* overlaps with Jessica's utterance *but ho- hot water bottles help* which introduces the hot water bottle theme. Also note how Claire's *help so much* is timed to follow Becky's *hot water bottles help*, which means it overlaps with Hannah's slightly more elaborate version of this statement. This short extract illustrates the pattern of balancing and mirroring very clearly: talk progresses through turns which are explicitly oriented to what has just been said, and which match it through repetition of grammatical patterns and of key words and phrases. Sequences of turns, then, are very much variations on a theme, which is what I have tried to capture in the $X_1 + X_2 + X_3$ notation. And since different speakers are usually associated with these sequential turns, this pattern also exemplifies sharing.

This extract from the talk of Hannah and her friends also illustrates what Bea calls 'bleshing' or 'melding' – that is, the way women friends combine as speakers to arrive at a common position: we share in the construction of talk to the extent that the individual voice loses significance. Everyone contributes to what is said, and who says what is not important. This means that sometimes we even say the same words at the same time (as Hannah and Becky do in the example above). I won't comment on this phenomenon further here: there will be many examples in this and other chapters to illustrate it, and bleshing and melding in women's talk will be the specific focus of chapter 6.

Let's look at another simple example of the $X_1 + X_2 + X_3$ pattern, this time from the opening section of a conversation involving me and Helen, where I begin by saying I'm worn out.

'Tiredness'

Turn 1:	very tired/ (Jen)
Turn 2:	oh are you? – I've got- wonder if that's what it's been for me actually/ (Helen)
Turn 3:	I've had this headache/ (Jen)
Turn 4:	yes I've had that/ and my eyes/ you know my eyes are the first place to go/ (Helen)
Turn 5:	yes/ (Jen)
Turn 6:	dreadful pains in my eyes/ (Helen)
Turn 7:	oh actually it's not a pain/ they're just sort of tired/ (Jen)
Turn 8:	well yes/ but sort of viral- in a sort of virusy way/ (Helen)
Turn 9:	oh god/ (Jen)
Turn 10:	you know all the bones round here ache/ (Helen)

In this sequence, Helen and I tell each other how we're feeling, in particular how tired we're feeling. The mirroring process continues for ten turns, moving from the more general topic of being tired to the specifics of how our eyes feel. This example is less straightforward than the previous one, since at one point – when I say *oh actually it's not a pain* – I do not mirror Helen. At this point, Helen adapts her account of her eyes to bring it more into line with mine, showing the work friends do to remain aligned.[8] In other words, the topic develops from both of us agreeing we're tired, to both of us agreeing we've been having headaches, to the rather more difficult negotiation about the state of our eyes. While Helen says that she has 'dreadful pains' in her eyes, I say that my eyes are 'just sort of tired', which Helen then claims has a 'virusy' aspect to it, a statement about her eyes which I concur with (*oh god*). Here is the example in its conversational form:

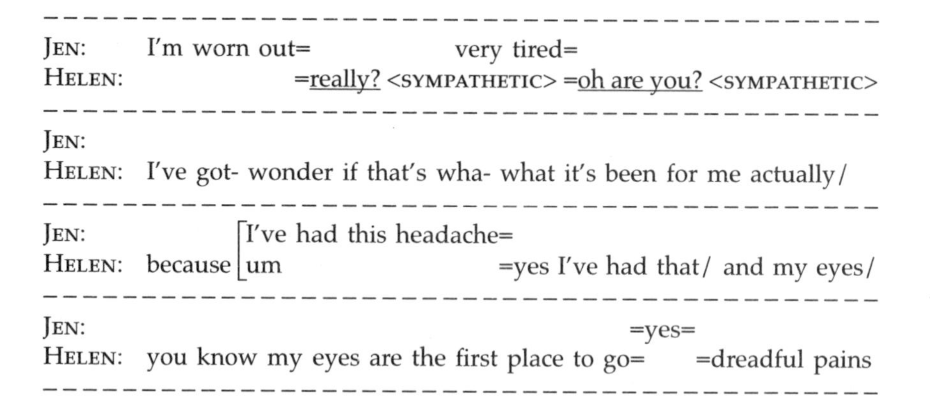

JEN:	I'm worn out=	very tired=
HELEN:		=really? <SYMPATHETIC> =oh are you? <SYMPATHETIC>

JEN:	
HELEN:	I've got- wonder if that's wha- what it's been for me actually/

JEN:	[I've had this headache=	
HELEN:	because [um	=yes I've had that/ and my eyes/

JEN:		=yes=
HELEN:	you know my eyes are the first place to go=	=dreadful pains

JEN:	oh actually it's not a pain/ they're just sort
HELEN:	in my eyes/

JEN:	of tired/
HELEN:	well yes/ . but sort of viral- . in a sort of virusy

JEN:	oh god/
HELEN:	way/ but . you know all the bones round here ache/

This sort of exchange is a (relatively trivial) example of what Bea was referring to when she said 'we complain to each other'. It certainly represents the kind of talk that Jo described as typical of women friends: 'you know if you're feeling bad you can just be grotty and have a moan'. Jo saw this as one of the comfortable aspects of women friends' talk but she also felt ambivalent about it, in case it meant we didn't also 'giv(e) of . . . [our] most exciting- the best and most interesting self'. The sequence above, involving me and Helen, seems to me typical of the opening stages of friends' conversations, when we check how each other is. As Helen said when I interviewed her: 'I think we always do that first . . . it's like making sure everything is alright, everything is in place'. This kind of talk functions as a way of re-establishing contact and of re-affirming the friendship – whatever the topic, the mirroring symbolizes our connectedness.

Certainly the subsequent talk in this conversation between Helen and me moves a long way from mutual complaining, covering problems Helen is having with a course she is running at the local college of further education, my own success (in my role as parent governor) at convincing the headteacher of the local school that he should give one of his staff responsibility for monitoring equal opportunities, and our shared experiences at a recent open evening at the school.

Balance involving mirroring stories

Frequently, balance and mirroring are done through the production of matching stories. In the topic 'Periods', after the sequences of mirroring turns which we've looked at, the friends take it in turns to talk at greater length about the mood swings which they associate with premenstrual tension. Their stories all pick up the same theme and the four friends support each other through confirming that these sorts of moods are experienced by all of them. The sequence of stories can be summarized as follows:

'Periods'

PMT_1: if I'm in a bad mood, my mother always thinks it's PMT (Becky)
PMT_2: I often feel as if I'm going to cry (Claire)
PMT_3: I sobbed in the bath – everything seemed to be going wrong (Hannah)
PMT_4: I cried in a Careers lesson because I had backache and no one noticed (Becky)

This summary does not do justice to the mirroring work that is going on in this long sequence of stories, since 'story' gives the impression that there is a sequence of four monologues. In fact, all four girls participate in this section of the topic 'Periods', making side comments, joining in to share the telling of particular points, adding minimal responses (*yeah* and *mhm*).[9]

If we go back to example 1 ('Taboo and funerals') in the earlier part of this chapter, we can see that the three stories which open this topic fit the $X_1 + X_2 + X_3$ pattern: Meg tells a story, Sally responds with a story from her experience – about her neighbour – and then Bea responds in turn with a story from her experience – about her father.

'Taboo and funerals'

TF_1: I met a student who is doing research on the question: Is it taboo to miss your mother's funeral?' (Meg)
TF_2: my nextdoor neighbour is flying to Australia for his mother's funeral (Sally)
TF_3: I didn't fly to the USA when my father died (Bea)

Each story mirrors the previous one in maintaining the theme of parents and funerals, but each one varies because it arises from the personal experience of the story-teller.

The topic 'Illness' also illustrates the way stories are balanced as women friends mirror each others' contributions. This topic is initiated by Karen who tells a story about her father and his recent attacks of abdominal pain. Despite the humour of parts of her story, it is apparent that she is worried about these attacks. Here's the second part of this story:

'Illness', Story 1 (Karen)

Anyway Doris phoned me Friday
and he's only had one attack in the last two weeks
and she's- I said, 'He told me it was wind'.
She said, 'Well I know you're going to think this is crazy
but since he's had his new teeth he's only had one attack'.

I said, 'Pardon'?
She said, 'Well if you think, if you've got teeth that don't fit properly you can't chew.
So you take your f-'
You know what it's like when you don't chew your food,
and since he's had these new teeth he's had the one attack.

Pat responds with a story which not only mirrors Karen's, but which is designed to reassure her, that is, to confirm her hypothesis that her father's problem is to do with his digestion rather than his heart. Here is Pat's mirroring story.

'Illness', Story 2 (Pat)

You know Bob Parry who used to live next door to us at Norton Road, the butcher,
he had- oh years ago, he had two or was it three terrible attacks where he passed out.
And the first time it happened it was in the middle of the night.
He woke up in bed with this excruciating pain in his chest,
staggered out of bed and collapsed
and went unconscious on the floor,
and he and his wife obviously thought he's had a heart attack
[...]
and it- that was indigestion.

Pat's story mirrors Karen's: hers, like Karen's, involves an older male protagonist, and he too has an acute attack involving pain in the chest/abdomen. In Pat's story, the diagnosis is known: the pain was the result of indigestion, and was not a heart attack.

Topic development and mirroring

The discussion sections of topics can also display balance and mirroring, in that participants' contributions to discussion are carefully matched. I want to show here how topics develop, through sequences of mirroring stories and through discussion sections where mirroring is an important aspect of the way speakers explore issues. A simple example (because it involves only two speakers) comes from one of the discussion sections in Pat and Karen's talk on the topic 'Illness'. Here is the fourth story in the sequence of stories about illness, followed by the opening part of their discussion.

'Illness', Story 4 (Pat)

Lynn was out shopping with her [mother] the other day.
She did it twice in an hour. (KAREN: *oh I wouldn't like that*)

She fell over in- was it Welwyn or somewhere they were,
in the street,
and Lynn said she was walking along,
she heard this crash
and didn't know what had happened for a minute,
looked round,
and there was her mum on the ground behind her.
She went to pick her up,
and of course her mother just cussed and swore at her
and said, 'Oh don't make such a bloody fuss,
sshhh, everyone's looking', and all that nonsense.
Lynn said they went into a shop
and she did it again –
'Don't make such a fuss', and all that.

Discussion

KAREN: I think if someone was me I'd be on the bloody phone and get an ambulance there straight away/ <LAUGHS>
PAT: well . yeah/ . I wouldn't just keep walking around/
KAREN: I don't think so/ no/ I mean-
PAT: not with a person with a history of high blood pressure/
KAREN: no/
PAT: at her age/
KAREN: and even so I think if you're with somebody who suddenly falls over/ if nothing else you'd get into a restaurant or somewhere where you could sit down/

Once the discussion section starts, turns are short and the two friends match each other's contributions carefully. Karen responds to Pat's story about Lynn and her mother by saying what she would do in Lynn's position (implicitly criticizing Lynn for allowing herself to be overruled by her mother). Pat matches this with her *well yeah I wouldn't keep walking around*. Karen agrees with Pat's agreement, and Pat adds a reason for their position: *not with a person with a history of high blood pressure*. Karen agrees with this reasoning, and Pat adds a further reason, Lynn's mother's age. At this point, building on their various contributions, Karen sums up their position by asserting that, whatever the circumstances (even if the person involved wasn't elderly and with high blood pressure) you would at least find somewhere to sit down.

The topic 'Pleasure in others' failures' provides another good example of mirroring during the development of a topic both at the level of stories and in terms of contributions to discussion. Here I will just reproduce Meg's opening story, a mirroring story from Bea, and part of the subsequent discussion. (The punchline of the first story depends on understanding the nomenclature of British university degrees: a first, or first-class degree, is the highest level awarded; a 2.1, or upper second class degree, is very good; a 2.2 is average, and therefore not a sign of great achievement; and a third, or third-class degree, is below average.)

'Pleasure in others' failures'

Story 1 (Meg)

[Stan's] one of those few- one of the few people in the world that I feel deeply spiteful towards,
and it's all to do with his son and my son.
My son's a little bit older than his son,
but when they were both young lads about fourteen or something,
he said to me, 'Well you know Jacob isn't of the same calibre as Max,
and Max is /ei/ genius <SLOW AND PRECISE>
and er you know thi- not many people are blessed with having a genius as a child'.
[...]
but it was true that Max's incredibly creative child,
he could do absolutely everything,
he w- he made fantastic Meccano models,
and he was the brightest boy they'd ever had in his- in the previous school,
and he went to Birkenhead School ((on a)) scholarship.
[...]
Anyway Max got a 2.2!

Story 2 (Bea)

I feel like that about a friend of mine who lives in New York
who's- well she refers to her son as her little star,
and that doesn't help.
and when I arrived at the- at the – at her apartment to stay,
and she and her husband were both out at their exciting jobs in publishing,
and this lad of s- of seven or eight let me in,
and asked if he could make me some coffee. (SALLY: *oh he IS a little star then*)
You know he IS a little star,
and he's so perfect that you just want to jump up and down 'im
and see if he'd squish you know,
[...]
and I'm so hoping that something marvellous will happen
and he'll run away from home
and – or you know something will squelch this...

Bea's story is interrupted by the arrival of Mary (who'd been delayed). We all explain to her what we're talking about and she joins in the discussion. The following is a brief extract.

Discussion

MARY:	but I don't like feeling like that=	
MEG:		=no I don't like feeling like that/
JEN:		=oh it's horrid/

MARY:	you know/			[but I do do it/	[a lot/
MEG:		but um	[((I think it's	xx))	yeah/ =yeah/
BEA:			well it seems	like we all do feel like	that=
SALLY:					=yes/

MARY:	yeah/	
MEG:	oh I feel it a lot/ I feel it most- more than I don't feel/	
OTHERS:		<LAUGHTER- - - - - ->

This topic elicits some surprisingly frank self-disclosure from these friends – the two stories given here are good examples. The subsequent discussion involves us working together to try and understand these feelings, which we see as problematic. Taking pleasure in others' failures is bad enough; taking pleasure in the failure of other people's children seems worse. Mary's assertion *I don't like feeling like that* is seized upon by Meg and me. Meg mirrors Mary's assertion, repeating it word for word, while I paraphrase (and intensify) her words, a more subtle form of mirroring. This set of turns is then balanced by the acknowledgement that we all indulge in these wishes: Mary and Bea express this in overlapping utterances and Meg mirrors their statements, adding the disarmingly honest comment that she ill-wishes others more often than not. This produces laughter from the rest of us.

'Exchanged vulnerable talking': balance, mirroring and self-disclosure

In many of these examples, mirroring turns or stories involve mirroring self-disclosure. In her interview, Rachel described the mirroring self-disclosure that occurs in the talk of women friends as 'exchanged vulnerable talking', a very apt phrase. She spells out what she means as follows: 'You can say whatever you think or whatever you feel, and you . . . expect it back . . . and it comes back'. The example above illustrated this clearly, in particular the way that self-disclosure makes us vulnerable. Admitting that you take pleasure in others' failure lays you open to criticism: that you are a horrible person, that you need to learn to control your feelings. But in the safety of each others' homes, we can risk making ourselves vulnerable, because only then can we find out whether our friends share our experiences and our feelings.

If we look back at the examples in this chapter, we can see how well Rachel's description fits. In their talk about 'Periods', for example, Hannah, Becky, Claire and Jessica self-disclose about backache and about mood swings associated with premenstrual tension. By doing this they gain each other's support, and understand that they are not abnormal. Their reciprocal self-disclosure bonds them to each other and increases the solidarity of the group. Other topics we have looked at, notably 'Taboo and funerals' and 'Musical instruments' with its following topic 'Relationships and equality', involve participants in a great deal of self-disclosure. It is because turns and stories mirror each other, and because a balance is maintained between participants, that the vulnerability arising from self-disclosure can be contained safely. Both at the level of the individual utterance, and at the level of whole stories, women say whatever they feel, and 'it comes back', in the form of a mirroring utterance or a mirroring story.

'We'd draw some general conclusions from it': rounding off discussion

Now we've looked at examples of mirroring at various different levels, I want to illustrate the way women friends round off discussion of particular themes. Meg's observation (in the interview) that a sequence of matching chunks of talk is usually followed by what she calls a 'conclusion' seems to refer to the final phase of discussion rather than to discussion in general. She claimed that, after a few mirroring turns, 'we'd draw some general conclusions from it and- and some sort of philosophical sort of- and it could be in the form of something profound or it could be just a joke like "Oh God we'll be like that one day ourselves" '. Her distinction between more philosophical and more jokey endings is certainly supported by the data. The first two examples below are both more philosophical: the first of these comes from the topic 'Pleasure in others' failures'. Bea comments on the feeling they're talking about, and summarizes its basic components. Meg then attempts to name this feeling, and three of the five friends share in the attempt to define it:

BEA: isn't it awful the way you DO get set up with some people though/ where you- you- you actually take pleasure- instead of taking pleasure in the triumphs of their children/ . . . you think 'yeah/ she fails!/ innit great!'/ <GROWLY VOICE>

[. . .]

MEG: Tom [. . .] says there's a German word to describe that/ [. . .] one of

---

MEG: those complicated German nouns which explains the fact that you

---

MEG: feel . a perverse displeasure in other people's successes/ [. . .]

JEN: oh it's the other way round ((I feel))/ it's sort of pleasure

---

JEN: [in other people-
BEA: [a perverse pleasure in= =yeah=
MEG: =in their downfall= =yeah/

The second example comes at the end of one section of the long topic on 'Relationships and equality', in which Sue, Liz and Anna debate whether it's preferable to be part of a couple or to live independently. (All three friends have been married, but Anna and Liz are both divorced and live on their own.) Liz and Anna round off this discussion section with a cynical assessment of men's inability to let go at the end of a relationship.

LIZ: what IS it with these men though that they- they have to do that?
ANNA:

LIZ: I mean [they don't- they- they particularly- [they don't
ANNA: [it's a typically male thing though that they- [they-

LIZ: particularly want you any more/ they've done- [I mean they've
ANNA: [no but they don't

LIZ: decided- [no they don't want anybody else
ANNA: want anybody else to have you [either/

LIZ: to have you/ but they also want to still own you=
ANNA: =yeah/

Often, however, women choose a more condensed, joke-type conclusion. For example, at the end of the discussion about Sue's husband and his saxophone playing (from the topic 'Musical instruments'), Sue rounds off discussion as follows:

LIZ: I don't think- don't think you should knock it cos I think it's really

---

LIZ: good [that he's got an interest/
SUE: [it's good but why isn't it quiet?

Note that her joke, the plaintive question *why isn't it quiet?*, allows her to voice criticism about her husband's playing in a covert way, and seeks support for her veiled complaint by inviting laughter. In the next example of a joking conclusion, Pat embroiders on Karen's theme of how ridiculously young some doctors seem to be. (This example comes at the end of the brief discussion section following Karen's account of her check-up, from the topic 'Karen's recent operation'.)

[Talking about doctors and youthfulness]

KAREN: I suppose if you're ill you don't care do you?
PAT: I suppose not/

KAREN: there are/
PAT: but there are- um there are limits aren't there?

Note how both these jokey endings use a question or questions. Questions normally expect answers, but this kind of question invites laughter, or the exchange of rueful glances, or only a brief verbal response, rather than any kind of thorough-going answer. The joke, in both these examples, proves to be a successful bid to round off discussion by asking a question that is unanswerable. In the first example, Sue knows, as do her friends, that expecting a musical instrument to be quiet is a contradiction in terms. In the second, Pat accepts Karen's suggestion that ill people aren't in a position to mind if their doctors are very young, but makes the irrefutable platitude *there are limits aren't there?*, which succeeds as a joke because it forces us to consider a world where there were no limits and where doctors were, perhaps, under twelve years old. (Pat has earlier said: 'Lynn and I have got this joke [about a new doctor]/ we say he looks . . . extremely young/ and then we always say "About five"/', a contribution which makes them both laugh.)

Sometimes joking and more philosophical comments are combined. The following extract comes from the end of the discussion about the 'obedient husband' who isn't allowed to play his guitar (part of the topic 'Musical instruments'). The discussion is part of a long sequence of discussion sections which, as I've discussed earlier, merge into talk on the topic 'Relationships and equality'. Interestingly, the joke here depends on making links with the earlier topic 'Rabbits'.

ANNA: =yeah [=((he
LIZ: oh [bless him= [he does] n't have much of a life=
SUE: [he's- [((he's just))] =he

ANNA: doesn't [by the sounds [of it/
SUE: doesn't <LAUGHS> real [ly/ [((it's a)) bit like a RAbbit/

LIZ: [he is really isn't he? [she should
SUE: ((yeah)) <GIGGLE> I think [I should bring him- [I think I should

---

ANNA: [introduce them/
LIZ: get him- <GIGGLING> [I wonder why she doesn't [get him a run in
SUE: bring him home for [weekends <LAUGHS>

ANNA: introduce them=
LIZ: the garden <GIGGLING- -
SUE: =((and then you'll be able to bring

ANNA:
LIZ: - - - - - - - - - - - - - - - - - - -> get [him a few
SUE: him home at)) week ends and let him go out in a run/ [yeah/

ANNA:
LIZ: lettuce leaves/ he'd be quite happy/ ['thank you Ginny'/
SUE: [ohhh! <AMUSED> oh DON'T/

ANNA:
LIZ: it's strange isn't it the life some people lead/
SUE: poor thing/ <CHUCKLES>

Discussion of the obedient husband finishes here. Anna's next utterance, *I wonder if anybody's ever done a study of sort of coupledom,* launches a new discussion section (if not a new topic – see earlier discussion). The joke here is framed by Liz's philosophical remarks: at the beginning she says, *he doesn't have much of a life,* and the discussion ends with her words *it's strange isn't it the life some people lead.* Note the mirroring work that goes on here: Liz's opening remark, for example (*oh bless him, he doesn't have much of a life*), is mirrored by Anna and Sue simultaneously (Anna says, *he doesn't by the sounds of it,* and Sue says, *he doesn't really*). Sue then introduces the rabbit theme, and this joke is collaboratively sustained by all three friends, who pick up points that had been mentioned earlier in the discussion of the school rabbit that Sue has brought home from school for the weekend.

Conclusion

This general overview will serve as an introduction to the conversational material. I've tested here some of the claims made in the interviews. In particular, I've examined the claim that women's talk develops in a series of carefully matched chunks, each one reflecting key points in the previous one at the same time as adding something new to the general theme. This gradual process of building up conversation enables speakers to self-disclose more easily: friends keep pace with each other as they move on to new revelations. The evidence of the conversations is that balance and mirroring are crucial organizing features of women friends' talk. It seems that the 'ethic of reciprocity' which I argued was fundamental to women's conception of friendship is also fundamental to the way talk is constructed.

5

'D'you know what my mother did recently?': Telling our stories

As earlier chapters have made clear, talk has a very special role in women's friendship: when women friends meet, they talk. And when women friends talk, they tell each other stories. Story-telling plays a central role in friendly conversation between women, as it does for most people, whatever their background. The writer Ursula Le Guin argues that 'Narrative is a central function of language'. She also claims that narrative is 'an immensely flexible technology, or life-strategy, which if used with skill and resourcefulness presents each of us with that most fascinating of all serials, The Story of My Life'.[1] Her account rings very true for me. My oldest friend and I always begin our weekends together (we live sixty miles apart and meet once every two or three months) by asking, 'Who's going to tell their story first?' By 'story' we mean an autobiographical account of everything that has happened to us in the weeks or months since we last saw each other. The fact that we have spoken on the phone in between is ignored. What counts is the face-to-face, blow-by-blow account. In other words, we tell each other the latest episode of the Story of My Life. The reason this friend is precious to me is that she actually wants to hear my story, just as I genuinely want to hear hers. Through the exchange of stories, we share in the construction and reconstruction of our personal identities, our 'selves'. Doing this is part of what being a friend entails.

My sense of the significance of stories in our lives and in our friendships is confirmed by what women said when they were interviewed. In Hannah's words, what she and her friends talk about is 'our experiences in our lives'. Women understand that keeping in touch with each other's lives is important. As Meg put it: 'There's a certain sort of degree of shared experiences which you- you like to draw on and if you don't see each other you're forever having to kind of you know re-establish not your friendship as such but where . . . you're up to. Often you miss telling people about quite important events and say, "Oh, didn't you know that? I thought you knew that", um that kind of thing'. Talking about 'our experiences in our lives' and telling people 'where you're up to' both entail telling stories.

The conversational data also provides evidence that girls and women are aware that they tell stories, as the following quotations illustrate:

- 'did I tell you this story?' (Anna, 30+ years)
- 'I was telling her this as a funny story' (Jen, 40+ years)
- 'go on anyway – you tell your story' (Liz, 30+ years)
- 'tell that story about the dog and the blood that makes me feel so scared' (Jessica, 13 years)
- 'can I carry on with my story now?' (Becky, 13 years)

and they talk about stories as follows: 'marvellous story', 'funny story', 'hard luck story'. Other aspects of the world around them are referred to in terms of stories – for example, films they've seen: 'it was a lovely story', and news items they've read in the papers or seen on television: 'the Kurd story'.

This chapter is the first of six which will explore different aspects of the conversations I've recorded. I've chosen to start with stories because they introduce some of the key themes of women's talk, and because, as I've said, they have an important function in keeping friends in touch with each others' lives, and in the construction of our identity (or subjectivity). But in terms of their structure they differ significantly from the surrounding conversation in which they are embedded. When someone starts to tell a story, we listen to them in a way that is quite different from normal. Think of the quiet that descends on an infant school classroom when the teacher says, 'Once upon a time . . .'. William Labov, who studied the language practices of Black adolescent males in New York City, was struck by the power of narrative to compel attention: 'they [narratives] will command the total attention of an audience in a remarkable way, creating a deep and attentive silence that is never found in academic or political discussion'.[2] A keyword here is *audience*. In friendly conversation, the idea of participants functioning as an audience while someone speaks is nonsensical for most of the time. In the conversations I've recorded, what is most noticeable is the noisy all-in-together quality of the talk (this will be the subject of the next chapter). Story-telling is the exception. When someone starts to tell a story, the other conversational participants withdraw temporarily from active participation and give the story-teller privileged access to the floor.

A typical story

The stories women friends tell each other are about personal experience, their own or that of someone close to them. (We've already had some examples in the earlier chapters: chapters 2 and 3 included some stories told by women when they were interviewed about their friendships, and in chapter 4, the section on mirroring looked at stories told by Pat and Karen about 'Illness', and stories told by the Oxton group about 'Pleasure in others' failures'.) The following is a typical story told by a woman to her friend about buying a dress. I'm following the normal convention used by those who work on conversational narrative, of presenting the story in numbered lines, each line corresponding to one of the narrator's breath-groups or intonation units.[3] This means that lines will typically consist of a grammatical phrase or clause. Falling final intonation is represented with a full stop, rising final intonation with a question mark. (I have edited some of these stories very slightly, to make them easier to read and to keep them to a manageable size. I've marked omissions with the following symbol: [. . .].)

Pat tells this story at a point in the conversation where she and Karen have started talking about their new dresses.

Sundresses

Well I saw those [dresses] um on Wednesday when I was up there,
and then my mother phoned me up and said,
'Oh I want to get a couple of these lengths which I've seen in Watford',
cos she's going to America in a couple of weeks' time,
[. . .]
5 and she said, 'I want a couple of sundresses
and can you just run them up for me'.
So I said, 'Yeah, I saw them myself',
and I said, 'Before you go and get them in John Lewis
go in St Alban's market,
10 cos I've seen dress lengths ready cut,
the lot . for four ninety-nine'.
And she said, 'Oh I haven't got time to go in St Albans.
I've seen the ones I want anyway in John Lewis's

and I don't think there were much difference in price'.
15 So I- and she was talking to me about them
and saying how nice they were,
and I said, 'Yeah well I nearly bought myself one'.
And then my Dad phoned up last night,
and he said, 'Go and get yourself one,
20 we'll give you the money'.
[...]
Didn't need asking twice.
But when I went up there
I was glad really,
cos in- where they had the finished lengths they only had the prints
25 and I was going to get one of those.
[...]
God I've wanted a plain black sundress for twenty years.
Now I've got one.

At the heart of any story is a series of narrative clauses – that is, clauses containing a verb in the simple past. This story starts with the verbs *saw* and *phoned*, but the key verb is *said: she said . . . so I said . . . and he said*. The narrative core of this story is a dialogue between the narrator and first her mother, then her father. This dialogue is framed by the opening event, the narrator seeing the dress lengths in the market, and by the final triumphant *now I've got one*. Notice that the narrator omits the key clause *and then I bought a sundress* – we are left to infer from the information given in lines 22–5 that this is what she did. The structure of this story is typical of oral narrative: clauses are organized in a temporal sequence which corresponds to the actual sequence of events. In other words, the basic structure is *a and then b and then c*. . . . At the beginning of the story, the action is suspended from time to time to provide background information. Pat tells Karen when the story began – *on Wednesday* – and where – *up there* (line 1). She introduces the key players – herself and her mother – and explains why her mother asked her to buy the dress lengths – *cos she's going to America* (line 4). Labov calls this part of a story *orientation*, by which he means those parts of the narrative which answer the questions who? where? when? Comments which *evaluate* the events described, such as *didn't need asking twice* (line 20), tell the audience how the narrator intends the events to be interpreted. (Here, Pat lets Karen know that she was very happy with her father's offer.) The last two lines operate as a sort of *coda*: they bring the story to an end and reorient us in the present.[4]

The language of oral narrative is much simpler than the conversation in which it is embedded. Most lines consist of one simple clause, e.g. *and then my Dad phoned up last night*, or of a simple clause with a chunk of direct speech as its direct object, e.g. *and he said, 'Go and get yourself one'*. Clauses are linked by simple coordinators (*and* and *so*), with an occasional subordinating conjunction such as *when* or *because* introducing a subordinate clause. The clauses are ordered in a temporal sequence which parallels the order in which the actual events occurred. Women's stories are full of detail – the names of people and places are given (e.g. *Watford, St Albans, John Lewis* (a department store)). Women also fill their stories with people's voices: in Pat's story we hear the voices of Pat herself, her mother and her father. What each of them said is presented as direct speech. It does not matter whether these people actually said what they are represented as saying; the narrator animates her characters as part of the creative act of telling a story. There is an immediacy in direct speech which would be missing if the speaker's words were merely reported. Compare *and he said, 'Go and get yourself one. We'll give you the money'* with a possible reported version *and he told me to go and get myself one, and said that he and Mum would pay for it*. Barbara Johnstone, in her analysis of the stories told by men and women in a medium-sized town in Indiana, North America, argues that that this way of presenting what happened is typical of women's but not of men's stories: 'women's stories typically create a storyworld populated with specific named people engaged in interaction, while the storyworld created in men's stories is more often silent, and the characters are more often nameless'.[5] As the other stories in this chapter will demonstrate, the representation of talk is a key component of women's stories. This is further evidence of the high value placed on talk in women's subculture.

The routines and rituals of everyday life: the topics of women's stories

What is the story 'Sundresses' about? It's really two stories in one: first, the narrator tells the story of agreeing to make her mother a couple of sundresses to take to America; secondly, she tells the story of buying one for herself after her father offers her the money for it. It's a story which affirms the importance of family ties: mothers turn to their daughters for assistance; parents treat a daughter to a dress. It is also a story which asserts the importance of everyday life – of going to the market, of making clothes, of talking to parents on the phone. This aspect of the story – its everyday quality – deserves attention. As I said in the Introduction, it is one of the strengths of ethnography that it validates everyday experience. This story and most of the others which will appear in this chapter are concerned with 'the routines, rhythms and rituals of everyday life'.[6]

By contrast, the oral narratives of male speakers described in classic accounts by sociolinguists and folklorists are about danger and violence, conflict and conquest.[7] In fact, William Labov claims that his famous 'Danger of Death' question is a surefire way of getting at oral narrative, if used sensitively. He (or one of his co-workers) would ask: 'Were you ever in a situation where you were in serious danger of being killed, where you said to yourself "This is it"?'.[8] The personal narratives told by women in conversation with their friends are not about dangerous or death-defying events. Perhaps this is another reason that women's talk has been devalued: women's stories may be seen by folklorists working in the male tradition as boring, as unexciting.[9] But it is self-evident that women friends would not continue to tell these stories to each other, year in, year out, if they found them uninteresting. We find such stories more than interesting – they fascinate us. Val told me in her interview that one of the things she values about her friend Cathy is her ability as a story-teller:

> She is the most vivid talker I've ever met . . . it's better than- than observing it, getting it through her eyes. It's her skill with the language, she's really really really entertaining, and with this massive network of friends she's got who are always up to nefarious things . . . I get every little detail, and it's like having a- a telescope into a completely alien world . . . she can relay to me all this that's come up, and who did what and which brother ran off with which aunt, and I'm there, I can see it.

Women's personal narratives differ from men's both in the everyday nature of their settings and subject matter, and in the absence of heroism. Women frequently tell stories which focus on things going wrong, rather than on achievement. But this isn't true of all stories, as 'Sundresses' illustrates. Pat's story is, in its own way, a story of triumph – after twenty years she finally owns a black sundress. Her story invites her friend to share her triumph. The sharing of successes and failures, however minor by worldly (or masculine) standards, is of central importance in women's friendships. But triumph or achievement in women's stories tends to be restricted to the domestic environment: friends will be asked to share in celebrating achievements such as buying a dress, varnishing the kitchen table, buying a bargain of a christmas tree, or to share in the achievements of those close to them – a daughter winning in an interschool quiz, a father making a rabbit hutch (all examples from stories in the conversations). The centrality of such events in women's lives is reflected in their stories of why their friends are precious to them. When describing what she liked about her friend Gianna, Mary described the following incident. The background to the story is that, because Gianna is Italian, Mary had assumed that she would be a brilliant cook. One afternoon she'd gone round to Gianna's house to find her 'sticking odd bits of pastry into a case because she'd rolled it out and it had all broken up so she thought "oh to hell with it" and she stuffed all the bits of pastry into a pastry case'. What she liked was that Gianna 'had got no sense that anybody English would worry about sticking bits of pastry into the pastry case to make a quiche bottom . . . I found that endearing'. This story is made to carry all the weight of why Mary is friends with Gianna, but significantly it revolves around a domestic incident which others might view as trivial.

Triumph

By contrast with the story about sundresses, the following story tells of one of those rare occasions when a triumph occurs in the world outside. But it is the narrator's mother who is presented as triumphing, not the narrator herself. (So, unlike the other stories quoted in this chapter, this story is a third person narrative, with *she* as the main protagonist, rather than *I*.)

'My mother and the jogger'

She took- she's got these two Dobermans who are really unruly but very sweet.
She took them for a walk on the beach one day,
and this was at the height of the Rottweiler scare,
and this jogger's running along the beach at Liverpool,
5 and Sophie, her dog that she can't control,
decided to run along after the jogger
and bit him on the bottom.
And this man was going absolutely mad,
and my mother started off by being nice to him
10 and saying, 'I'm terribly sorry, she's only a pup and she was just being playful', and so on,
and he got worse,
so the more she tried to placate him,
the more he decided he was gonna go to the police station and create a scene about it.
So she said, 'Let me have a look',

15 and she strode over and pulled his- <LAUGHS> pulled his tracksuit bottoms down,
and said, 'Don't be so bloody stupid, man, there's nothing wrong with you,
You're perfectly all right'.
At which point he was so embarrassed he just jogged away. <LAUGHTER>

This is a story of achievement: it celebrates a woman who demonstrates agency, a woman who takes control. Moreover, this woman inverts the normal order of things, since at the end of the incident it is the man who is embarrassed and the woman who is triumphant. This is one of the reasons the story is so funny: it overturns normal expectations. But the mother, who appears in other stories, is presented as an eccentric – a woman capable of doing the outrageous: she is not necessarily a role model. The laughter with which this story is greeted arises not just from amusement and admiration, but also from shock.

The next story is more typical in terms of women and triumph in the outside world. This story is firmly embedded in the world of the family, a world where women are permitted some agency. And notice that the narrator's chief emotion is one of wonder: *it was really really strange*, she comments at the end.

'Finding the family home'

Ooh I didn't tell you about my trip to Derby did I?
Last weekend with Aunty Sheila and Jessie.
It was so funny.
This was- I took my aunt, my father's sister, really our only surviving relative that we know about, to Derby,
5 because that's where she and my father grew up.
[...]
And then just on the off-chance she took me to this little village called Fairfield.
Now my father always used to talk about Fairfield Hall
where my great-grandfather lived when my dad was a child.
[...]
So we went to Fairfield,
10 and we went to look for Fairfield Hall.
[...]
And I'd pictured this great big house on top of a hill with a big gravel drive,
and it wasn't like that at all.
It was just a very very nice Georgian- very big Georgian country house with a relatively short gravel drive,
and nothing . particularly like I'd imagined.

15 And we had a look,
and thought it was very interesting,
and we were all getting back into the car,
[. . .]
and Aunty Sheila said, 'Are you not going to knock on the door then'?,
and I said 'No'.
20 'No, I don't think so'.
And then I thought- but then I thought, 'Hang on a minute – why not'?, you know.
The worst that can happen is they could be really rude and slam the door shut and yell, 'Go away'.
So I said, 'OK let's go and see'.
[. . .]
So we walked up to the front door,
25 and I- I rang the bell,
and this man answered the door who was about my aunt's age,
and I said, 'I'm sorry to bother you but are there any members of the Lamb family still living here?',
and that was the family surname then,
and he looked at me, and he said, 'Why do you ask'?,
30 and then he looked at my aunt and he said, 'Are you Tezhy'?,
and Tezhy was her nickname as a little girl.
It was short for Treasure, really obnoxious.
You can imagine.
She- she was a little girl in the thirties with those silly ((xx)) dresses and a big bow on the side of them.
35 And this happens to be Bruno
Who's like a great uncle of mine.
Bruno Skinner his name was.
And he recognized Aunty Sheila,
and he said, 'Come in, come in',
40 and he took us into the house.
[. . .]
I just thought it was really strange to sit in this room in this house that had been in the family for like a hundred years,
and to think that my dad had played there as a child,
and my grandfather and all these people- all these people who I've got photographs of,
and I've only heard about their lives through snatches of stories.
[. . .]
45 and it was really really strange.

As you'll have noticed, this story isn't narrated in a triumphant way, even though it is about finding a long-lost relative. Throughout, the orientation is far more one of 'things happened' rather than 'I did this'. This is in part because the story has two different perspectives: on one hand, this is the story of an old woman, Aunt Sheila, who is taken back to her old home and is recognized by an uncle she hasn't seen since childhood. At the same time, it is Anna's story of discovering part of her father's past and of making the connection between the house in the present and all the relatives who had lived there in the past. The narrative flips between these two perspectives, between Aunty Sheila's experience of what happened, and Anna's. There is also slippage between Anna's presentation of herself as in control (e.g. *I took her*, line 4), and places where she presents Aunty Sheila as the active character, with Anna in the role of experiencer rather than doer (e.g. *she took me*, line 6). This is why what might have been the punchline – great-uncle Bruno's words 'Are you Tezhy'? – comes across as slightly muted, as the story of the uncle recognizing Sheila/Treasure mutates into Anna's own narrative of the strangeness she felt, sitting there in that house that had only existed in her imagination before. So while this is a story of achievement, it is presented in a tone of wonder rather than of heroism, and the story is not unlike others told by women friends in that it focuses on the family. Crucially, this is a story about identity: Anna tells this story to her friends as part of her serial story about herself, this one particularly offering some answers to the question 'Who am I?'.

Disaster

More typically, women's stories revolve around times when things go wrong. The following is an extract from a long story about being struck down with acute cystitis on a flight to Rome.[10] The narrator realized on the morning of the flight that she wasn't feeling well and suspected it was cystitis. She got her colleague Shirley to get her something from the chemists, which she took at the airport. She also drank lots of water, because she remembered that this was important if you had cystitis. (The full version of 'Cystitis' is 208 lines in length; it appears as appendix A at the end of the book. Stories told by women friends vary enormously in length, from two or three lines to over a hundred. They are certainly not 'overwhelmingly of a throw-away variety, with the teller quickly recounting some incident which took place . . . in order to make a point relevant to the embedding conversation', as has been claimed in some accounts of conversational story-telling.)[11]

'Cystitis'

So while we were waiting at the airport- our plane was delayed- I actually drank three litres of water.
We were there for like an hour and a quarter
and I just kept drinking and drinking and drinking.
We got on the plane and of course I couldn't stop going to the loo.
5 Then it got worse and worse and worse.
I spent the whole plane journey to Ro- to Rome in the toilet.
Three quarters of the way through the plane journey I- I literally couldn't leave I was in such pain
Shirley came banging on the door.
'Are you all right? Are you all right?'
10 She was trying to get the air hostess to come and see to me
and Alitalia I will never fly again
they were just dreadful.
And she kept going up to these air hostesses saying, 'My friend's in the toilet and she's ill.
Will you do something',
15 and they wouldn't do anything.
And finally we were coming in to land,
and by this time I was passing blood,
and I was really terrified out of my mind,
cos I'm not a sickly person and I never get ill,
20 and if something like that happens it just freaks me out.
I was- I didn't know what to do.
So I had to go and sit down because we were about to land,
but it was like every two minutes I thought, 'I've got to go to the- the toilet, I've got to',
25 so I was hysterical practically.
And finally we sat down coming in to land,
and there's a girl sitting on the other side of the gangway to me,
quite a pretty Italian girl,
and this air steward is bending down talking to her,
30 a male air steward chatting her up basically,
and he looks across at me.
He says, 'What's the matter with you? are you not very well?',
and I thought, 'Finally getting through here',
and I said, 'Yes I'm not'.
35 And he said- and he said, 'What's wrong?',
and he can hardly speak a word of English,
so I've got to try and explain,
and all the passengers are listening.
So I told the girl,
40 and she translated for him,
and he said to me, 'Would you like to see a doctor when we land?

I can arrange for that if you want'.
So I said, 'Well OK,
but I don't want to be taken away in an ambulance or anything like that,
45 but yes, if you can arrange and radio ahead and and arrange for me to see
  a doctor, that'd be great'.
He said, 'Yes no problem'.
He said, 'There won't be an ambulance or anything'.
Three minutes later we land,
50 and there are men running down the gangway towards me.
They- they bodily lift me out of my seat,
and there's the blue flashing light outside the plane.
I couldn't believe it.

This story is in the great tradition of funny stories women tell each other where appalling things happen to them – the humour lies precisely in presenting oneself as at the mercy of incomprehensible forces. In Anna's case, the incomprehensible forces are, first, her own body (a potent source of humour for women) and secondly the unhelpful airline staff. Everything that happens in the story happens *to* her, and is outside her control. First, her illness forces her to spend most of the flight in the aeroplane toilet. This kind of excruciatingly humiliating and embarrassing detail is very much part of women's disaster narratives. Secondly, the air steward's poor English and general tactlessness mean that Anna is put in a position where she has to describe her symptoms knowing all the surrounding passengers can hear her. (This aspect of the story gains its humour from our culturally given understanding that you don't share the details of your malfunctioning urinary tract with strangers.) Finally, despite her having been given assurances to the contrary, she is whisked off in an ambulance, thus losing both her luggage and her companion. By the time Anna reached line 49 in the extract above, her two friends were helpless with laughter. Anna's friends' laughter is not callous: it arises from a heartfelt recognition of the world Anna describes, where women feel they are at the mercy of alien forces. Such stories underline the message that heroism is rarely an option for women: acting alone usually ends in disaster. (Anna's enforced separation from Shirley is portrayed as a significant factor in the continuing nightmare.)

Frightening experiences

Research which looks at gender differences in personal narrative has found that women's stories are more often about experiences that are embarrassing or frightening than about personal skill or success.[12] This is precisely what I have found in the stories told by women in the course of conversation with friends. The cystitis story involves both embarrassment and fear, and so is particularly powerful. The following is a perhaps more typical story about a frightening experience, where a woman describes her walk home from the pub (the Talbot) at night. The group of friends have been talking about the (recent at the time) Yorkshire Ripper murder case, and about women's fear of being alone, especially at night.

'Walking home alone'

I went to th- for a drink the other night on my own,
and met Janet and Paul.
And . when I was coming out through the Talbot to that back way,
a bloke in the car park sh- shouted across to me,
5 and he said, 'Have you got a car?',
and I said, 'Er what?',
and he said- he said, 'Have you got- Can you give me a lift up there?',
and I said, 'I haven't got a car'.
And I nipped up that back lane up the- the bo- up Talbot Road,
10 and all the way up I thought he was going to come,
cos he went the other way up- up Rose Mount,
and I thought he was going to cut along . whatever that road's called.
And . my heart was in my mouth all the way up Poplar Road.
And what I did was I walked right next to the houses.
15 Normally I ra- walk on the other side of the road,
but I thought, 'If e- anyone comes near I'm just leap in this house
and batter on one of these doors,
"Let me in!"'. <LAUGHTER>
But at the very top of the road there was a little kind of gap with-
20 where you have to cross over,
and I thought I'd had it. <LAUGHTER>

What is interesting about this story is that nothing happens – Meg, the narrator, gets home safely. But the point of the story (and it comes after another story told by her friend Sally on the same theme) is that the world outside is dangerous, especially at night, and that being alone is frightening. Even though nothing happens, you still have to negotiate all kinds of imagined dangers as you walk home. Notice again how direct speech is used to bring this story to life. The exchange in the car park introduces us to the unknown man, who makes a request that is experienced as threatening by the narrator. Her walk home is described both with detailed reference to place names (*Talbot*

Road, Rose Mount, Poplar Road) and with her dramatization of her thoughts and the words she imagines she would shout if anyone came near her ('*Let me in!*'). It's noticeable that her friends laugh at the two points where she expresses her inner thoughts. Laughter, as we'll see later, is a sign not of amusement but of recognition. Through their laughter, Meg's friends demonstrate a shared worldview: they, too, have experienced the feelings she describes.

Embarrassment

Embarrassment, like fear, is a common theme of women's stories. It is particularly common in the stories girls tell each other. This isn't surprising, given the tensions and dilemmas associated with that difficult rite of passage in British culture known as adolescence. The girls' conversations are full of laughter: much of this arises from their having fun, but some of it arises in the context of embarrassing stories which they tell each other. The laughter functions as a way of releasing tension. Becky, in the first of these stories, glosses the episode she describes as 'funny'. It is funny in that, both at the time it happened and when it is recounted as a story, the event reduces all the girls involved to hysterical laughter. But it is clearly also a story about embarrassment.

This first story is told by Becky with Claire's help (Claire's contributions are in italics) about an incident involving Becky, Claire and the school librarian which took place in school on a day when Hannah wasn't there:

'Knicker stains'

It was so funny when you weren't there one day.
Well, we were in the library, right?
3 and we were in that corner where all the erm the picture books are.
Claire's putting on some lipstick,
I was putting on some lipstick,
6 and and and they said, 'oh what are you doing in that corner?',
and she said we were smoking ((xx)),
no I said we were checking for people who were smoking,
9 and he said- and he said, 'Are you sure you weren't having a quick smoke yourself?',
and I said, 'Yes, I must admit it',
and I meant to say, 'Look at my nicotine stains',

12 and I held up my fingers like that,
and I said, 'Look at my knicker stains'.
((xx)) we were rolling about the tables.
It was so funny.

Notice how the evaluative clause 'it was so funny' frames this story, appearing both as a prelude to the story and as the final line. The heart of the story consists of the narrative clauses in lines 6, 7, 9, 10, 12 and 13. Each of these contains a simple past tense verb (*said, held up*) and they are temporally ordered (we understand *and* to mean *and then . . .*). The telling of this story is followed by chaotic talk and laughter, with Jessica saying that she had told the story to her mother, and her mother too had been reduced to hysterics, but had added a comment: 'she said that we weren't very good librarian monitors or whatever we were meant to be'. This functions as a rather delayed coda, and signals the end of the topic.

This story is about a funny (or embarrassing) slip of the tongue, and depends for its impact on Becky telling us what she *didn't* say, *Look at my nicotine stains*. The punchline, the words she actually said, *Look at my knicker stains,* only has such an impact because we know what she was trying to say. Overtly, the friends treat this as yet another ridiculous story which they can laugh over – it fits the tradition I mentioned earlier of a female protagonist finding herself in an impossible or humiliating or embarrassing position. But I don't think it's reading too much into this brief story to argue that it is also revealing about what is going on under the laughing surface of their talk. The girls are at a watershed in their lives, moving willingly or unwillingly from girlhood to womanhood. When they were younger, words like *knickers* were part of everyday playground currency, like *bum,* superficial coinage, always good for a laugh. Now as social pressures force them to take notice of their bodies, as their bodies become the object of the adult male gaze, words like *knickers* are becoming fraught with sexual overtones and are losing their innocence. *Knicker stains* is an extraordinary slip of the tongue in the way it reveals the girls' anxiety about their changing bodies, and about their fears of loss of control in all aspects of their lives. The impact of the slip of the tongue is also heightened by its co-occurrence with the direct command *look at*. It is inappropriate for less powerful speakers, like Becky, to issue commands to more powerful speakers, like the male librarian here. Becky's intended command *look at my nicotine stains* is only acceptable because it reinforces her powerless position, both as a pupil and as someone who has broken a school rule: by holding up her nicotine-stained fingers, she intended to incriminate herself. These words were meant to be part of a confession – she meant to admit her guilt and thus to acknowledge the librarian's power to punish her as he saw fit. But by transposing the object of this command from *nicotine stains* to *knicker stains*, Becky finds herself in the totally unacceptable position of giving a direct command to a high status male, a command which tells him to do something with strong sexual overtones. It is not surprising that the girls seek refuge in laughter. It is hard to imagine any other escape route from this highly charged situation.

The next story, told by Claire two years later, when the girls are fifteen, narrates an experience which is explicitly described as 'embarrassing', when Claire visited a friend's house and saw her friend's brother naked.

'I just saw everything'

Did I tell you about-
remember I t- I was- I went into the Stefanides' house,
and you know they've got a mirror up as you go into that- in the room up the stairs,
and I went in,
5 and I looked in the mirror,
and Mem was standing there naked,
[. . .]
and and Gina was cutting his toenails, <SCREAMING>
and I walked in,
and he was- and he had his leg up on the- on the sofa,
10 and I just saw everything. <LAUGHS>
[. . .]
I ran out.
I was- well I was really embarrassed.

Claire in fact produces the end of this story (lines 11 and 12) after some taunting from the others, in particular from Hannah, who says, 'You loved it'. So we see here girls of fifteen demonstrating an awareness of a range of possible reactions, from *I loved it* to *I was really embarrassed*, and colluding with each other in arriving at the more appropriate, socially sanctioned one. The subject of this anecdote – a female seeing a naked male – raises a lot of questions. Representations of the naked female body are commonplace in our culture. Women's bodies are the subject of drawings and paintings, past and present; they also appear routinely in advertisements for products as disparate as motor cars and shampoo. This is without mentioning the many pornographic and semi-pornographic publications which explicitly trade in representations of naked women. Claire's story reminds us that the reverse situation – where the naked male body is exposed to the female gaze – has a very different meaning. It is men who have the power of the gaze, while it is women's role to be the object of the gaze. There is a profound asymmetry here, which helps to explain why a woman or girl seeing a naked man (or boy) is so transgressive: Claire feels she needs to deny the power of the gaze – *I ran out, I was really embarrassed.* The detail of her story, however, particularly the line *I just saw everything,* suggests that this was only one of her responses, and that adolescent curiosity about the male body was another powerful force at work.

It is surely significant that in a relatively small corpus like this one, I have found a parallel story told by an adult woman to her friend. Here the accompanying emotions are more complex, though embarrassment is one of them. Karen tells this story to Pat (Pat's words are in italics).

'Getting undressed'

It was a couple of weeks ago,
I forget now which day it was,
3 but I was sitting in my living room
and without meaning to I was looking out into the garden
and I was looking straight into Lever's house,
6 that's the one up in Bentley Close on the corner,
and I saw him get undressed in his living room.
There's no reason why you shouldn't get undressed in your living room if you want to, (*yeah*)
9 and I thought, 'My God' (*yeah*)
'if I can see him',
he can see you,
and I don't always just get undressed in the living room. <LAUGH>

Again we have a narrative in which the central 'happening' is that a female sees an unclothed male. Notice how Karen, like Claire, disclaims any agency: she says she was looking into the garden *without meaning to.* In other words, she denies having the power of the gaze. What's more complex here is that Karen reveals that her chief anxiety arises not from her (unintentional) infringement of Lever's right to privacy, but from her anxiety about her own privacy. She infers that if she can see him, he can see her. This switches the focus directly onto women as the object of the male gaze. Karen wants to avoid this position. Karen's story is embedded in conversation about some trees she has just planted in her garden. When she tells Pat that she's planted nineteen trees, Pat asks jokingly 'What are you doing? growing your own forest?'. Karen's story functions as an explanation: the trees are to act as a screen, to prevent her from being overlooked. While Karen takes the appropriately modest position of desiring privacy, her comment in line 11, *and I don't always just get undressed in the living room*, hints at more sophisticated (sexual?) activities and recasts her desire for privacy in a more adult, less fearful frame.

Collaboration in story-telling

I stated near the beginning of this chapter that telling a story gives a speaker special rights to the floor. This is true, but women friends prefer a way of talking which emphasizes the collaborative and which is antipathetic to monologue. So although storytellers are granted a more privileged floor, this often lasts only for a brief period at the beginning of a story. Christine Cheepen, who observed this phenomenon in conversations she'd recorded, calls this more collaborative form of story-telling 'dialogic': 'This dialogic form of story telling means that the distinction between "story-teller" and "audience" becomes blurred, because what is happening in such a situation is that the speakers are collaborating in a story-telling'.[13] All the stories quoted in this chapter have been edited, and the editing has in large part consisted of suppressing the other voices, to make the stories more 'story-like'. I don't think this has falsified my analysis, but I now want to acknowledge the collaborative nature of women friends' talk, and from now on stories will include the other voices.

To show you how women friends collaborate in story-telling, here's a longer and fuller version of the last story, 'Getting undressed'. (Pat's words are again in italics.) (Another collaboratively-developed story, 'Obedient husband', which will be discussed in the next chapter, is given in full in appendix B.)

'Getting undressed'

cos you know how we said we were overlooked
th- that day we sat in there, (*yeah*)
3 I thought, 'Damn this',
and then the other day I was sel-
cos that was the only thing wrong with it, wasn't it?

6 yeah well I- it was a couple of weeks ago,
I forget now which day it was,
but I was sitting in my living room
9 and without meaning to I was looking out into the garden
and I was looking straight into Lever's house,
that's the one up in Bentley Close on the corner,
12 and I saw him get undressed in his living room.
There's no reason why you shouldn't get undressed in your living room if you want to *(yeah)*
and I thought, 'My God' *(yeah)*
15 'if I can see him'
he can see you
and I don't always just get undressed in the living room. <LAUGH>
18 You know I mean OK I'm sure he's not *peeping* peeping or anything,
but he- but it just-
you accidentally saw him
21 that's right
oh I don't blame you
I think it needs screening trees round it.

While Pat allows Karen to tell the narrative core of this story (lines 6–12) without intervention, once the key narrative clause has been reached – *and I saw him get undressed in his living room* – she joins in. From line 13 onwards the story is jointly constructed by the two friends, to the extent that Pat provides the verb *peeping* to complete Karen's *I'm sure he's not . . .*, and it is Pat who recapitulates the main point: *you accidentally saw him,* and who provides a coda: *oh I don't blame you I think it needs screening trees round it*. This coda is very interesting: Pat now realizes that Karen's reason for planting the trees is serious. Her earlier joking remark about growing a forest is no longer appropriate – she wants to emphasize that she sympathizes with what Karen is doing, and that she sees her action as a sensible step to protect her privacy. The trees are no longer referred to as *a forest* but as *screening trees.*

In the stories they tell, women present an everyday world where their mundane activities are celebrated and where their problems and anxieties can be shared. They do not present themselves as heroes, and they are more often done to than doing. Barbara Johnstone in research I've already mentioned argues that men's and women's stories depict strikingly different storyworlds. She writes: 'women's stories tend to be "other oriented", underplaying the protagonists' personal roles and emphasizing social community and mutual dependence, while men's stories are "self-oriented", serving to build up their tellers' own personal images'.[14] It is precisely those stories where women are on their own that are the most bleak: Meg's only hope as she walks home up the dark street ('Walking home alone') is that people living in the houses there will respond to her cries for help; Anna ('Cystitis') presents herself as unable to get the help she needs and cut off from her friend. Apart from the mother in 'My mother and the jogger', in those stories where women do take action – 'Sundresses', 'Finding the family home', 'Getting undressed' – the action is not foregrounded. Moreover, what happens is presented as *reactive* rather than *proactive*. In other words, in all three of these stories the protagonist takes action in response to some other action. Pat buys herself a sundress after her father tells her to; Anna visits the old family home under pressure from Aunty Sheila; Karen plants trees in her garden after realizing she could be overlooked. Even in 'My mother and the jogger', the mother's action is reactive: she only pulls the jogger's tracksuit bottoms down to prove that he is unhurt after he refuses to accept her apologies for her dog.

Sharing pleasant experiences

One of the primary aims of women's story-telling is to share experience, and women use stories to share pleasant experiences with each other, as well as experiences that are more painful. I want to end this chapter with a story told by Mary which is a classic example of the way women relish the detail of everyday life, and which shows how women friends construct stories together. The basic story is very simple and can be summarized in one sentence: 'I got stopped by a train in the docks yesterday'. The narrative core of the story consists of five lines:

I was stopped by a train.
Have you ever been stopped by a train in the docks?
I got stopped by a train in the docks yesterday.
I've never been stopped by a train before.
It was lovely.

The first four lines are variations on the opening statement *I was stopped by a train*. This is a kind of summary or *abstract*[15] of the story and tells the listeners what is to come. The second line turns the statement into a question, a question which adds the important information that the event narrated took place *in the docks*. This question leads into her repeated statement *I got stopped by a train in the docks yesterday*, in which she orients the story in time by adding the adverb *yesterday*. Her incredulous tone is explained in the fourth line, where she tells her friends that this had never happened to her before. Every one of these four lines uses the same verb: *was/got stopped* followed by the same phrase *by a train*. Three of the four lines have *I* as their (grammatical) subject. This kind of repetition occurs frequently in women's story-telling, as in their talk generally. (Repetition will be discussed in detail in chapter 9.) The fifth line breaks the pattern. This line – *it was lovely* – gives the narrator's viewpoint and thus gives meaning to the previous four lines. The audience now knows how to evaluate the story.

When Mary asks if any of her friends has ever been stopped by a train in the docks, Sally says *yes* (as Mary continues her story). As Mary elaborates on her basic story, Sally joins in, and the two friends construct the rest of the story together, with others present adding minimal responses (*mhm* or *yeah*). The full extract is given below. (Sally's words are in italics; I have omitted the one or two instances of *mhm* and *yes* contributed by other participants.)

Grain trains in the docks

1 I was- I was- I was stopped by a train.
2 have you ever been stopped by a train in the docks?
3 [I got stopped by a train in the docks yesterday.
[*yes oh yes frequently*
4 [I've never been stopped [by a train before.
[*yes* [*yeah*
5 it was lovely
6 cos it was- it was going across um Duke- Duke Street bridge
7 the [middle one
[*that's right yeah*
8 *and the guy just gets off*
9 [that's right [and walks
[*((xx))* [*and ((sort of stops))*
10 and there's this bloke walking in front of the train
yeah *that's-*
11 and you can hear this [clanging noise
[*yeah*
12 [cos one of the chains is clanging on-
[*yeah*
13 and it sounds very romantic
yes
14 like it's like the far- the West
15 you know this clanking noise
16 and all it is- is- is this bit of metal that's clanking along the ground
17 but I [didn't realise
[*oh it's LOVEl-*

18 but I've seen all these train tracks
19 [it's the grain trains [yes
it's the grain trains [*I think* [*to go to the-* *yes*
20 it was the bulk carriers
yes *yes*

Mary's opening narrative tells of a single experience and uses the past tense. Sally, who has seen trains in the docks 'frequently', continues the story with the line *and the guy just gets off* which Mary adds to: *and walks*. The story ceases to be about one single event in the past, and moves into a timeless present, usings verbs like *gets off* and *walks* and *sounds*. In line 19 the two narrators sum up the experience they are describing: *it's the grain trains*, while in the last line Mary shifts her audience back into the specific past of her experience yesterday: *it was the bulk carriers*. This last line marks the end of the story both because it reorients the story in the past, switching from *is* to *was*, to match the opening lines, and because at the same time it paraphrases the previous line, thus tying the (more general) middle section to the rest of the narrative.

Conclusion

We've looked at nine stories in this chapter, a small fraction of the stories told in the conversations in my corpus. For women friends, story-telling serves several functions. At the level of conversational organization, stories are often used to introduce new topics (as we saw in the last chapter). But more importantly, story-telling functions to bind these women friends together, through creating a shared world. 'In an important sense, a community of speakers is a group of people who share previous stories . . . and who jointly tell new stories'.[16] Women friends constitute such a community, and through our story-telling we create and re-create our identities and experiment with possible selves, in a context of mutuality and trust. Conversational narrative is our chief means of constructing the fictions that are our lives and of getting others to collude in them. But story-telling also allows us to 'order or re-order the givens of experience', and while stories undoubtedly reinforce the dominant culture, they also provide 'a relatively safe or innocuous place in which the reigning assumptions of a given culture can be criticized'.[17] As we have seen in this chapter, the stories that women friends tell each other reinforce our sense of ourselves as objects, as powerless, as reactors rather than actors. But they also hint at alternative ways of being, of women as doers, observers as well as observed, who see ourselves as powerfully allied through our shared knowledge and our shared experience.

6

'The feminine shape . . . is more melding in together': The organization of friendly talk

Bea summed up her view of the way women talk with the words, 'the feminine shape . . . is more melding in together'. 'Meld' is defined as 'to merge, blend; to combine, incorporate' (*Shorter Oxford English Dictionary*), and is thought to be a twentieth-century American formation from the words 'melt' and 'weld'. Bea also used the word 'blesh' in her description of how women talk. This word too is a combination of two other words – 'blend' and 'mesh'. The idea of merging or blending seems to be central to both 'blesh' and 'meld' (and the two words are themselves examples of bleshing and melding). Bea's claim is that some kind of merging or blending is a key feature – or even *the* key feature – of women's style of talking.

This is an important claim, and one which can, I think, be substantiated by the conversations I've recorded. Overall, what is most noticeable about the talk of women friends is that the construction of talk is a joint effort: all participants share in the construction of talk in the strong sense that *they don't function as individual speakers*. In other words, the group takes priority over the individual and the women's voices combine (or meld) to construct a shared text. A good metaphor for talking about this is a musical one: the talk of women friends is a kind of jam session. The dictionary definition of *jam session* is 'A meeting of musicians for the spontaneous and improvisatory performance of music, especially jazz, usually for their own enjoyment' (*Penguin Macquarie Dictionary*). The key words here – *spontaneous, improvisatory* and *enjoyment* – are all central to any account of what is going on in the talk of women friends. In fact, we could adapt the definition to read: '*Jam session* – (of speech) A meeting of women friends for the spontaneous and improvisatory performance of talk, for their own enjoyment'.

The previous chapter focused on solo performances, where women used narrative to tell each other about their own experience or the experience of others. All jam sessions – whether of the musical or the conversational kind – include solo as well as ensemble or all-together sections. But the heart of good conversation for women friends is group talk, where speakers are typically 'melding in together'. I will start to pin down exactly what melding entails in linguistic terms by looking at two phenomena characteristic of women friends' talk: jointly constructed utterances and overlapping speech.

Jointly constructed utterances

In the conversations I've recorded, two or three or more women friends will work together so that their voices combine to produce a single utterance or utterances.[1] The previous chapters have already provided many examples, from both the interviews and the conversations, of the ways in which women friends speak as a single voice. I shall draw on these as well as on the whole range of conversational material to illustrate my argument.

To begin with, let's look at some very simple examples where the last word of an utterance is provided by a different speaker.

1 *[Sue and Liz discuss where they like to talk]*

SUE: I mean in someone's house it's easier to talk than=
LIZ: =out/

---

2 *[Karen worries that she is overlooked by a neighbour]*

KAREN: I mean OK I'm sure he's not=
PAT: =peeping/

---

3 *[Helen and Jen speculate on the effect an individual's absence could have on a group]*

HELEN: they won't be so=
JEN: =homogeneous/

---

4 *[Discussion of students fooling around in class]*

ANNA: the lecturer doesn't want to say anything though

LIZ: =adults/
ANNA: because they're supposed to be=

These four utterances are all constructed by *two* speakers. They are remarkable because they are identical to utterances produced by a single speaker. In other words, in each case two speakers combine with each other, blend their voices, to produce a single utterance. This will be easier to see if I present these four examples as single utterances, using the symbol // to indicate a switch of speaker:

1 I mean in someone's house it's easier to talk than//out
2 I mean OK I'm sure he's not//peeping
3 they won't be so//homogeneous
4 because they're supposed to be//adults

This level of collaboration can only be achieved when speakers pay extremely close attention to each other, at all linguistic levels. For example, in the three examples above, the woman who contributes the last word has had to follow the *meaning* of what the other speaker is saying. She has also had to follow the *grammatical structure* of what is being said. Often she also matches the *intonation pattern* and *rhythmic quality* of the other speaker.

Jointly constructed utterances may involve more than just the final word of an utterance, as examples 5–8 illustrate.

5 *[Discussion of open evening at local school]*

JEN: they said they kept bumping into all sorts of people=
HELEN: =that they knew/

---

6 [Discussion of Christmas play at local primary school]

KAREN: once those cameras start flashing particularly with

KAREN: the infants=
PAT: =it puts them off/

---

7 [Discussion of victims and blame]

MEG: women who are victims of rape are often thought to um

MEG: somehow .
MARY: oh have caused the rape/

---

8 [Discussion of child abuse]

BEA: I mean in order to accept that idea you're

BEA: having to .
MARY: mhm/ completely review your view of your husband/

In all these examples, two women jointly construct an utterance, negotiating quite complex grammatical constructions. For example, Helen adds a relative clause *that they knew* to the noun *people*; Pat completes the utterance Karen began by replacing *once those cameras start flashing* with the (anaphoric) pronoun *it* and then adding a predicate *puts them [the infants] off*. In example 7, Mary has to deal with difficult tense choices: she produces *have caused the rape* rather than *cause the rape*, as someone who is a victim must already have been abused or attacked. Example 8 is perhaps most notable for the level of understanding it demonstrates in terms of the meaning of what is being talked about: Bea and Mary here operate very much as one speaker and express the group voice on the position of the mother of an abused child. All these examples demonstrate the way speakers monitor what each other is saying to the extent that the construction of utterances can be shared. Women friends exploit this ability to talk in a more melded way than is typical of other, less intimate, groups of speakers.[2]

Joint construction involving simultaneous speech

A variant on the pattern occurs where two speakers produce part of an utterance together, rather than one speaker beginning and another completing the utterance. Examples 9–11 below are the most simple kind, where two speakers both say the last words of an utterance.

9 *[Anna describes her friend Shirley's reaction to her cystitis on their trip to Rome]*

ANNA:	if she'd been in my position I think I'd have been

ANNA:	a bit m[ore sympathetic/
SUE:	[more sympathetic/

10 *[Pat tells Karen about her neighbour's attack of acute indigestion]*

PAT:	he and his wife obviously thought he'd had a [heart attack/
KAREN:	[heart attack/

11 *[Talking about the school play]*

PAT:	and every line they played for a laugh . [got a laugh/
KAREN:	[got a laugh/

Saying the same words at the same time may involve more than just the last words of an utterance, as the next example shows. This example comes from a conversation between two women, me and Helen, when we're discussing a local political crisis which we both know about. (Jane Bull was the leader of the local council at the time of this conversation.)

12 *[Helen and Jen discuss local political crisis]*

JEN:	and apparently [Jane Bull ((xx))
HELEN:	[well in fact Jane Bull's very threatened/

JEN:		[she had this grammar school
HELEN:	because did you- did you hear	[she had this grammar school-

JEN:	meeting/
HELEN:	yes/

In this example, I begin to talk about Jane Bull, and Helen picks up this theme to produce *Jane Bull's very threatened*. When Helen begins to say why Jane Bull is threatened, I join in and we say together *she had this grammar school*, an utterance which I complete with the word *meeting*. This is a good example of the extent to which utterances can be jointly constructed. This chunk of talk cannot be said to belong to either of us: we are drawing on our shared knowledge of local events to produce talk collaboratively. In this example, it is also quite clear that the main goal of talk is not information exchange since we both know what the facts are and are aware that each other knows.

Incomplete utterances

If the potential exists for speakers to share in the construction of utterances, then we would predict that from time to time utterances will be incomplete, since speakers know that others can anticipate what is to come, and others may choose *not* to complete the utterance verbally, but instead may choose to indicate that they understand by nodding or smiling or saying *yes*. This is precisely what we find in conversations between women friends. In the first example here, Meg is summing up the discussion about taking pleasure in others' downfall:

13 [Schadenfreude]

MEG: funny how . you can be so mean about- it's obviously jealousy isn't it?

Meg doesn't specify exactly what (or who) people are so mean about but leaves it for her friends to fill in for themselves. Her subsequent tag question – *it's obviously jealousy isn't it?* – continues as if the preceding text were perfectly coherent; that is, it assumes her friends have processed the preceding statement successfully. (Note that this tag has falling, not rising, intonation: Meg does not expect a reply. Tags like this will be discussed in chapter 8.)

In the next example, Mary doesn't complete her utterance in the context of a discussion about whether there is ever an occasion when you would not attend a funeral.

14 [Funeral discussion]

MARY: but if there's no spouse I mean/ and there's very few relatives left/

MARY: it doesn't really seem much of a- <LAUGHING>
SALLY: mhm/
JEN: it does seem-
MEG: but it does-

MARY: =mhm/
JEN: =mhm=

What's extraordinary about this example is that other speakers' comments repeat this lack of completeness: Mary is heard as saying something like 'it (there) doesn't seem much of a point', while my paraphrasing acceptance *it does seem-* presumably means something like 'it does seem pointless'. Meg repeats this, leaving out *seem,* and Mary and I both add minimal responses. The important thing is that all of us clearly understood what was being said, even though not all the words were actually uttered.

Incomplete utterances were also a feature of the interviews. Example 15 comes from the interview with Hannah and Becky.

15 [Hannah and Becky talk about their friendship]

BECKY: I think we'll probably be like that for the rest of our lives/
HANNAH:

BECKY: [like . we might not see each other for YEARS/ and then-
HANNAH: [yeah I mean you could- and

BECKY: yeah/ I think it'll be really nice/
HANNAH: then just sort of-

Here, Becky's utterance *we might not see each other for years and then-* is unfinished. Hannah collaboratively adds *and then just sort of-*, an addition which still leaves the utterance incomplete. At this point, Becky says *yeah, I think it'll be really nice,* demonstrating agreement with their (non-explicit) position.

In the next example, Pat and Karen continue the discussion of privacy and screening trees which was begun in the story 'Getting Undressed' (see previous chapter). Karen mentions that she had recently driven past her old house, where she had planted trees several years earlier.

16 [Screening trees]

KAREN: we drove down Kingshill the other day / and there's lovely conifers

KAREN: up- up in the front/ they've all grown/ [. . .]

PAT: yeah I think it's worthwhile doing that/ [i.e. planting trees]

KAREN: that's right/
PAT: because as you say your neighbour has got um privacy/

KAREN: yeah well
PAT: because of the trees you planted/ how annoying/

KAREN: that doesn't matter does it? . after all they did pay forty-
PAT:

KAREN: five thousand seven hundred and fifty pounds for the house/ so I
PAT:

KAREN: should think my twelve quids worth of trees- <LAUGHS>
PAT: <LAUGHS>

Here, Karen's utterance *so I should think my twelve quids worth of trees* is left incomplete. The laughter jointly produced by Karen and Pat immediately after this part-utterance signals their shared understanding of her wry comment. It is an interesting side effect of our capacity to anticipate the conclusion of utterances that we have the option *not* to complete an utterance.

Sharing in the search for the right word

Nearly all the examples I've given so far have involved only two speakers (though one or two examples have shown other speakers playing a more minor role). I want to look here at three examples which involve more than two speakers. Each of these examples of jointly constructed talk arises in conversation where speakers are struggling to find the right words. In the first example, Kate (aged 16) has just asserted that gay pop groups should be more popular:

17 [Discussion of gay pop groups]

Kate:	I'm gonna go round going 'Yes support gay pop groups cos I don't

---

Kate:	approve of this . raci-' I mean wha- what's that thing where [. . .]

Kate:	if you're g- an- anti-gay? what's [that ((mean))? [gayist/
Gwen:	[gay/ [anti-gay/

Kate:	[you're gayist/ =prejudiced/
Sarah:	[you're ((xx))- you're prejudiced=
Emily:	=prejudiced= yeah/

Here, after several false starts, the group settles on the word *prejudiced* offered by Sarah, with three of the four friends saying the word in turn. This pattern of repetition (in this case, of an individual word) is another important feature of women's talk and will be the subject of chapter 9.

In the next example, Sue, Liz and Anna are eating and begin to discuss salads of different kinds. Liz and Anna help Sue to find the word she wants:

18 [Food talk]

Sue:	you know at Tony's dad's they do this lovely salad with

Sue:	parmesan and . you know that traditional Italian- what's

---

Sue:	the other cheese? parmesan- no/<TUTS> soft
Anna:	Dolcellata?

Sue:	s- no the squidgy stuff that they put on pizzas/
Anna:	Gorgonzola?

Sue:	=Mozarella/ Mozarella and- and
Anna:	Mozarell [a/ yeah/
Liz:	[Mozarella= mhm/

Sue:	it's just the best thing ever/

All three speakers contribute to this chunk of talk, and once the right word has been found their minimal responses (*yeah* and *mhm*) demonstrate that they all take responsibility for what is being said. In this example, the three friends remember the word *mozarella*. In example 19, below, Meg, Bea and I fail to remember the word *Schadenfreude* (just as Kate, Sarah and Emily failed to recall the word *homophobic* in example 17 above), but we work together to refine our sense of the concept we are discussing.

19 [Topic: Pleasure in others' failures]

MEG: Tom [. . .] says there's a German word to describe that/ [. . .] one of

---

MEG: those complicated German nouns which explains the fact that you

---

MEG: feel . a perverse displeasure in other people's successes/ [. . .]

JEN: oh it's the other way round ((I feel))/ it's sort of pleasure

---

JEN: [in other people-
BEA: [a perverse pleasure in= =yeah=
MEG: =in their downfall= =yeah/

These three women friends work together to form the utterance *it's sort of pleasure//a perverse pleasure//in their downfall*. The fact that two of the three add a minimal response – *yeah* – at the end of this co-constructed utterance provides evidence that they are happy both with what is said and with the way it has been said. (The appearance of acceptance tokens such as *yeah* at these points is a consistent feature of the texts, and one which will be discussed in greater detail later in the chapter.)

Finally, in this section, I want to look at an example involving five speakers, who work together to find the right words in a more extended way. This extract comes from the topic 'Apes and language', which was triggered by my asking whether anyone had seen a TV documentary on this subject the previous evening. The responsibility for singing the main tune is passed from Mary to me, from me to Bea, and from Bea to Meg. Between us we construct an account of what apes are capable of linguistically.

20 *[Topic: Apes and language]*

	MARY:	I mean they can shuffle words around and [make a different meaning/
	BEA:	[draw up a conclusion
2	BEA:	((xxx))-
	JEN:	they put two words together to form a compound/
	MEG:	yeah/
	MARY:	[that's right=
	BEA:	=mhm/
	JEN:	to mean something that they didn't have a [lexical item for/
4	MARY:	[that's right/ for [a brazilnut/
	BEA:	a stoneberry for a- [a brazilnut/
	JEN:	[which is-
	HELEN:	right/
	JEN:	[well th- they can't POSSib[ly <HIGH>
	MEG:	yes/ and [lotionberry for [vomit/
	HELEN:	mhm/ [gosh/ [((was it?))
6	BEA:	=lotionberry for what?
	JEN:	be imitating their trainers=
	MEG:	yeah/ she'd- sh-
	MEG:	she'd- she'd sicked up one morning on yoghurt which would have
8	MEG:	had raisins in it/ and er she said that ((it looked))- they
	MEG:	asked her what er- what the vomit was/ and she said
10	MEG:	lotionberry/
	BEA:	ah/
	HELEN:	amazing/

Notice how carefully we time our supporting utterances to fit what each other is saying, indicating our continued involvement in the talk and our acceptance of what is being said. In particular, staves 1–5 involve four speakers cooperating in expressing a complex idea: Mary begins with the statement *I mean they can shuffle words around and make a different meaning;* I paraphrase this with the words *they put two words together to form a compound to mean something that they didn't have a lexical item for;* Bea gives the example *a stoneberry for a brazilnut,* an utterance which is co-completed by Mary, and Meg then adds a second example *and lotionberry for vomit*. All these examples show how women friends collaborate in the construction of text.

Overlapping speech

Overlapping speech is an important feature of women friends' talk, and one that immediately strikes anyone who listens to a recording of women friends' conversation. Women friends combine as speakers so that two or more voices may contribute to talk *at the same time*. This kind of overlapping speech is not seen as competitive, as a way of grabbing a turn, because the various contributions to talk are on the same theme. We've already seen how jointly constructed utterances can involve simultaneous speech, when two women complete an utterance simultaneously. More typically, overlapping speech occurs when two speakers say the same thing but at slightly different times. Here is a fuller version of example 8:

8a [Discussion of victims and blame]

BEA: I mean in order to accept that idea you're

BEA: having to . [completely
MARY: mhm/ . completely review your [view of your

BEA: change your view of your husband/
MARY: husband/

Bea overlaps Mary's completion *completely review your view of your husband* with her own completion, which echoes Mary's words, apart from the substitution of *change* for *review*. In other words, two speakers complete the utterance *in order to accept that idea you're having to . . .*, but their completions are not produced simultaneously.

Overlap also occurs when two speakers complete an utterance simultaneously but complete it differently, as in the two following examples.

21 [Talking about aging parents]

LIZ: and I mean it's a really weird situation because all of a

---

SUE: [you become a parent/ yeah/
LIZ: sudden the [roles are all reversed/

---

22 [Talking about newly painted door]

PAT: it wouldn't be so bad if the door was in the middle of the house/
BARBARA:

PAT: you know if it [had a window each side/
BARBARA: [yeah so it was balanced/ yeah/

A slightly different kind of overlapping speech occurs when co-participants ask questions while another participant is speaking (see examples 23 and 24 below).

23 [Topic: Taboo and funerals]

SALLY: well she lived in Brisbane/ ((they were at Brisbane))/

SALLY: so he's going over there- = Australia/ so he's going to
MARY what – Australia?=

SALLY: the funeral/

---

24 [Talking about Oxford student murder]

LIZ: it was the boyfriend/ yeah she was under the
ANNA: has he

LIZ: floor boards =yeah/
ANNA: been charged?=
SUE: =mhm/

In example 23, Mary checks that Sally is talking about Brisbane in Australia, while in 24, Anna's question about whether the boyfriend has been charged overlaps with Liz's account of where the body was found. Overlapping speech also results when friends comment on what each other is saying. Examples 25–7 illustrate this.

25 [Discussion of Twin Peaks]

- -

ANNA: it's all about this . you know sort of Canadian border town/

- -

SUE: [I thought it was a nice whodunnit/
ANNA: where [everybody's really sort of respectable and nice and that/

- -

26 [Becky talks about crying in school]

- -

BECKY: and I cried not for very long/ j- just sort of . [a few
JESSICA: mhm/ [I hate

- -

BECKY: tears/ =I know/
JESSICA: it when no one notices=

- -

27 [Mature students at college]

- -

SUE: there's one mature student there/ and she lives in/ [and
ANNA: [oh god/

- -

SUE: they're really quite horrible to her/
ANNA: yeah it must be tough to live in halls/

- -

Comments are often more extensive than these three brief examples, and can involve other participants in an elaborate descant over the main tune. Here's a longer example, from the discussion of the obedient husband.

28 [Talking about obedient husband]

- -

SUE: she pushes him to [the abs-
ANNA: [he'll probably stab her with the

- -

SUE: [she pushes him to the limit/ yeah I
LIZ: =yeah grrr <VICIOUS NOISE>
ANNA: bread knife one [day= she'll wake

- -

SUE: think he will/ I think he'll rebel/
LIZ: ='here you are Ginny'/ <LAUGHS---------->
ANNA: up dead= <LAUGHS---------->

- -

This is a brief extract from a long episode where Liz and Anna embroider on Sue's story. Note how Liz and Anna's contributions, taken in isolation, involve no overlap: their turns are carefully coordinated to alternate in a continuous commentary on what Sue is saying. Note also how as Sue tells her story she responds to the others' contributions. Her two consecutive utterances, *she pushes him to the limit/ yeah I think he will/*, are incomprehensible unless we interpret the second as a response to Anna's *he'll probably stab her with the bread knife one day*. I shall return to this extract later.

In the conversations of women friends, the most remarkable examples of overlapping speech occur when speakers pursue a theme simultaneously, saying different but related things at the same time. In the following example, the topic of conversation is Anna's mother. It's agreed that, while she is eccentric, she is a very good cook. Sue and Anna express this in different words simultaneously.

29 [Anna's eccentric mother]

<table>
<tr><td>SUE:</td><td>but she cooks nice food=</td><td></td><td>[you know . she cooks really</td></tr>
<tr><td>ANNA:</td><td></td><td>well</td><td>[she's a- she's a really good</td></tr>
<tr><td>LIZ:</td><td>=yeah/</td><td></td><td></td></tr>
</table>

<table>
<tr><td>SUE:</td><td>inventively/</td></tr>
<tr><td>ANNA:</td><td>cook/</td></tr>
</table>

Example 30 is very simple: Anna and Liz are here talking about the same topic – the boy, Dominic. They choose to organize their talk so that their contributions about Dominic overlap rather than occurring in sequence.

30 [Talking about shy boy at piano teacher's]

<table>
<tr><td>ANNA:</td><td>I make a point of tal</td><td>[king to him every week/</td></tr>
<tr><td>LIZ:</td><td></td><td>[he's just done his grade one as well/</td></tr>
</table>

This example comes from a passage where Anna and Liz are establishing that they both know this boy, a passage that involves several brief overlaps:

31 [Piano lessons]

ANNA:	there's a lovely little boy who goes before me called
ANNA:	Dominic= [he's got red hair/ [have you seen him? he's just
LIZ:	=Domi [nic yeah/ [he's gorgeous/
ANNA:	[so sweet/ and he's ever so shy/ so I make a point of tal [king to him
LIZ:	[yeah/ [he's just
ANNA:	every week/ [that's right/
LIZ:	done his grade one as well/ has [n't he?

A final example of this pattern will show how carefully speakers are attuned to each other; this means that a topic can be pursued by two speakers at the same time.

32 [Discussion of the way history is taught at the local comprehensive school]

HELEN:	they ask them really to compare . their life now with the 19th
HELEN:	century/ it's very good sort of introduction [to history itself/
JEN:	yes/ [and they have news-
HELEN:	[yes very good/ and they went round the park/ and did
JEN:	papers and [stuff/ and ((it's))- and they use ((list))
HELEN:	all sorts of stuff/ I was really impressed by that/
JEN:	primary sources/ yes/

In this example, Helen and I are both familiar with the way history is taught at the local school, and both admire it. We both have things we want to say which contribute to the topic, and we choose to say them at the same time. This brief extract shows us making a series of points about the way history is taught, at the same time as responding to each other's points: for example, Helen's point that the comparison of life now with life in the nineteenth century is a good introduction to history is supported by a *yes* from me, while my point that they use newspapers is acknowledged by Helen with *yes very good*. This example shows how easily speakers can speak and listen at the same time. Simultaneous talk of this kind does not threaten comprehension, but on the contrary permits a more multilayered development of topics.

In terms of the jam session metaphor I used at the beginning of this chapter, while jointly constructed utterances can be compared to several instruments playing the same tune, overlapping speech is more like several instruments playing different tunes which fit together harmonically. In the terminology of classical music this latter pattern is called polyphony.[3] All the examples in this section on overlapping speech (examples 21–32) exemplify the pattern of polyphonic talk, where two or more different but mutually reinforcing things are said at the same time.

The collaborative floor

In order to talk about the way women friends 'meld in together' in conversation, I need to look briefly at theories of conversational organization. There are nonconversational speech events such as sermons or lectures or sports commentary where just one speaker speaks. For these speech events, it is very easy to describe the relationship between the speaker and what is said (the text) as they are in a one-to-one relationship. Once you have speech events involving two or more speakers, the picture gets complicated (and informal conversation between equals is the archetypal speech event involving two or more speakers). You still have one text (the talk that these two or more people produce) but you have no obvious way of predicting the relationship between the speakers (multiple) and the text (single). Instead of a one-to-one relationship, there's a many-to-one relationship.

This aspect of talk – the way speakers cooperate to produce orderly rather than chaotic talk – is usually discussed under the heading *turn-taking*. Researchers who work on turn-taking try to work out the underlying rules which can account for the orderly management of talk.[4] After all, most of the conversations we take part in succeed in involving all participants and in producing coherent talk. How do we do this? In order to explain how speakers cooperate in talk, analysts use the concept of the conversational *floor*. This rather abstract concept refers to the conversational space available to speakers. This particular sense of the word *floor* derives from conventional usage; the phrase 'holding the floor', for example, describes how a speaker at a particular moment occupies the conversational space. 'Seizing the floor' refers to the way one speaker can butt in and start talking without letting another speaker finish.

Carole Edelsky, in her ground-breaking paper 'Who's got the floor?', refines the notion of floor by suggesting that we need to distinguish between two different kinds of floor, which she calls the *single* (or singly-developed) *floor* and the *collaborative* (or collaboratively-developed) *floor*.[5] The main characteristic of the single floor is that one speaker speaks at a time. In other words, in a single floor speakers *take turns* to speak. By contrast, the defining characteristic of the collaborative floor is that the floor is thought of as being open to all participants *simultaneously*.

Edelsky's paper arose from her analysis of five university committee meetings involving seven women and four men, some of whom were close friends as well as colleagues. She observed that these meetings fluctuated between talk which was more firmly oriented towards the business they were meant to discuss, and talk which strayed from the agenda. The chief goal of committee meetings is to get through a certain amount of prespecified business. The kind of talk achieving this goal involves a single floor with one speaker speaking at a time, sometimes at considerable length. But there is another goal at meetings where members of a committee work together on a daily basis and are in some cases friends as well as colleagues: the goal is to maintain good social relations. This more interpersonal goal is achieved through the collaborative floor.

The single floor depends on the notion of the conversational *turn*: speakers take turns to occupy the conversational floor. We are all of us experienced participants in the single floor, since this is the model of conversation tacitly held by all members of our (English-speaking) culture.[6] As children, we are told not to butt in and to 'wait for our turn'. One of the skills we develop at school is the ability to participate in single-floor talk, since schools also assume a norm of one-speaker-at-a-time.[7] It is probably not surprising that a culture which tends to favour the individual over the community should assume an individualistic model of how conversation works. But this model can only be applied satisfactorily to asymmetrical talk (talk involving speakers who are not equals) such as adult–child, doctor–patient, or to very formal talk (usually in the public domain) such as business meetings. In informal talk between equals, speakers will often develop a collaborative floor, where the individual speaker becomes far less significant and what is said is jointly accomplished by all speakers.

In this chapter I've shown how women friends make frequent use of jointly constructed utterances and of overlapping speech. These are both classic components of a collaborative floor. Collaborative floors, in Edelsky's account, typically involve shorter turns than single floors, much more overlapping speech, more repetition, and more joking and teasing. This summary implies that the collaborative floor simply involves more or less of something which is regularly found in a single floor. But I want to argue that the collaborative floor is radically different from the singly-developed floor, since it is qualitatively as well as quantitatively different from one-at-a-time turn-taking. This is precisely because the collaborative floor is a shared space, and therefore what is said is construed as being the voice of the group rather than of the individual.

'Quizzes': An extended example

To illustrate how a collaborative floor works in practice, we need to look at an extended example. We have already seen one – the jointly constructed story 'Getting undressed' in chapter 5 (page 111). That story involved only two speakers, but it was remarkable for the sensitive timing of their contributions: they were able to keep the thread of narrative and evaluation moving without a pause. (Note that this collaborative story-telling did not involve overlapping speech – overlapping speech is less common in conversations involving only two speakers, but it certainly occurs; see example 32.)

The example I shall focus on in this section involves six women friends (the Oxton group). This stretch of talk begins with a very brief story told by Janet about her daughter Vicky's performance in a quiz, consisting of one narrative clause: *Vicky drew with Robin Lee last night.* The reason this story is of interest to the assembled friends is that Robin Lee is a teacher at the local comprehensive school where many of our children were pupils. Janet is obviously proud that her sixteen-year-old daughter has managed to equal the score of an adult teacher in a quiz. But the anecdote itself serves mainly as the trigger for a discussion about quizzes in general. Here is the opening section, where Janet tells her story (twice, because she repeats it in the process of clarifying what sort of quiz she is talking about).

33 [Topic: Quizzes]

	JANET:	ooh I must tell you/ Vicky- you know the quiz Vicky goes to			
2	JANET:	on Wednesday?=		=she drew with Robin Lee=	=last night/
	MEG:		=mhm=		
	MARY:		((xx can't guess))		
	HELEN:				=oh=<LAUGHS>

- -

JANET: <LAUGHS> ((she
MARY: <LAUGHS>
HELEN: it's quite lucrative this idea as well/ not only is it-
SALLY: <LAUGHS> ((xxxxxxxxxxx))
JEN: what d'you-

- -

4 JANET: got)) two fifty/ it's a- it's a pub-
MEG: <CHUCKLE>
HELEN: in a- [in a pub
JEN: [what d'you mean it's- it's-

- -

JANET: they have this little quiz/ and apparently Mr Lee goes
HELEN: <LAUGHS>

- -

6 JANET: now/ and Vicky was absolutely deLIGHTed/ she BEAT him/
HELEN: <LAUGHS>

- -

JANET: well she didn't beat him/ [she came- she drew/
MEG: [you'd love those Jennifer/

- -

Once all six friends are clear that the topic of Janet's story is a pub quiz, we launch into talk around this topic, combining factual information about quizzes we have participated in with fantasies about becoming a team ourselves.

- -

8 JANET: yeah/ they're
MEG: I'm in a . a qui-[quiz league/ we have a marvellous time/
JEN: [yes I know/ I was once in one

- -

JANET: starting one at the Talbot apparently tonight=
MEG: mhm/
JEN: down- =well the La-

- -

10 MEG: we could put
JEN: don't you remember the Labour Party had one once/ I was

- -

JANET: =yes we could/ Ox[ton Ladies/
MEG: ourselves up as a team= [the Ladies group/
MARY: <SNORTS>
HELEN: mhm/
JEN: in a team with Don Frazer/

- -

12	JANET:	<LAUGHS>
	MEG:	yes why not?
	MARY:	
	HELEN:	<LAUGHS>
	SALLY:	<LAUGHS>

In this opening phase of the discussion, notice how some turns occur simultaneously (but parallel in thematic terms): Meg's *I'm in a quiz league/ we have a marvellous time/* overlaps with my own *yes I know I was once in one*, and also with the start of Janet's *they're starting one at the Talbot [pub] apparently tonight*. Other turns are carefully timed to occur in sequence: Meg's suggestion *we could put ourselves up as a team* is followed by Janet's *yes we could/ Oxton Ladies*. This joke about our title as a putative quiz team is jointly produced by Janet and Meg, who say *Ladies* at the same time, even though they phrase the possible title slightly differently. (The evidence that this is accepted as a joke by all present is reflected in the laughter and snorting of Sally, Helen and Mary as well as Janet.) At this point, Meg sums up the general view about our future as a quiz team, while Mary initiates a new phase of talk with a question:

MEG:	[((that would be fun wouldn't it?))
MARY:	[what sort of questions do you get asked on these quizzes?

In a collaborative floor, speakers can construct talk in this way, rounding off one point while moving on to a new one, *at the same time*. Participants in a collaborative floor are not baffled by this: no one in the conversations I've recorded ever protests at the overlapping talk, and the fact that topics are developed coherently suggests that participants follow this multi-stranded, polyphonic talk with ease. Mary's question leads into a free-for-all, with everyone keen to suggest what sort of questions are typical of quizzes. Here is a brief example:

14	JANET:	'Where's the biggest pyramid?' was what they had last night=
	MARY:	='What's

JANET:	='where's the biggest'= =pyramid/where/
MARY:	the biggest pyramid?'= = where?=
SALLY:	((shocks xx))

-

16	JANET:	[it's in MExico=			
	MEG:		=is it?	oh one of those Aztec .	
	MARY:	in E[gypt	=oh in Mexico is it?		
	SALLY:	((is it Ok-xx?))-	=right/		mhm/

-

MEG:	numbers/		
JEN:		((xx)) one of those trick ones=	
MARY:			=God I'd be hopeless at that/
HELEN:		mhm/	mhm/

-

The overlapping talk in stave 16 arises as Mary and Sally hazard a guess about where the biggest pyramid is, Janet gives the answer, and then Meg, Mary and Sally react to Janet's answer. The topic is sustained for some time more, with questions on geography and literature being singled out for discussion. This is a fascinating piece of talk because the six speakers (a large number) manage to maintain one floor (rather than splitting into two or more conversations). While the talk may appear anarchic at times, this is clearly a collaborative floor: speakers are keenly aware of each other's contributions, and all utterances relate to the same topic, with particular points being jointly developed.

Collaborative floors in the interview setting

I've talked about the place of a collaborative floor in conversation between friends, but now need to discuss the role of the collaborative floor in the interview setting. So far in this chapter I've used only one example from the interview material (example 1, a jointly constructed utterance). Here are two more brief examples, both involving overlapping speech:

34 [Becky and Hannah reflect on who they can talk openly to]

-

BECKY: I mean I've got friends that- . . . sometimes I feel

-

BECKY: like I have to put on a bit of a – you know say the-

-

BECKY:	you know	[say the right words and things you know/
HANNAH:		[say the right things/ . yeah/

-

35 [Dinner parties]

SUE:	sometimes you have a dinner party and there's four of you or

---

SUE:	whatever=	and	[it's pleasant and it's very nice/
ANNA:			[yes but it becomes chit-chat/
LIZ:	=couples yeah/		

In example 34, Hannah says *say the right things* at the same time as Becky says *say the right words and things*: this example shows that meaning is what matters, rather than the exact words. These friends are collaborating to produce talk, and this involves the joint completion of an utterance and overlapping speech. In the second example, example 35, Sue and Anna talk simultanously: their utterances both develop the theme of the unsatisfactory nature of dinner party talk.

These examples represent a very particular type of collaborative floor. They arise in a setting – the interview – where participants are *not* equals, but have specific roles: interviewer or interviewee. But where there is more than one interviewee, and where the interviews are carried out in a relatively informal manner, then speakers will often share the role of interviewee and will combine to answer the interviewer's questions. In the two examples above, we see combinations of two or three speakers sharing in the construction of talk in answer to my questions. It is recognized that this collaborative pattern of talk may occur in the interview setting.[8] But what has not been recognized is the relationship between the phenomenon of several interviewees answering as one speaker, and the collaborative floor established in the talk of friends and intimates. What happens in the interview setting is that interviewees can choose to establish a collaborative floor. When they do this, a collaborative floor (where two or more interviewees share the floor to answer questions) is embedded in a single floor (where the interviewer and the interviewees take turns to speak). In the interviews I recorded, this happened frequently. In other words, where I interviewed two or three friends together, they nearly always chose to function as a single voice.

More remarkably, the single floor of interviewer–interviewees is sometimes completely abandoned in the interviews I carried out, and an unambiguous collaborative floor is established. This would happen where a particular question led into general discussion which I couldn't resist joining in, or where the answer involved accounts of events in the past which I'd been part of. The example below is one of the second kind: I had shared in the experience Bea is describing, so I join in the answering of the question.

36 *[Bea explains why the kitchen was the place she talked with women friends when the children were young]*

BEA: I think one of the reasons it used to be the kitchen was- didn't we

---

BEA: use to try and keep the children in the sitting room where the toys

---

BEA: were/ and then we would be . [away from them and hide in the kitchen=
JEN: [we escaped!

BEA: ((xx)) =yes where the kettle was=
JEN: <LAUGHS> =where the kettle was= =not to
MEG: =yeah exactly=

BEA: =yeah but now we've- we've recovered
JEN: mention the gin bottle= we've-

BEA: the sitting room=
JEN: =that's right, it's our territory again=
MEG: =yes/

In this example, Bea, Meg, and I jointly elaborate on an answer to my question, 'Where do you talk'? This extract is unambiguously a collaborative floor: we construct utterances jointly – *(we would) hide in the kitchen//where the kettle was* and *but now we've//we've//we've recovered the sitting room* – and we talk at the same time, on the same theme: *we would be away from them* and *we escaped!* are uttered simultaneously.

The test of acceptance

An important piece of evidence to support the idea of the collaborative floor comes from the fact that no one in the conversations and interviews I've collected protests about these patterns of talk. No one ever says, 'Let me finish what I'm saying', or 'Don't interrupt me'. In singly developed floors, where the rule is that one speaker speaks at a time, any overlapping speech or any attempt by a speaker to complete another's utterance will be construed as a bid to seize the floor. But 'interruption' is not an appropriate term for what speakers do in a collaborative floor: the idea of trying to 'seize the floor' becomes redundant, because the floor is already occupied by all speakers. A collaborative floor is a shared floor.

In fact, far from protesting, women friends involved in a collaborative floor explicitly welcome each other's contributions to talk. If we look at fuller versions of some of the earlier examples, what is noticeable is the way friends incorporate each other's contributions into the general stream of talk. This seems to be routine melding work.

1a [Two friends discuss where they like to talk]

SUE: I mean in someone's house it's easier to talk than= =out/
LIZ: =out=

2a [Karen worries that she is overlooked by a neighbour]

KAREN: I mean OK I'm sure he's not= =peeping or anything/
PAT: =peeping=

3a [Helen and Jen speculate on the effect an individual's absence could have on a group]

HELEN: they won't be so= =yes yes/
JEN: =homogeneous=

5a [Discussion of open evening at the local school]

JEN: they said they kept bumping into all sorts of people=
HELEN: =that they

JEN: [they li- they knew and liked/
HELEN: [knew/ yes/

6a [Discussion of christmas play at local primary school]

KAREN: once those cameras start flashing particularly with

KAREN: the infants= =it puts them off=
PAT: =it puts them off= =yeah/

In the examples 1a, 2a and 6a, incorporation is carried out by repeating the collaborative completion, while in example 3a it is carried out by accepting the completion with the agreement token *yes*. In example 5a, I amend *they liked* to the more complex *knew and liked*, incorporating Helen's completion *they knew*. Acceptance of an incorporation is also often overtly signalled with a *yes*, as in 5a and 6a.

Speakers also add utterances to each other's utterances, and these are also incorporated into the jointly constructed text:

37 [Novel reading]

SUE:	and I kind of	skipped to the last chapter/ to make sure	that
LIZ:		yeah/	yeah/

SUE:	I was right=		=and I was/
LIZ:		=and you were=	

In example 12, when Helen switches from co-constructing the utterance *she had this grammar school meeting*, she signals her continuing involvement in what is being said by her contributions *yes* and *that's right*.

12a [Topic: Local political crisis]

JEN:		[she had this grammar school
HELEN:	because did you- did you hear	[she had this grammar school-

JEN:	meeting=	and it was a disaster=	
HELEN:	yes/	=that's right/	=that's right/

When speakers participate in a collaborative floor, and when the topic under discussion is well known to both speakers, then who says what is unimportant. In example 12, Helen could have said *she had this grammar school meeting* on her own, or she and I could have said the entire chunk together. What matters is that what is to be said gets said. And when it is said like this, friends demonstrate how 'in tune' with each other they are.

Minimal responses

A significant part of a collaborative floor is the use of minimal responses. These brief utterances – *yeah, mhm, that's right* – occur in all forms of talk. But they occur more frequently in collaborative floors than in singly developed floors. This is because, once the floor is construed as occupied by all speakers at all times, speakers have an obligation to signal their continued presence in, and acceptance of, the shared floor. So minimal responses signal that speakers are present and involved. These seemingly minor forms have very important, and very different, functions in these two different floors. When talk is more formal (for example, the vast majority of talk occuring in the public domain), and a singly developed floor is established, then minimal responses say: 'I am listening – and I thus acknowledge your right to hold the floor. I will wait for my turn'. When talk is informal (for example, between friends in private) and a collaborative floor is established, then minimal responses say: 'I am here, this is my floor too, and I am participating in the shared construction of talk'.

We've already noted how important minimal responses are for indicating that speakers accept each other's contributions to talk. Let's look at the full version of example 8 – minimal responses are underlined:

8b [Topic: Child abuse]

BEA: I mean in order to accept that idea you're

BEA: having to . completely
JEN: yes/
MARY: mhm/ . completely review your view of your

BEA: change your view of your husband=
MARY: husband= =that's right/
SALLY: =yes/
MEG: yeah/ mhm/

This extract comes from a conversation involving five women friends and all five women play their part in this chunk of talk. While Bea and Mary co-construct the 'main tune', the other three women indicate that these words represent their position, too. But minimal responses have multiple meanings: for example, my *yes* in the above example is not just supportive – by agreeing with what Bea is saying before she has said it all, I show that, like Mary, I can anticipate what the rest of this utterance might be.

It's been observed by many researchers that women make frequent use of minimal responses.[9] It's also been observed how sensitively women use minimal responses.[10] If you look back at the examples in this chapter, you can see how speakers time their responses, as a rule, to come just at the end of a chunk of talk (at the end of a phrase or clause, for example). And this point is so accurately predicted that the rhythm of the 'main tune' is not affected. Examples 38–40 below are typical examples of well-placed minimal responses.

38 *[Talking about material for sale in local market]*

Karen: it was the prettiest material I've ever seen in my life=
Pat: =mhm/

39 *[Talking about taping themselves]*

Clarie: much better than a diary=
Becky: =yeah/

40 *[Discussion of male bias in research]*

Mary: it's staggering isn't it?=
Meg: =mhm/

Example 41 is a slightly longer extract which demonstrates that minimal responses are not restricted to clause-final position, but may be used as a sign of encouragement at other points.

41 *[Child abuse]*

Meg: you remember that little boy [. . .] that was um . carried
Sally: mhm/

Meg: off= =and sexually abused=
Sally: =yes=
Bea: yes/ =yes/

In this instance, Meg hesitates and Sally says *mhm,* at which point Meg picks up the thread of her utterance. This example also shows how complex multiparty talk is: speakers are engaged not only in monitoring, and supporting, each other's contributions, but also in coordinating their minimal responses. In this example we see Sally and Bea cooperating as active listeners.

When a speaker tells a story, minimal responses occur much less frequently. Story-telling, as we saw in chapter 5, gives the speaker a peculiarly privileged role; listeners normally listen in silence, with minimal responses only appearing at or near the end of the story. In conversation, the telling of an anecdote often functions to introduce a new topic; the utterance of minimal responses signals listeners' acceptance of the new topic. Typically, all co-participants will join in at this point (whereas, as in examples 38–41, at other points in conversation, one participant's *mhm* stands for all participants). In the example below, Becky comes to the end of her anecdote; her three friends all make a minimal response, which relieves the tension engendered by Becky's self-disclosing story, as well as expressing their support for the new topic she has introduced (feelings about boys).

42 [Becky confesses her past crush on Damien]

BECKY: and I just suddenly have seen how awful he is and

BECKY:	horrible=		
CLAIRE:		=yeah/	
JESSICA:		=yeah/	
HANNAH:			yeah/

Through signalling the active participation of all participants in the conversation, minimal responses play a significant role in the collaborative construction of text and of the maintenance of a collaborative floor.

Laughter

Laughter is a significant component in the talk of women friends. It occurs in response to a variety of different aspects of talk: at the end of self-disclosing and painful stories, at funny or idiotic moments in discussion. Laughter may arise in response to what someone else says, or speakers may laugh at the end of an utterance, or even during an utterance. It can signal amusement, surprise, horror, sympathy or catharsis. Example 42 above continues as follows:

BECKY:	and I just suddenly have seen how awful he is and

BECKY:	horrible=				<SCREAM OF LAUGHTER>	
CLAIRE:		=yeah/		but like um-		but they're so
JESSICA:		=yeah/			<LAUGHS>	
HANNAH:			yeah/		<LOW CHUCKLE>	

CLAIRE:	stupid right?

Becky's self-disclosure initially triggers supportive minimal responses from her three friends, but when she bursts into a scream of laughter, releasing the tension that has built up during her account of her past infatuation with Damien, Jessica joins in with a matching loud burst of laughter, while Hannah chuckles more meditatively. Claire is left to sum up the reason for Becky's embarassment and the justification for their hilarity: how could you possibly ever 'fancy' one of the boys when they're 'so stupid'?

The opening section of the extract 'Quizzes' is full of laughter. This is much more light-hearted than the laughter of Becky and her friends above. As the topic of quizzes is established, laughter signals that this topic is going to be treated as an opportunity to have fun. The main point of Janet's opening anecdote is that the normal pattern has been reversed, with a teacher being held to a draw by a pupil. The upturning of normal expectations is a classic comic theme. In this case, it sets the scene for continued fooling. Key points, such as the suggestion of an Oxton Ladies team, are greeted with laughter, as are moments of mock panic like Mary's *I'd panic at the thought of asking the questions* and Sally's despairing *I heard it tonight* [i.e. a question and answer on *Transatlantic Quiz* on the radio] *and still didn't know*.

Like minimal responses, laughter plays a special role in the construction of a collaborative floor. It allows participants to signal their continued involvement in what is being said, their continued presence in the collaborative floor. If we assume that a collaborative floor is at all times open to all speakers, then clearly speakers need strategies to signal that they are participating, even when they don't actually produce an utterance. Laughter, like minimal responses, fits this requirement perfectly. It allows people to signal their presence frequently, while not committing them to speak all the time.

In the following extended extract from a conversation between three friends, laughter is extensively used. I've already quoted a very brief part of this extract in the section on overlapping speech (example 28, page 130). Even in this brief example, we saw how Liz and Anna laughed together at the climax of their violent fantasizing about what the obedient husband might do to his wife. The overall impression given by the long and complex stretch of talk of which this example was a tiny sample is that all three friends are talking most of the time, but this impression is due in large part to the significant amount of laughter produced by participants simultaneously with each other's utterances.[11] The full extract is interesting from several points of view. It is, firstly, a good example of a collaborative floor. Secondly, it subverts the norms of story-telling, since Sue might expect to tell her story to an attentive audience, but instead, after an initial phase when she recounts the bare bones of the story, she has to contend with a raucous descant from Liz and Anna, who work together to weave a commentary around Sue's account of an 'obedient' husband. Thirdly, it is interesting because there is a constant slippage between narrative (Sue is the only person with access to the facts of the story she is recounting) and discussion (the central point of the story – that the wife forbids the husband to play his guitar – becomes the focus of wide-ranging speculation about what marriage means).

Here's the opening narrative, which Sue tells to Liz and Anna.

Obedient husband

I told you I went round to a friend's who had ((a)) guitar.
[. . .]
The wife right- his wife would not let him have a guitar.
She said no <A AND L LAUGH>
and he's so obedient.
She's- she said, 'You're not having a guitar',
so he didn't have one,
he just didn't play it ever.
And then for christmas she allowed him to have a guitar
as long as he didn't play it in front of her.

This opening narrative provides a variety of themes which all three friends seize on. First, the notion of the wife 'allowing' the husband to have a guitar prompts discussion of power structures in relationships. Secondly, the related theme of 'obedience' is explored, particularly in terms of whether this is an appropriate quality in a husband. Thirdly, the theme of musical instruments is a rich source of talk, as Sue's husband John plays the saxophone, and Sue is known to have mixed feelings about this.

The complete version of 'Obedient husband' can be found in appendix B. Here I will present just part of this episode of talk, to illustrate the way laughter functions in friends' talk. After Sue finishes her introductory narrative, all three friends start to talk, and a collaborative floor is established.

Obedient husband (1)

SUE: he's just so nice/ he thinks she's wonderful/ and I
ANNA:
LIZ:

2 SUE: would be worried if I was her . you know= to- to push him-
ANNA:
LIZ: =what/ that you weren't

SUE: she- she pushes him to [the abs-
ANNA: [he'll probably stab her with
LIZ: matching up?

4 SUE: [she pushes him to the limit/ yeah I
ANNA: the bread knife one [day= she'll wake
LIZ: =yeah ggrrr/ <VICIOUS NOISE>

SUE: think he will/ . I think he'll rebel= <LAUGHS>
ANNA: up dead= <LAUGHS-------------------
LIZ: ='here you are Ginnyy'/ <LAUGHS--------->=have a s-

6 SUE: <LAUGHS>-------------------------------
ANNA: -->
LIZ: have a cut throat/ <CUTTING NOISE> <LAUGHS>-----------------

SUE: but that- this particular night she let him play the guitar/
ANNA: <SNORT> <LAUGHS---------------------->
LIZ: ------------------->

8 SUE: and it was so nice you know/ and she like she bans him= this
ANNA:
LIZ: <LAUGHS ---> =<CACKLES>

SUE: is what I f-=
ANNA: =I wouldn't put up with it/ I'm sorry
LIZ: =he'll probably pick it up one day and go

10 SUE: =I wouldn't/ no/ but you've got to see it to
ANNA: though/ would you?=
LIZ: [ckxxx] <MIMICS BREAKING NOISE>

	SUE:	believe it because he's just . obedient/ and she- [and she
	ANNA:	
	LIZ:	[why did

12	SUE:	just- [what/ obedient?
	ANNA:	
	LIZ:	you use that word? that's a dreadful [word/ obedient/

	SUE:	yes ((x)) yes but he is/ that's what
	ANNA:	
	LIZ:	makes him sound like a pet rabbit/

14	SUE:	he's like/ he's obedient/ [he just does as she says/
	ANNA:	[oh how aaww-ffuull/
	LIZ:	

At the climax of this extract (staves 5–6), all three women are laughing at once. Sue establishes that Rob is 'nice', that he adores his wife – *he thinks she's wonderful* – and that she forbids him to play the guitar. Anna and Liz, clearly appalled by this scenario, begin to fantasize about what the husband might do if he were to rebel. Their laughter expresses many things: their amusement at the cartoon-like violence they conjure up with their scenario of the husband stabbing the wife, their sense of the unlikelihood of this fantasy, given Sue's assertion that Rob is like a pet rabbit, and perhaps also a sense of their own daring at expressing such violent ideas. (The three women friends use sound effects to great effect in this part of their conversation, though skill with sound effects is widely recognized as a feature of boys' talk, and is not usually associated with the talk of adult women.)[12]

As collaborative talk, this extract is very interesting. The three speakers construct a collaborative floor where Sue plays the main tune, while Liz and Anna either jointly construct a commentary on what Sue is saying, or take it in turns to comment. Their laughter increases the impression of all three friends participating all the time. In the extract above, there are 14 staves: of these, 9 (64 per cent) involve two or more speakers speaking at the same time; 13 (93 per cent) involve two or more speakers speaking or laughing or adding sound effects at the same time. Laughter seems to be an intrinsic component of friendly talk among women. This being the case, the impression given by this chunk of conversation of extremely involved participation from all three speakers is accurate.[13]

To demonstrate that this is not an isolated example, here is another extract from this same stretch of conversation. The three friends have begun to consider more seriously the suggestion that the husband can't be as obedient as he seems to outsiders. Sue tells Liz and Anna what her husband, John, thinks.

Obedient husband (2)

SUE: John says at home he must- he must rebel/ he must/
LIZ: there's a limit- yeah must be/ yeah he must/

SUE: John can't bear to think-
ANNA: John probably wants to help him
LIZ: ((cos)) John- <LAUGHING> John can't bear

SUE: d'you know what
ANNA: rebel/ 'Come round for lessons in rebelling'
LIZ: he gives him- yeah give him-

SUE: the funny thing is- yeah/
LIZ: 'Buy a saxophone – I'll give you the number

SUE: yeah/ he would/ he's got this twi- he's got this
LIZ: where you buy one'/ <LAUGHING>

SUE: nervous twitch/ exactly/ he's got this
ANNA: I'm not surprised/ <LAUGHS-------------------
LIZ: oh/ <LAUGHS---------------------------------

SUE: nervous t- <LAUGHS> he's got this real nervous twitch/ and John says
ANNA: --------------------->
LIZ: ------------------------------->

SUE: 'I'm going to ask him about it'/
ANNA: <LAUGHS>
LIZ: <SHRIEKS OF LAUGHTER>

This example is made up of 8 staves – all of these, apart from the last one, involve two or three speakers talking and laughing at the same time. In the first stave, Sue and Liz talk polyphonically on the theme that the husband must rebel at home, but timing their utterances so that the key word *must* is uttered simultaneously. But with this theme established, Liz and Anna again cooperate to fantasize on the nature of this rebellion, taking turns to imagine John in the role of agent provocateur, while Sue continues with her (factual) account, bringing in the new point that the husband has a nervous twitch. This brings the house down, especially when Sue weaves the theme of John as agent provocateur into this new theme.

Talk as play

These brief extracts from a conversation between Sue, Liz and Anna on the topic of an obedient husband show us three women having enormous fun. They use the topic as an excuse to play with ideas about marriage and obedience, and also to play with words and with their skill at collaborative talk.

As I showed in chapter 3, women friends often deny that they 'do' much together, since they don't class talk as 'doing'. Research on men's friendships emphasizes the importance men place on shared activity such as playing football or pool, going to watch a match, going to the pub.[14] When we were children, we called these sorts of activities 'play', and playing was what we did with friends. It seems that men's 'play' is activity-oriented, while women's 'play' centres on talk. I am arguing here that women's melding talk takes the shape it does *precisely* because it is play. Talk-as-play is inevitably structured differently from talk-as-serious-business. To begin with, the main goal of talk-as-play is the construction and maintenance of good social relations, not the exchange of information (though this will also be one of the functions of friendly talk, as there in an informational component to all interaction). The second goal of talk-as-play is that participants should enjoy themselves. The fun of talk arises as much from *how* things are said as from *what* is said.

This exposition of the functions of women's friendly talk brings us back to the idea of talk as a kind of jam session. Women friends arrive at each other's houses and, after a brief warm-up over a glass of wine or a cup of tea, start playing. Solo passages alternate with all-in-together ensemble passages. We improvise on each other's themes, share painful and funny experiences, laugh at ourselves and with each other. The construction of a collaborative floor symbolizes what friendship means to us: as we create utterances together, as we say parallel things on the same theme at the same time, we are demonstrating in a concrete way the value we place on sharing and on collaboration. Our individual voices merge and blend in a joint performance. Laughter occurs frequently not just because people say funny or shocking things, but because we take huge pleasure in the talk we create and in our skill at 'melding in together'.

7

'You know so I mean I probably . . .': Hedges and hedging

In this chapter, I explore the use of the linguistic devices known as *hedges* by linguists, words and phrases like *maybe* and *sort of* and *I mean* which have the effect of damping down the force of what we say. The term is derived from the everyday usage of 'hedge', as in 'to hedge your bets', where 'hedge' means roughly 'to avoid taking decisive action'. When we hedge linguistically, we avoid saying something definite and so we keep our options open. Hedges are a valuable resource for speakers, and there is growing evidence that women use them more than men.[1] They are used frequently and sensitively by women friends, and one of their functions is to help in the 'struggle for words' which Rachel raised in her interview as being a significant feature of friends' talk.

To clarify what I mean by a hedge, let's look at an example where many of them appear. This excerpt is a rare example of a failed story, 'failed' in the sense that Meg's story is greeted with discomfort and disbelief by her friends, and in the sense that Meg eventually falls silent and doesn't get to finish the story. She is telling Bea, Sally and me about meeting an old friend she hasn't seen for a while. After explaining who Jean is, she starts to tell us about her reaction to Jean's appearance. (The example is slightly edited and hedges are underlined.)

Meeting an old friend

- -

MEG: anyway ((xx)) <u>I think</u> **Jean's** got a a a a a body hair problem/

- -

OTHERS: <LAUGHTER>

MEG: no-
BEA: well I have quite a lot of body hair/ how much has she got?

MEG: well-
BEA: you mean like it was coming out- . like it was coming
JEN: but where ((xx))-

MEG: yeah/ . no I saw it on her chest honestly/ and um o-
BEA: out- oh/

MEG: on- I- I do look at this from a- with an objective clinical eye/ er

---

MEG: but I did see what- what amounted to sort of chest hair/ . black/

MEG: she's a very dark- sort of dark skinned and sallow complexion and a

---

MEG: lo- I mean I- I mean I hope I'm just reporting this without any

---

MEG: edge to it/ . you know so I mean I probably-

BEA: you mean you really feel that she's turning into a gorilla?

OTHERS: <LAUGHTER>

Meg's account of her friend, which precedes this extract, is uncontroversial for the most part. It comes to a climax with the statement *I think Jean's got a a a a a body hair problem*. Body hair on women is a controversial topic in our culture. Meg's use of the hedge *I think*, combined with her stammering, suggests that she is anxious about how her remark will be received by her friends. As it turns out, she is right to be anxious: Bea immediately challenges her: *well I have quite a lot of body hair* and asks *how much has she got?*. Meg starts to justify her statement, but becomes more and more inarticulate as she senses that her story is not going down well with her audience. The more she becomes embarrassed, the more frequently she hedges. By the end of her turn she is reduced to almost continuous hedging: *you know so I mean I probably-* and she then stops talking altogether. The situation is saved by Bea, whose outrageous comment *you mean you really feel that she's turning into a gorilla?* releases the tension.

It is unusual to find so many hedges one after the other as we find in Meg's last, incomplete utterance, but this is a rare example of a woman realizing that what she is saying is not acceptable to her friends. Most of the time in conversation with friends, what we say is accepted. But we still need to use hedges. The rest of the chapter will illustrate the various different ways hedges are used in talk between friends, and will explore the reasons for women's use of these forms.

The multiple functions of hedges

The expression of doubt and confidence

The basic function of hedges is to signal that the speaker is not committed to what she is saying. In other words, when we hedge an utterance, we are saying that we lack confidence in the truth of the proposition expressed in that utterance. So when Meg says, *I think she's got a body hair problem,* she signals by the use of the hedge *I think* that she is not totally confident about the truth of the proposition *she's got a body hair problem.*

In the following example, Hannah and her friends are talking about Australian soap operas on television, and start to discuss Australian accents. Claire mentions a girl at their school, Julie, who comes from Australia but doesn't sound Australian.

- -

CLAIRE: but you know Julie right? she's Australian/ she-

- -

CLAIRE: [she hasn't got an Aus- yeah/ she hasn't got an Australian accent/
BECKY: [is she Australian?

- -

JESS: who?
CLAIRE: [Julie/ <u>it's the way she speaks man</u> <LAUGHS> <TAKES OFF
BECKY: [Julie/

- -

CLAIRE: JULIE'S ACCENT> I doubt it/
BECKY: <u>maybe</u> she had elocution lessons/

- -

Claire's parody of the way Julie speaks leads Becky to say *maybe she had elocution lessons*: this is an attempt to justify Julie's accent, but the inclusion of the hedge *maybe* in this utterance signals Becky's lack of commitment to the proposition *she had elocution lessons*. In effect, she says, 'Here's a possible explanation, but I'm rather doubtful about it'. Her doubt is mirrored by Claire who responds *I doubt it.*

Similarly, Anna's repeated *maybes* in the following example tell her friends that she is doubtful about the propositions contained in these two utterances:

[Anna arrives in a state after a row with her boss]

ANNA: maybe he's right/ maybe I am a crap manager/

Besides forms like *I think* amd *maybe,* the auxiliary verbs *may* and *might* are important hedges which we regularly use to hint at doubt. In the following example, Helen expresses her doubt about the numbers of people likely to attend an adult education course for school governors she is running.

HELEN: but what it means about next week is we may not have enough for two groups 'cos I had two apologies in advance/ [. . .] and you know some other people may have commitments/ so I don't think we're going to run two groups/

She uses the auxiliary may twice in this extract; both times it signals her lack of commitment to the proposition expressed in the utterance. Her final statement *so I don't think we're going to run two groups* reiterates her doubt about there being two groups. Notice the way different hedges – *may, you know, I don't think* – combine in this chunk of talk to communicate the speaker's uncertainty.

The final example is taken from a point in conversation between Sue, Liz and Anna where Anna has just finished telling a story about her eccentric mother, who begged a lift on a milk float after being stranded at the station in the early morning on her way to a funeral. The hedge *probably* is used by all three speakers to hedge the proposition 'Anna's mother told the milkman (that she was going to a funeral)'.

ANNA: bet the milkman couldn't believe it/
LIZ: [yeah
SUE: [did he know she was going

ANNA: =well she probably told them/
LIZ: probably told [him=
SUE: to the funeral? [probably/ yeah/

ANNA: you know what she's like/ <CHUCKLES>

In this example, the three friends mirror each other's relative confidence about what Anna's mother did, through their choice of the adverb *probably*, which is closer to confidence than to doubt.

Sensitivity to others' feelings

One of the strengths of hedges is that they can be used not just to modify the force of the propositional content of an utterance, but also to take account of the feelings of the addressee, that is the person or people being talked to. When we talk, we communicate not just propositions and attitudes to propositions, but also attitudes to addressees. This latter function of language is called the *interpersonal* function.[2] When Meg began to talk about her old friend Jean to her friends, before she introduced the body hair theme, she used the highly hedged utterance: *she looks very sort of um – kind of matronly really*. The hedges *sort of, kind of, really* in this utterance signal that Meg is not firmly committed to the proposition *she looks matronly*. This is not because Meg herself doubts the truth of the proposition, but because she is unsure how her friends will respond to this unflattering description of another woman. Meg does not want to offend us, her addressees, by assuming our agreement. By using the hedges, she protects us from the full force of the controversial claim.

Of course, she also protects herself: Meg's use of hedges here allows her to wriggle out of the accusation that she has said something mean if she needs to. For example, given the negative connotations of the adjective *matronly*, if Meg is later accused of describing Jean as old or overweight, she can deny it. What she said was *kind of matronly*, not *matronly*. This use of hedges to protect the speaker as well as the addressee is one of their major functions.

The idea that we need to protect ourselves and those we are speaking to draws on a model of communication that has developed the notion of *face* (as in 'to lose face') and the related concept of *face needs*.[3] We all have face needs – that is, the need to have our personal space respected (known as *negative face*) and the equally important need to be acknowledged and liked (*positive face*). In English, hedges are extremely useful in terms of protecting negative face: they help us to avoid imposing on people. A classic example is the standard formula for asking someone a favour: we say, 'Could you possibly lend me a fiver?', using the hedges *could* and *possibly*, not the peremptory (and face-threatening) 'Lend me a fiver'. They also protect positive face, by facilitating the expression of controversial views. For example, the hedges Meg uses when talking about Jean's appearance allow her to retain her friends' good opinion of her, since she did not actually say *she looks matronly*.

To clarify the way hedges protect the face needs of all participants in talk, let's look at an example where Sue complains about her husband's music. Her complaint is framed in terms of her daughter, who is asleep upstairs. The hedges in this extract allow Sue an acceptable way of complaining about her husband, and allow Liz to join in this discussion without committing herself to the dangerous line of unmitigated agreement with Sue. (It is permissible – though dangerous – for a wife to criticize a husband, but extremely risky for others to do so.)

[Background music gets louder]

SUE: I mean how can you live with this?
LIZ: well I know it's difficult when

SUE: [oh it drives you insane/
LIZ: you've got a man around [but-

SUE: I mean Emma's sleeping next door to this/
LIZ: she'll probably

SUE: [well I don't know I mean-
LIZ: get used to it . real[ly quickly/

Sue protects her positive face (her need to have her friend's affection and respect) by not taking too strong a line: the hedges mean she can retreat from this critical position if necessary. At the same time, by using hedges she is able to voice her irritation at John's thoughtlessness, and to receive support from Liz. Liz is also tentative, since she wants to support Sue but doesn't want to be seen to be taking too critical a position. She uses hedges to protect her own face and Sue's as well. Sue's rhetorical question *how can you live with this?* also functions as a kind of hedge. (I'll discuss women friends' use of rhetorical questions in the next chapter.)

In the following example, Karen obviously feels the need to hedge the assertion that she's never been worried about whether her doctor was male or female in case Pat doesn't agree. (In this way, she protects her own face – she could retreat from her statement – and she also protects Pat's.)

KAREN: well I suppose it is I've never really had any worries like that/

PAT: no/ it wouldn't bother me but perhaps-

KAREN: mind you as they're getting younger . I might feel [differently/
PAT: [yes/

In fact, as we can see, Pat mirrors Karen's assertion with the utterance *it wouldn't bother me* – that is, it wouldn't bother her to have a male doctor. But she then starts an utterance which she doesn't complete: *but perhaps-* which suggests that she thinks there might be circumstances where you would be bothered. Karen then gives an example of such circumstances – where (male) doctors are getting younger, and Pat agrees with her. Note the use of the modal auxiliary *might* in Karen's utterance, which hedges her statement of her feelings.

Searching for the right word

Hedges are also useful devices for signalling that we are searching for a word, or having trouble finding the right words to say what we mean. This can be reasonably trivial, as in the following example where Becky tries to describe a sensation she gets in her nose when she is premenstrual:

BECKY: it feels like your nose is just sort of . expanding/

The hedge *sort of* alerts her friends to the fact she is trying to find the right word; it also signals that the word we eventually use may not be the perfect choice. Note the pause after *sort of*, which is commonly found when hedges function in this way. The hedge indicates that the speaker is still active even though a pause might follow: other speakers can then give the speaker time to hunt for the mot juste.

While *sort of* and *kind of* are the two hedges most frequently used to stall for time while the speaker searches for a word, other hedges such as *really* and *you know* occur here too. The following is an example with *you know.*

[Talking about TV programme about apes]

BEA: he [orang-outang] had you know- he had five very adequate . manip- whatever you would call hands and things/

In her interview, Rachel commented explicitly on this aspect of women's talk: 'Talking with women I'm- I'm much happier about struggling around how to say things'. Rachel observes from her own experience not only that women friends engage seriously in the struggle for accurate self-expression, but also observes that women have the conversational skill to support each other in this struggle: 'and also women give you time to struggle with it', an observation borne out by the data. Friends did not butt in when someone was searching for a word, though, as we saw in the last chapter, the search for the right word can be carried out collaboratively, where a woman appeals to her friends for help.

In the following example, Helen is talking about her younger daughter. She is trying to describe the bad situation that had existed at her daughter's primary school, and contrasts this with how well she's settled down at her new secondary school:

HELEN: she really loves it/ and she's somebody that was <u>really</u> being . <u>sort of</u> labelled as somebody that wasn't <u>really</u>- was anti-school almost at Riversdale Road [primary school]/

Helen searches for a word to describe what was happening to her daughter at Riversdale Road school, and settles on *labelled*. Notice that in this example, the pause precedes the hedge *sort of*, but Helen's struggle for words has already been signalled by the hedge *really*. As she continues to describe this situation she begins an utterance *somebody that wasn't really-*. Her search for words leads her to the term *anti-school*, which expresses what she is trying to say, but which means she has to rephrase her utterance, changing *wasn't* to *was*. The hedges here also arise from the sensitivity of the topic, and from Helen's need to protect her own face. It is characteristic of hedges that they perform several functions simultaneously: they are extremely versatile linguistic forms.

In the next example, *sort of* is again used multifunctionally, as Gwen hypothesizes about what Emily's mother was like as a teenager.

EMILY: you know what? my Mum thinks I'm much more sensible than SHE was at our age [. . .]
GWEN: what did she do at your age? [. . .] was she all- all <u>sort of</u> <u>a bit of a</u> raver?
EMILY: <u>I think</u> she was/

Not only is Gwen searching for an appropriate word to describe the sort of wild teenager she is imagining, she is also being careful to protect herself in case her remark turns out to be unacceptable to Emily. (As it turns out, Emily accepts the term *raver* as a description of her mother as a teenager.) Note how Gwen's utterance is full of signs of struggle: she hesitates on the word *all*, continues with *sort of* then hedges even further by premodifying *raver* with the phrase *a bit of a*.

The final example shows Helen struggling to find the right word, and also protecting herself in case she has made a mistake. *Sort of* in this example is primarily used to signal that this might not be the ideal word, and that finding the right word is difficult.

[Final part of discussion of Apes and language]

```
-----------------------------------------------------------------
BEA:   what's a paradigm?
MARY:                          that . ac[c e p t e d     .     view of the world=
JANET:                                  [((purely an)) idea/
-----------------------------------------------------------------
HELEN:  =a sort of model/
-----------------------------------------------------------------
```

This is another example of friends working together to find the right words. As the speaker making the third attempt at a definition, Helen wants to signal that her contribution does not imply disagreement with what Mary and Janet have already suggested, but that she is building on what they have said and is herself not wholly satisfied that this is the right word.

The search for the right words is often part of women's struggle to think about things in new ways, and to come to new forms of understanding. This is an important aspect of the talk women friends do, and hedges play an important part in facilitating such talk. I'll return to this subject, the role of talk in developing new knowledge, in the final chapter (chapter 11).

Avoiding playing the expert

The use of hedges before a key word is sometimes used deliberately by speakers. Rather than meaning that the speaker is searching for the right word, hedging can be a strategy to avoid the appearance of playing the expert. By 'playing the expert', I mean that conversational game where participants take it in turns to hold the floor and to talk about a subject which they are an expert on. This is a game which seems to be played most commonly by male speakers.[4] Women, by contrast, avoid the role of expert in conversation: in a collaborative floor, it is very important to minimize social distance between participants, and hedges appear to be a useful strategy to achieve this goal. In the first example here, Helen arrives early at my house and takes the opportunity to talk to me about my imminent visit to her college to run a workshop on the school curriculum as part of her adult education course for school governors. In other words, she has arrived at my house in her capacity as 'friend' but talks about something which brings into play her professional persona as Senior Lecturer in Further Education. She uses hedges skilfully to dilute the force of what she is saying, to make it look as if her words aren't at her fingertips, and thus to avoid expert status.

[Explaining what stage the group has reached on the course]

HELEN: so they'll be re- you know they'll be feeling quite sort of ready for that/

In the example below, the speaker (Meg) is a psychologist who is familiar with the process being described in the discussion on child abuse. Her use of *sort of* makes her appear less fluent, and thus avoids opening up distance between participants.

[Discussion of child abuse]

MEG: they can sort of um test that out by . showing people sort of video tapes/

The final example comes from a discussion of apes and language which was triggered by a science programme the previous night on TV. As a linguist, this is a topic I enjoy, but although I have things I want to say, I don't want to play the expert; I certainly don't want to give my friends a linguistics lecture.

[Jen is defending the position that apes can use language]

JEN: but I still think- well basically what my thinking is/ is that the people like Terrace [a psycholinguist] represent the group that on the whole does not want to admit that other species have the language whatever it is ability/ and that's- and I think I'm always opposed to that group/ cos I think it's the- the whole dangerous thing of saying 'We're a superior species'/

The hedges in this example, combined with vague language (i.e. the vague phrase *whatever it is* in *the language whatever it is ability* and the word *thing* in *the whole dangerous thing*) mean that I avoid sounding like an expert. There is also disfluency: both false starts and repetition of words. All these aspects of the way I talk about the topic combine to make me sound less authoritative. (The evidence that this succeeded is demonstrated by the lively collaborative discussion on the topic 'Apes and language' that followed: see example 20 in the previous chapter.) The preservation of equal status and the maintenance of social closeness are both important principles in friendly talk between women.

Women and hedging

Why are hedges a significant feature of the talk of women friends? Their use, it seems to me, is crucially related to three aspects of our talk: we often discuss sensitive topics; we practise mutual self-disclosure; and finally we establish, and therefore need to maintain, a collaborative floor. I'll look at each of these factors in turn.

Negotiating sensitive topics

Women friends talk about a huge range of things, but this range includes a significant proportion of topics that can be labelled 'sensitive'. By 'sensitive' I mean that they are topics which are controversial in some way and which arouse strong feelings in people. These topics are usually about people and feelings. If we look at the topics which were talked about in the four conversational extracts analysed at the beginning of chapter 4, we can see that some are more sensitive than others. For example, the discussion of 'Periods' in the conversation involving Hannah and her friends is a good example of a sensitive topic (because menstruation is a taboo topic for many people in most contexts in our culture), whereas the topic following that, a brief one focusing on Claire's experiences at the gym ('Gymnastics'), is not. In the conversation involving Sue, Anna and Liz, the topics 'Antiques' and 'Rabbits' were 'safe' topics, involving talk about things and animals rather than about people and feelings. The topic 'Relationships', by contrast, is highly sensitive, dealing with personal relationships and issues such as appropriate behaviour in marriage. Other sensitive topics arising in these four conversations were: 'Brothers and boys and the male body' (Hannah and co), 'Karen's recent operation' and 'Illness' (Pat and Karen), and the long sequence 'Taboo and funerals', 'Child abuse', 'Loyalty to men' and 'Fear of men' (Oxton group).

Here are just three brief examples of hedged utterances from one of these sensitive topics, 'Child abuse'.

1 *[Trying to work out why girl victims of sexual abuse are often treated unsympathetically]*

BEA: what happens to women sexwise is their fault/ and I mean I think it's just that taken down . extending it to little girls/

2 *[Talking about the incestuous family]*

MARY: I mean I think it was your theory wasn't it? that- that it runs in families/

3 *[Talking about the incestuous family]*

MARY: I mean is it- is it to do with the mother?

Here, even though the five of us involved in talking about child abuse do not bring any direct personal experience into our discussion, at the same time we have all been little girls, all of us have children, and the subject provokes powerful feelings. The hedges in this talk of child abuse function chiefly as an interpersonal resource: we use them to protect each other and ourselves. Bea tries out an explanation of attitudes to girl victims in terms of attitudes to adult women and argues that this (unsympathetic, patriarchal) view of women is applied (inappropriately) to female children. Her hedges signal doubt (she is not totally committed to this position), sensitivity to her addressees (who might find the position controversial), and sensitivity to her own need to protect her face. In example 2, Mary is very careful not to pin a (possibly controversial) theory on one of her friends, and allows room for the friend (Meg) to reject the claim. In example 3, Mary's *I mean* softens the force of the highly controversial suggestion that mothers are in some way implicated in child abuse. Mary doesn't just hedge this claim, she also phrases it as a question, which effectively hedges it further. (I will discuss the use of questions as hedges in the next chapter.)

While each of these examples is unique, with hedges being used for a subtly different combination of reasons, in all three cases one fundamental reason for the use of hedges is that the topic itself is highly sensitive, and anything said needs to be mitigated. In other words, talk on sensitive topics is too difficult if statements are made bluntly: we all need to protect ourselves and each other from the naked force of such subjects.

The following example is a longer extract, to show how hedges are used over a series of utterances to soften the force of what is said, and to show how they combine with each other. In this extract, Helen is telling me about a girl, a friend of her daughter's, who had left the local school after winning a scholarship to the local girls' independent school. Helen and Fran (her daughter) have always been very fond of Catherine, but have despaired about her appearance: in their view, Catherine's parents have very old-fashioned ideas. Fran had recently seen Catherine at a United Nations inter-school quiz, and Helen is telling me about this meeting. Helen uses several hedges at various points in this chunk of conversation: one of their functions is to protect my feelings, in case I am unhappy at this way of talking about Catherine (after all, every positive statement Helen makes implies a criticism of Catherine's past appearance, and also assumes a world view where 'looking good' is important for women, a position I am known to be critical of).

HELEN: Fran said she looked really lovely/ she was . at last wearing sort of modern clothes/ cos they don't have to wear uniform/ she looked really pretty/ she'd had her hair sort of done/ and she looked really sort of- you know Fran said she felt very warm towards her because she looked so nice and human at last/

I respond by hypothesizing that Catherine's parents' attitude has mellowed because they accept the school's views on dress. Helen then feels confident to continue as follows:

- -

HELEN: she's all toned in grey and things/ but I mean you know Fran

- -

HELEN: said she looked . really much more relaxed/ mhm/
JEN: it's a beginning/

- -

By hedging her claims, Helen shows sensitivity to my feeling in her presentation of this controversial account of a young woman's appearance. She also displays her awareness that this is a difficult subject: she is trying to say something nice about Catherine, but the more she continues, the more she is in fact revealing a covertly judgmental attitude. (The adjective *human* – in *she looked so nice and human at last*

– is particularly revealing in terms of what it implies about Catherine in the past.) By using hedges, Helen succeeds in negotiating this sensitive topic, and in fact, succeeds in getting me to share her position: when I join in with *it's a beginning* I am colluding in a discourse which promotes an ideology insisting on women taking care over their appearance.

The discussion of sensitive topics is a regularly occurring feature in the talk of women friends. These topics trigger the use of hedges, because without hedges it would be difficult – if not impossible – to talk about sensitive matters. (For comparison with a 'safe' topic, see Pat and Karen's relatively unhedged discussion of screening trees, example 16 in the previous chapter.)

Self-disclosure

When we talk with our friends, we trust them enough to tell them stories about ourselves that we would not risk telling people less close to us. Disclosing personal information is always risky, but is an important element in close relationships, because self-disclosure normally produces matching self-disclosure from others, which promotes close bonds. Self-disclosure is a key component of the talk of women friends. We confide in each other, tell each other our hopes and fears, reveal moments in our lives when we have behaved 'badly'. As we saw in chapter 2, the ability to be ourselves, warts and all, with our friends is something we value very highly. But because self-disclosure involves highly personal material, utterances need to be softened, and hedges are a vital resource in making disclosure possible.

Helen's talk about Catherine above, although overtly about her daughter's views, discloses a great deal about her too, since she clearly shares her daughter's views. So the hedges appear both because the subject matter is sensitive, and also because this extract is in effect a chunk of self-disclosure. A very clear example of self-disclosure is Becky's confession to her friends that for some time she 'fancied' Damien. (The final part of this example was discussed in the previous chapter.) Becky initiates the topic by saying, 'I stopped sort of fancying him quite recently'. The hedge *sort of* is doing a lot of work here: it signals that Becky feels vulnerable about the topic 'fancying'; it also signals that 'fancy' may not be the best word for what she is talking about. She seems to want to self-disclose to her friends, yet at the same time she distances herself from her subject matter – her 'fancying' of Damien – by hedging. This utterance also presupposes that Becky fancying Damien is shared knowledge. Once Becky realizes that not all her friends know about this, she has to fill in the gaps in their knowledge with the following bit of self-disclosure (hedges underlined):

BECKY: and then when we came back [from holiday] I sort of fell in love with

---

BECKY: him again/ and then the real sort of clincher was ((xx))
JESS: <QUIET LAUGH>

BECKY: and I suddenly- because I've suddenly sort of fancying-

---

BECKY: you know people say love's blind/ I think I thought he was perfect/
JESS: oh but d'you think-

BECKY: apart from the ((obvious things))/ and I just suddenly have seen
JESS: mhm/
CLAIRE: yeah/

BECKY: how awful he is and horrible= <PEAL OF LOUD LAUGHTER>
JESS: =yeah <MATCHING LAUGH>
CLAIRE: =yeah/ but like um-
HANNAH: yeah/ <LOW CHUCKLE>

Becky's self-disclosure makes her very vulnerable: it is embarrassing enough at the age of fourteen to admit to feelings like 'love' and 'fancying'; it is worse when the object of your affections is a boy in your year at school, someone who you now think is 'awful' and 'horrible'. She hedges what she says, to protect her own face and that of her friends. Even so, this is such a sensitive topic that the hedging is not enough: Becky's embarrassment erupts at the end of her self-disclosure and triggers sympathetic laughter from her friends.

There are some topics which are so sensitive that self-disclosure would be unthinkable without some means of damping down the force of what is said. The final example comes from a discussion of the Yorkshire Ripper case. Meg discloses that after police appeals for help she forced herself to consider whether her partner might be the murderer. This leads to reciprocal self-disclosure from Sally, who admits to having gone through the same process. This is obviously a difficult fact to admit for both women: they make themselves very vulnerable. They need to protect their own face as well as that of their addressees. The strength of hedges is that they facilitate the expression of highly charged material; Meg and Sally unburden themselves to their friends, and are reassured to discover that they are not alone in having gone through this process.

MEG:	I remember at the time thi- you know really thinking 'now could this
SALLY:	
MEG:	be M-' I think it was Mike/ [. . .] and I actually made a special point
SALLY:	
MEG:	of thinking 'could it be him?'/ and I wondered if other women
SALLY:	
MEG:	at the time . thought-
SALLY:	oh god yes/ well I mean we were living in Yorkshire
MEG:	
SALLY:	at the time/ and I . I mean I . I mean I did/ I sort of thought well
MEG:	
SALLY:	'could it be John'?/

It is inconceivable that this kind of self-disclosure could take place without the use of hedges.

Collaborative floors and the need for open discussion

Another reason for the relatively frequent occurrence of hedging in the talk of women friends is that, as I've argued in the previous chapter, the floor is collaborative and speakers share in the construction of talk. This means that to a large extent it is the group voice that counts rather than the voice of the individual. Consequently it is important for women friends to avoid expressing themselves in a hard-and-fast way.

Hedges play an important role in facilitating open discussion – that is, in promoting discussion where speakers avoid absolutes and where utterances are mitigated. The example given earlier of Pat and Karen discussing their doctors illustrates very clearly what I mean by the phrase *open discussion*.

[Discussion about whether it matters if your doctor is male or female]

KAREN: well I suppose it is I've never really had any worries
PAT:

KAREN: like that/ mind you/
PAT: no/ it wouldn't bother me/ but perhaps-

KAREN: as they're getting younger . I might feel [differently/
PAT: [yes/

Karen's initial statement is hedged, which means that she is not seen as taking a firm line, but would be prepared to moderate her views if necessary. Pat is free to agree with her or to nudge the discussion on with a 'yes but . . .' response. She begins by agreeing, but then starts a second utterance which does the work of suggesting alternative points of view without actually stating them. The inclusion of the hedge *perhaps* here means that Karen is free to take up this new line or to stick with her original position: both are possible because Pat is tentative about proposing a new point of view. Karen responds to Pat's tentative fragmentary utterance by making a suggestion of a possible world where she might 'have worries', and Pat agrees with this step. So between them the two friends move through the following series of moves:

Position 1: we have no worries about the sex of doctors: male doctors are OK
Position 2: there are circumstances where a male doctor might be a problem
Position 3: as we get older and doctors are younger than us, a male doctor might be difficult

On the face of it there is nothing very remarkable about this sequence of moves. But in fact it takes great skill for such a sequence to come about. If speakers didn't hedge their assertions, it would be difficult for other speakers to bring in different points of view without sounding antagonistic.

This is precisely what happens when speakers use bald statements. In the following example (which was recorded by chance because Anna's brother, Mark, put his head round the door to say hello to his sister and her friends), Mark and Anna start arguing about the merits of wild rice.

ANNA: wild rice is nice/ you've never tasted it [so ((xx))-
MARK: [well the Indians don't

ANNA: they probably do/
MARK: eat it so why the bloody hell should you?

ANNA:
MARK: they don't/

This exchange is adversarial rather than collaborative (and follows earlier provocative comments by Mark). Anna makes an unhedged statement about wild rice – *wild rice is nice* – and challenges Mark on the grounds that he has no right to judge since he hasn't ever tasted it. Mark, far from building on what has gone before, interrupts her in order to introduce a totally new claim (a Y to Anna's X): 'Indians don't eat wild rice'. Anna disagrees with this position (notY), but hedges her counterclaim with *probably*. Mark responds with the unhedged, bald refutation *they don't*, which just restates his original claim. It is problematic to call the sort of talk illustrated in this dialogue between Anna and Mark 'discussion' as there is no possibility of speakers shifting their ground. Without hedging, speakers take up uncompromising positions and this produces conflict. Speakers are not able to adapt or moderate their views in order to develop a more subtle, jointly agreed position. Such 'discussion' is sometimes ennobled with the term 'debate', but where all that is done is that one speaker automatically gainsays another speaker's statement, little can be achieved and talk quickly becomes futile.

In contrast with this, let's look at another example of the way women friends use hedges to promote open discussion. The topic 'Funerals' involves five women in the discussion of sensitive issues. Through the judicious use of hedges, they manage to express different points of view without coming into conflict. For example, Bea discloses that she did not attend her father's funeral because going to America at that point in her life was too difficult, and Sally agrees with her that it is madness to travel a long way for a funeral. Meg and Mary, however, both assert that there are no circumstances which would make them consider missing their mother's funeral. When the bare bones of the friends' positions are stated like this, it sounds as though they must involve conflict. In fact, the presence of hedges means that these women avoid taking up inflexible positions; here are a few examples taken from key points in the development of this topic (in the sequence in which they were uttered). Note how much of this discussion is carried out in hypothetical terms: I have included *would*, the auxiliary expressing hypothetical meaning in these utterances, since hypothetical forms can also function as a hedges.

- I said, 'Well I wouldn't go, Steve'/ and [. . .] as you say it was just taboo/ (Sally)
- she [my mother] said no/ I mean no point in coming/ (Bea)
- I mean it's not as if I'm particularly religious/ (Sally)
- if there's a spouse then perhaps they would want you to go/ (Mary)
- but I think I would be hurt and angry if they [brothers and sister] hadn't [come to the funeral]/ (Meg)
- I think going half way round the world is a different kettle of fish/ (Jen)
- well it really depends on the- I mean I think it really depends on the attitude of the survivors who are there/ (Bea)
- I think I would go now because probably- because I would want to go/ (Bea)

Because no one takes up a hard-and-fast position, the discussion moves along gradually, with different points of view being assimilated and accepted, so that eventually the group as a whole arrives at a position. This is expressed as follows:

JEN: there's two things aren't there/ there's the- the other people

---

JEN: like your mother or father who's left/ and- or- or siblings/

JEN: and there's also how how you feel at that time about .

JEN: the easiness of going/
MARY: mhm/
BEA: mhm/
MEG: mhm/
SALLY: yeah/

Note how this summary is explicitly accepted by all members of the group, and that the summary takes account of both the main positions.

Hedges are vital to the maintenance of a collaborative floor. They help to preserve openness, and they also help to avoid closure and conflict. In singly-developed floors, where speakers talk one-at-a-time, and where turns and ideas are seen to 'belong' to individual speakers, discussion will develop in a less melded way, or will not develop but will get stuck when speakers take up diametrically opposite positions. In a collaborative floor, the group voice takes precedence, which means that speakers need to avail themselves of linguistic forms like hedges which enable them to make personal statements without blocking others from make their own personal statements.

Hedging: a misunderstood activity

Ever since Robin Lakoff included hedges in her account of women's language,[5] there has been a tendency to see these linguistic forms as stereotypically feminine. This view has arisen from the assumption that the only legitimate use of hedges is to indicate doubt or uncertainty. Where hedges are used as an interpersonal resource by speakers, to be sensitive to the face needs of those we are speaking to as well as to protect our own face, they have been misunderstood and labelled 'weak', 'tentative', 'unassertive', characteristics associated with conventional femininity. Lakoff claimed that such usage was typical of women 'precisely because they are socialized to believe that asserting themselves strongly isn't nice or lady-like, or even feminine'.[6]

There are many assumptions being made here: first, that women are normally unassertive; secondly, that the use of hedges is linked with unassertiveness; and thirdly, arising from the first two, that women use hedges more than men. Ironically, while the last of these assumptions seems to have some basis in fact,[7] the first two are pure speculation. As I've argued in the central section of this chapter, there are good reasons why women exploit the multifunctional potential of hedges in their talk. Women's greater use of hedges can be explained in part by topic choice. The women's conversations I have recorded involve predominantly topics relating to people and to feelings, while men talking to other men avoid discussion of personal issues and seem to prefer to talk about things.[8] Another crucial feature of women's friendly talk is self-disclosure. It is the means by which personal experience, and the emotions associated with this experience, is shared. As I've illustrated, the preference for sensitive topics and the sharing of feelings through self-disclosure make speakers vulnerable as well as threatening the face of others. Hedges are a valuable resource for speakers in these circumstances, and women use them to mitigate the force of what is said and to protect each other.

The other main reason that women use hedges is that in talk with friends women prefer to establish a collaborative rather than a single floor. Little work has been done on all-male talk, and certainly I know of no research focusing on turn-taking patterns in the talk of men friends.[9] But Edelsky's pioneering work in this area involved a mixed group of women and men, which suggests that some men can and do operate in a collaborative floor. On the other hand, the predominance of the single, one-at-a time floor in public life, and the high value placed on this form of conversational organization in our culture, suggests that this is the pattern preferred by men. Certainly, in terms of connection and separateness (see chapter 3), the single floor is more separate and therefore more attuned to a masculine sense of identity.

Recognizing that women use hedges more than men does not entail recognizing that women are unassertive. There is nothing intrinsically unassertive about choosing to talk about sensitive subjects or about sharing feelings and experience. On the contrary, women's ability to exploit the multifunctional potential of hedges is a strength, not a weakness, and arises from women's sensitivity to interpersonal aspects of talk. Talk is never just the exchange of bits of information. Talk always involves at least two human beings, and thus involves interpersonal interaction. Hedges are a key means to modulate what is said to take account of the complex needs of speakers as social beings. In friendly talk, where *how* we talk is at least as important as *what* is talked about, hedges are a resource for doing friendship.

It is probably no coincidence that a form which is associated more with women's talk than with men's has such low status. Although I hope I have shown that hedges deserve to be highly valued, I think it is worth considering the hypothesis that women's facility with hedges does not arise by chance, but stems directly from our experience as a subordinate group. It is one of the keys to survival for members of less powerful groups in society that they pay close attention to the face needs of the powerful.[10] As a group with little power, women have had to develop extraordinary interpersonal sensitivity, to anticipate the needs and desires of more powerful others – that is, men. (This is known in folk culture as feminine intuition.) However, as women struggle for equality, for independence, for the right to self-determination, we need to re-evaluate aspects of our subculture called 'weak' by those who have had the power to label us and what we do. Hedges seem to me a prime example of a linguistic form which has been misunderstood precisely because of its association with women's ways of talking. But in talk, where we need to be sensitive to the face needs of others, where we need to qualify assertions to avoid total commitment to a particular point of view which we might want to withdraw from, where we engage in the struggle for the right words, where we want to avoid taking up hard and fast positions and want to facilitate open discussion, where we want to maintain a collaborative floor, then hedges are a vital component of talk.

8

'It was dreadful wasn't it?': Women and questions

All conversations include questions, and asking questions is something we all do routinely as speakers. In this chapter I want to examine the ways in which women friends use questions; in particular, I want to tease out the wide variety of functions that questions perform in women's conversation, in order to demonstrate what a versatile linguistic form the question is, and at the same time to show how skilful women are at exploiting this form.

What do I mean by 'question'? In written language, it's easy to spot questions, because we use the convention of putting a question mark at the end of a sentence if we want to mark it as a question (as I have done in the previous sentence). In spoken language, there are no question marks – as speakers we recognize questions by other means. But for simplicity, I have used the question mark symbol in my transcripts of the conversations to mark out those utterances which I am counting as questions (see 'Transcription Conventions', pages 11–13).

So what am I counting as a question? Here are four examples of questions from the women's conversations:

1 *[Talking about Janet's interview]*

MEG: did you get your jòb?

2 *[Talking about obedient husband]*

LIZ: whỳ did you use that word [i.e. 'obedient']?

3 *[Talking about Liz's son's school]*

ANNA: but otherwise you're háppy with the school?
LIZ: oh yeah/

---

4 *[Talking about TV programme on rabies]*

PAT: there's a cat with suspected rabies in Cumberland now ìsn't there?

I'm counting the first example (and examples like it in the conversations) as a question because some component of the verb phrase (the auxiliary *did* in this example) precedes the subject of the utterance (*you*) rather than following it. In other words, Meg signals that what she is saying is a question by using the order *did you get* instead of *you did get*. This switch of subject and verb, known as *inversion*, is a key way of marking questions.

The second example involves both subject–verb inversion (*did you*) and the WH-word *why*? Other WH-words are *what, where, who, when* and *how*. Utterances beginning with a WH-word are easy to identify as questions.

The third example demonstrates that an utterance may function as a question even though there is no subject–verb inversion and no WH-word present. What marks this utterance as a question is the rising intonation pattern which begins on the word *happy*. My assessment that what Anna says is a question is confirmed by Liz's response, *oh yeah*, which can only be construed as an answer to a question.[1] Anna could equally well have said *are you happy with the school* with inversion of subject and verb as well as rising intonation, but it is typical of speech that we often rely on prosodic features alone. (However, it's important to note that rising intonation is associated particularly with information-seeking questions, though even they frequently have falling intonation. The other three examples above all have falling intonation.)

The fourth example is a *tag question*, with the phrase *ìsn't there* 'tagged on' to the end of Pat's statement *there's a cat with suspected rabies in Cumberland now*. The tag switches the utterance from being a statement to being a question. Tags can have rising or falling intonation, depending on what the speaker is trying to convey; in this example, Pat's tag has falling intonation. Tag questions are deceptively simple constructions, and have become notorious because early commentators on language and gender claimed they were an archetypal woman's form.

Women talking to each other use questions in a wide variety of ways. Questions can be used to seek information, to encourage another speaker to participate in talk, to hedge, to introduce a new topic, to avoid the role of expert, to check the views of other participants, to invite someone to tell a story, among other things. In the next part of the chapter, I shall look at some of these functions, illustrating them with material from the conversations. I'll then deal with tag questions in a separate section, before analysing two extended examples to show how the various different uses of questions interact in continuous talk.

The various functions of questions

1 *Information-seeking questions*

When we think about questions, the kind of question that springs to mind is the classic information-seeking question such as *Did you buy any milk*? or *Where's the library?*. Information-seeking questions do occur in women's talk, but play a relatively low-key role compared with other uses of questions. This is because the primary goal of women friends' conversation is the maintenance and development of friendship; information-exchange is a secondary goal. The only exception to this claim is in the conversations of teenage girls, where information-exchange seems to have a higher priority, especially information about boys and about adolescent problems in general. Here is a brief extract from a conversation between Hannah and her friends (aged 15). (Questions are underlined in examples from this point on.)

[Discussing sanitary towels]

BECKY:	do you flush pads down the toilet? cos [Mum te- tells me
CLAIRE:	[yeah/

BECKY:	that I shouldn't do it/
CLAIRE:	I do/

Note how the above question overtly seeks information, but the questioner is also seeking reassurance that her behaviour is congruent with that of her peers. As the rest of this chapter will show, questions frequently function on several levels at a time.

The following is a typical information-seeking question from conversation between women friends:

[Topic: Karen's recent operation]

PAT: when have you got to go for another check-up?

Again, seeking information is only one of the things this question is doing. Here is the question with Karen's answer and a few more lines of conversation:

PAT: when have you got to go for another . [check up?
KAREN: [I haven't got to go/

PAT: why?
KAREN: sh- I- she- oh . it was- it was awful really/ well I went

---

KAREN: in there ek- fully expecting everything to be A1 OK/

PAT: and it wasn't/
KAREN: and it wasn't/

Pat's question, as well as specifically asking about Karen's next check-up, also functions to give Karen the chance to talk about herself and how she is feeling since her recent operation. Karen's answer to Pat is in two parts: the first part – *I haven't got to go* – is explicitly oriented to Pat's question; the second part – *it was awful really* – expands her answer, adding an evaluative component, and shows that there is more to be said. Pat then asks another information-seeking question, *Why?*, which invites Karen to explain what is 'awful'. (The doctor has told her that 'there's just one part inside that hasn't healed up'.)

There are few examples of information-seeking questions in women's friendly talk where information is the only goal of the question. One minor but important use of such questions is to clarify the meaning of a particular word.

[Claire has mentioned wildebeeste]

HANNAH: what's a wíldebeeste?
CLAIRE: it's kind of- it's like a deer/

[Final part of discussion of Apes and language]

BEA: what's a pàradigm?
MARY: that . ac[c e p t e d . view of the world=
JANET: [((purely an)) idea/

HELEN: =a sort of model/

The most salient factor in these questions is that the questioner does not know the answer to the question they pose. Hannah asks Claire what a wildebeeste is because she does not know; Bea asks for clarification of the term *paradigm* because she is not sure of its meaning.

Information-seeking questions tend to cluster at particular points in conversation, such as in the opening section where friends are catching up on each other's lives. In the following example, from one of the Oxton group's conversations, three information-seeking questions are addressed to Janet, who has recently had a job interview.

MEG: did you get your jòb?
MARY: oh did you go for a jòb? <HIGH, SURPRISED>

JANET: ((xxxx))
MEG: ((xxxx))
MARY: tell us about it/
JEN: WHÀT job?

They also occur at those points in conversation when some action is taking place simultaneously with speech, for example, the serving of food and drink. Here are two examples:

[Mary has just arrived and is offered a glass of wine]

JEN: do you want red or whìte?
MARY: oh white please/

[Anna, Sue and Liz are eating as they talk]

ANNA: do you want more garlic bread as wèll?= [two more/
LIZ: =not for me [thank you/

- -

SUE: oh bring them in just in case/ <LAUGHS>

- -

In both these examples, the person asking the question needs information: in the first example, I (Jen) don't know whether Mary would rather drink red or white wine; in the second, Anna doesn't know whether Sue or Liz want more garlic bread. But these questions are doing more than seeking information – they are crucially tied to action. All competent speakers will assume that Mary's answer led me to pour her a glass of white wine, just as Sue's response led Anna to go and get the remaining garlic bread from the kitchen.

2 *Conversational maintenance*

Questions play a crucial role in the maintenance of conversation. They allow participants in conversation to check where each other is, in particular to check that they are still in tune with each other. They are also a way in which participants in a conversational jam session invite each other to join in.

Sometimes a question invites a particular speaker to speak, as we saw above with Meg's question to Janet about her job, or the two following questions, where the addressee is actually named. In the first, Karen questions Pat about her christmas tree:

KAREN: did you get a róoted tree Pat?

and in the second, Meg questions me about my move to London:

MEG: so what are your plàns Jen? you– when you gòing?

Sometimes questions are addressed more generally to other members of the group (where there are more than two speakers):

[Discussion about Apes and language]

HELEN: but what do they [researchers] mèan by 'talking to herself'?

While these questions maintain conversation by drawing participants into talk, they also function to initiate or develop topics. For example, Karen's question to Pat leads into her telling a story about buying a tree too big to go in her house, followed by a long discussion about christmas trees, while Helen's question about apes talking to themselves moves discussion along at the same time as inviting others to clarify the point.

Women friends also ask each other questions to re-orient the conversation. The following example comes from part of a conversation where Anna had been talking about a friend's wedding dress, but conversation had drifted to talk of holidays. Liz then asked the following question, which refocused talk on the topic of the wedding:

LIZ: so you finally said that you weren't going to make this wedding dress anyway?

Not only do questions draw others in to talk, they also encourage speakers to continue talking. In other words, questions help to maintain conversation both by drawing in new speakers and by encouraging current speakers. Here are two brief examples; the first one we've looked at already in this chapter:

[Topic: Karen's recent operation]

PAT:		why?	
KAREN:	it was awful really/		well I went in there ek- fully expecting

PAT:		and it wasn't/	
KAREN:	everything to be A1 OK/		and it wasn't/

Here, Karen has started to talk, but Pat's prompt – *why?* – encourages her to continue. Similarly, in the next example, when I complain about tiredness, Helen encourages me to continue with her question:

JEN:	I'm worn out=		very tired/
HELEN:		=réally? <SYMPATHETIC>	

Another aspect of conversational maintenance is checking that communication is working. As we've already seen (in discussion of the collaborative floor), women ask each other questions to confirm that they've understood correctly and that they are following what each other is saying:

[Discussing Australian accents]

CLAIRE:	but you know Julie right? she's Australian/she-

CLAIRE: [she hasn't got an Aus- yeah/ she hasn't got an Australian accent/
BECKY: [is she Australian?

HANNAH: whó?
CLAIRE: [Julie/
BECKY: [Julie/

In this example, Becky asks *is she Australian?* to check what Claire is saying, and Hannah asks *who?* to clarify who is being talked about. In the next example, Mary uses a question to check that the Brisbane referred to by Sally is Brisbane in Australia.

[Funeral discussion]

SALLY: well she lived in Brisbane/ they were at Brisbane/

SALLY: so he's going over there- =Australia/
MARY: what – Australia?=

Cross-checking can even include checking that a word has been heard correctly:

[Talking about a boy at school]

CLAIRE: he can be such a ((xx)) but he's- he can be really sweet/

CLAIRE: a bastard/
JESS: a búzzard did you say? oh/

It's typical of collaborative talk that participants help each other to find the words they need. We've already seen (in the section on 'searching for the right word' in chapter 6) how speakers ask each other for help if they can't think of the right word. They ask each other for help by asking questions, as the following three examples illustrate.

[Talking about salads]

SUE: you know that traditional Italian- what's the óther cheese?

[Discussion of gay pop groups]

KATE: I mean wha- what's that thing where [. . .] if you're g- an- anti-gay/ what's that ((mean))?

[Talking about the TV soap Neighbours]

CLAIRE: and what's that one that speaks really weirdly? with Toby as

---

CLAIRE: his son/ um- Joe Mangel that's it/ Joe Mangel/
BECKY: Mangel/
JESS: Toby um-

CLAIRE: oh he's such a bad actor/

---

3 *Instigating stories*

Questions often occur as a prelude to stories. Sometimes a speaker will ask another speaker a question in a way which functions as an invitation to tell what has been happening to her. Meg's question to Janet about her job interview – *did you get your job?* – functions like this. Superficially, it merely asks for a yes/no answer – that is why I called it an information-seeking question earlier. But Janet interprets this question as an invitation to talk, and proceeds to tell her friends the story of her interview.

The story 'Getting undressed' (see chapter 5, page 110) also arose in response to a question. Karen told Pat that she had planted nineteen trees in her garden, and Pat responded with the following series of questions:

PAT: nineteen? what are you doing? growing your own forest?

In order to answer these questions, and to justify planting nineteen trees, Karen tells the story of seeing her neighbour undress in his living room.

Sometimes a story is hinted at, and then one of the participants will ask for clarification. The story 'Knicker stains' is foreshadowed in Becky's remark to Hannah *it was so funny when you weren't there one day,* and Hannah is further tantalized by Jessica's comment: *I told my Mum and she had hysterics,* which provokes her into asking the question *What?* followed by the unmitigated command *tell me then!*. Hannah's question (plus command) results in Becky telling the story of her famous slip of the tongue in the school library. ('Knicker stains' was discussed in detail in chapter 5, pages 107–9.)

But it is just as common for the question which initiates a story to be produced by the story-teller. In other words, narrators often begin their stories with a question which they then answer themselves. If we look at the stories discussed in chapter 5, the story 'My mother and the jogger' begins with the question *d'you know what she did recently?*; the story' I just saw everything' begins with the question *did I tell you about?- (remember I t- um I was- I went into the Stefanides' house)*; and the story 'Finding the family home' begins with the tag question *ooh I didn't tell you about my trip to Derby did I?*. In all these cases, the speaker answers her own question by telling a story. Note that other speakers do not intervene when narrators produce questions to introduce stories; the convention of starting a story with a question is well understood.

4 *Topic initiation*

This type of question overlaps with the last, since stories are often the way a new topic is introduced (as we saw in chapter 4). Questions can initiate stories, but more generally they are a way of leading into a new topic. Here are a few examples.

[Opening of topic: Being a teenager]

RUTH: would you say we're týpical teenagers?

[Beginning of topic: Quizzes]

JANET: you know the quiz Vicky goes to on Wédnesday?

[Opening of topic: Oxford student murder]

LIZ: ((wasn't it)) tèrrible about that Oxford student?

[Opening of topic: Twin Peaks *and David Lynch]*

ANNA: have either of you been watching Twin Pèaks?

[Opening of topic: Apes and language]

JEN: did you see Horìzon [BBC science programme] last night?

Questions can also be used to link one topic with another. As the 'Funerals' topic draws to a close, Mary asks Meg (who had initiated the topic with an anecdote about meeting someone who was studying taboo), *what was your bloke saying about taboo?*. Meg's rather hesitant response (*I didn't get much more from him than that/except he's looking at er ba- battering*) leads into the new topics of child abuse and the question of women's loyalty to husbands and partners.

5 *Topic development*

Questions are used in the development as well as in the initiation of topics. Speakers can use judiciously placed questions which are doing more than simply seeking an answer – the main goal is to extend the topic under discussion.

[Topic: School rabbit]

- - -

SUE: and I can't bear to see it shut in there/ all it wants to be is out/

- - -

SUE: and free=
LIZ: =mhm=
ANNA: =can't you um um re-whatsit it and let it go into the

- - -

SUE: no/ I don't think [it would survive in the wild/ [it's just
LIZ: [no it
ANNA: wìld? [wouldn't survive wòuld it?

- - -

SUE: not frightened/ <DISCUSSION CONTINUES>
LIZ: wouldn't/ no/

- - -

Anna's question in the example above extends the discussion of the rabbit and freedom. In the same way, Helen's question in the following example develops the topic of a local political crisis by checking my knowledge of it and introducing a new point:

[Helen and Jen discuss local political crisis]

- - -

JEN: and apparently [Jane Bull ((xx))
HELEN: [well in fact Jane Bull's very threatened/

- - -

JEN: [she had this grammar school
HELEN: because did you- did you hear [she had this grammar school-

---

JEN: meeting? <DISCUSSION CONTINUES>
HELEN: yes/

Questions which structure the shape of talk can occur at any point. In the discussion which forms part of the topic 'Relationships' (Sue, Liz and Anna), Liz skilfully begins to round off the discussion of the relative merits of being in a couple and independence with the following question:

LIZ: what IS it with these men though that they- they have to do that? [i.e. try to control you even though the relationship is over]

This question triggers remarks from Sue and Anna which conclude the discussion. Questions can also round off topics in a jokey way, as we saw in chapter 4 (pages 91–2). For example, Sue rounds off discussion of noise and her husband's music with the question *but why isn't it quiet?*, and Pat rounds off discussion about doctors being young with the (tag) question *there are limits aren't there?*. Questions like these invite laughter, or the exchange of rueful glances, rather than any kind of verbal response; they function to round off discussion because, although they are overtly questions, they are unanswerable.

6 *Hedging*

As we saw in the last chapter, questions are a useful resource for speakers who are trying to protect their own face and that of their addressees. Sue was able to express some of her frustration about her husband's habit of playing loud music in the room next to her daughter's bedroom through the use of questions (combined with hedges):

[Background music gets louder]

SUE: I mean how can you live with this?
LIZ: well I know it's difficult when

SUE: [oh it drives you insane/
LIZ: you've got a man around [but-

SUE: I mean Emma's sleeping next door to this/

[. . .]

LIZ: I don't think- don't think you should knock it cos I think it's really

LIZ: good [that he's got an interest/
SUE: [it's good but why isn't it quiet?

Sue's question *I mean how can you live with this?* is one that that Liz is not expected to answer. When Liz tries to look on the bright side, saying to Sue, *I think it's really good that he's got an interest,* Sue responds with another question: *it's good but why isn't it quiet?*. As I commented earlier, her jokey question allows her to seek support for her veiled complaint through inviting laughter.

Sometimes, speakers phrase their utterances as questions to hedge what they are saying even more strongly. This can be when a speaker wants to avoid offending another, as in the following example, where Gwen is being careful not to express her claims about Emily's mother too presumptuously:

[Talking about Emily's mother]

GWEN: what did she dò at your age? [. . .] was she all- all sort of a bit of

GWEN: a răver?
EMILY: I think she was/

or it can be when a topic is just very sensitive, and a speaker wants to be very careful about protecting the face-needs of everyone present:

[Talking about the incestuous family]

MARY: I mean is it- is it to do with the mòther?

The following, much longer, example shows how questions can be used in the discussion of controversial topics to introduce a different point of view without overtly disagreeing with another speaker. Where women friends are trying to establish and maintain a collaborative floor, it is crucial to avoid linguistic strategies that might lead to conflict. But this does not mean that different points of view cannot be expressed, just that they need to be introduced into discussion with care. Questions are one way of doing this. In the extract below, Sue, Liz and Anna are talking about the (contemporary) Gulf War, and about their fears of what Saddam Hussein might do.

SUE: I mean it's just frightening/ y-you get Israel into the- that's what

---

LIZ: oh yeah/ and then
SUE: he wants to do/ and all these other s- I mean they-

ANNA: it's just too horrible/ it's just too horrible
LIZ: everybody'll drag in/

ANNA: to contemplate/
LIZ: a- the- he's an absolute madman/ this is what

LIZ: fascinates me/ he's got all this support and-
SUE: yeah/

ANNA: <u>aren't they fanàtical? absolute fanàtics/</u>
----> SUE: <u>but àre they?</u> I mean I think

SUE: that people- (–) there's people like us there who think- there must

---

ANNA: [I don't know/ they all seem brainwashed/
SUE: be/ ordinary people who thin[k . 'I don't want him to do

---

ANNA: they all seem brainwashed/ well then <u>why doesn't</u> [<u>somebody-</u>
SUE: this'/ [but they

LIZ: yeah/
SUE: don't/ they're only showing you the brainwashed people/

LIZ: [there must be/
SUE: I mean there's people cowering in their homes the [same as we would

---

LIZ: I'm surprised somebody hasn't gone bang bang and that's it/
SUE: be/

ANNA: =I expect it must be too difficult . . .
LIZ: I really am=

In this discussion, two potentially conflicting points of view are voiced: first, that all Iraqis are fanatics and therefore capable of anything, second, that while Saddam Hussein might be a madman the ordinary people are people like us, who do not want war. Anna puts forward the first point of view; Sue's question *but are they [fanatics]?* raises the idea that there might be another perspective, but by using a question she does not commit herself to this point of view, and thus does not directly contradict Anna. Her question allows her to suggest rather than assert that it may not be true that all Iraqis are fanatics. The subsequent discussion shows Anna slowly modifying her position, through another question, *Why doesn't somebody [bump off Saddam Hussein]?*, which is picked up by Liz – *I'm surprised somebody hasn't gone bang bang,* a comment Anna responds to with *I expect it must be too difficult.* This latter statement reveals her as shifting to a point of view that acknowledges that ordinary people are powerless and that their apparent collusion in Saddam Hussein's military adventures does not necessarily mean they are all 'fanatics'.

7 *Rhetorical questions*

Several of the examples we have looked at have been rhetorical questions – that is, questions which do not expect an answer. Sue's question about her husband's noisy music *how can you live with this?* was a good example, as is Anna's question *aren't they fanatical?/ absolute fanatics/* in the example above. Women use rhetorical questions frequently and with great skill. They are a way of expressing general truths, which assert the group's world view and check that consensus still exists.

Often rhetorical questions are left unanswered, apart from a minimal response. Other participants agree with what is said and the conversation moves on. In the following example, the rhetorical question is answered with *I know,* showing that friends interpret rhetorical questions as a cue for agreement.

- -

JESS: why is it always that in school that your knickers start going

- -

JESS: [up your bùm?
BECKY: [I know/ I know/ I always get that/

- -

Rather than explain in detail why your knickers might start going up your bum in school, Becky chooses to respond by agreeing – *I know* – and by stating explicitly that she has had the same experience – *I always get that.* Through using rhetorical questions, friends invite each other to confirm the shared world of their jointly negotiated discourse.

In the following example, Sue is talking about her childhood, and about her parents' limited ambitions for her at school:

SUE: I remember when I got my O levels/ my dad was so proud/ and . he rung

---

SUE: everybody up to tell them/ and- but . that was the pinnacle really/
LIZ: yeah/

SUE: [that was it/ I mean what more
LIZ: yes/ there was no more after that/ [yeah

SUE: would you ne[ed than eight Ò levels? so- yeah/
LIZ: [need yeah/ it's just ignorance I suppose/

This is a complex example, since the rhetorical question voices Sue's father's world view rather than her own. Sue uses a rhetorical question to show that for her father this point of view is absolutely taken for granted. Liz's minimal response – *yeah* – expresses *not* her agreement with Sue's father's point of view, but rather her understanding of what Sue is saying, as her expansion of Sue's point – *it's just ignorance I suppose* – demonstrates.

The following, longer, example shows how rhetorical questions can occur one after the other, to build up a sense of outrage or incomprehension. Sue doesn't expect her questions to be answered. Initially, Liz struggles to provide some answers, but eventually subsides, allowing Sue to voice the moral indignation of the group. (Note how this topic is initiated with a question about a programme on television.)

[Topic: Abusive headteacher]

SUE: actually did you watch that programme about that .

LIZ: [no I didn't watch it/ I I
SUE: headmàster? who was convic- First [Tuesday it was/

LIZ: saw it was on/ I ((wouldn't)) watch it/ it was- it was
SUE: d'you know whàt Liz? I- what I don't

LIZ: in- it was-
SUE: understand/ for eight years he like- he sexually assaulted

---

LIZ: [but weren't they
SUE: beat up and everything these boys/ and [what I want to know is

LIZ: distúrbed?
SUE: how did the st- yes they were disturbed boys who were sent

LIZ: =yeah that's right/ yeah/
SUE: there for safety=

SUE: how didn't the r- the rest of the staff knòw? how didn't his

LIZ: %well apparently it can go
SUE: wìfe know? I just can't believe that nobody knew/

LIZ: on%/ yeah/
SUE: how could you live in a- cos they all lived there/ they all

LIZ: I don't know I ((expect)) –
SUE: lived in a boarding school/ how could- . how could- I could

SUE: understand the outside world not knowing/ but how could the

SUE: stàff not know?

8 *Avoiding playing the expert*

One explanation for some of the questions that women ask each other is that they are a way of avoiding playing the expert. Women avoid the role of expert in conversation in order to minimize distance between conversational participants, and questions, like hedges, are a good way of achieving this goal. The following is a brief example of what I mean. In this extract from the discussion about quizzes (discussed earlier in chapter 6), Janet feels comfortable with knowing the answer to the quiz question since she has been told it by her daughter, but the other women go out of their way to confirm that they don't know.

[Topic: Quizzes]

JANET: 'Where's the biggest pyramid?' was what they had last night=
MARY: ='What's

```
-------------------------------------------------------------------
JANET:                              ='where's the biggest'=        =pyramid/where/
MARY:   the biggest pyramid'?=                                =where?=
SALLY:                 ((shocks xx))
-------------------------------------------------------------------
JANET:          [it's in MExico=
MEG:            |                 = is it?            oh one of those Aztec .
MARY:   in E[gypt?               =oh in Mexico is it?
SALLY:  ((is it Ok-xx?)) -   =right/                                       mhm/
-------------------------------------------------------------------
MEG:      numbers/
JEN:               ((xx)) one of those trick ones=
MARY:                                              =God I'd be hopeless at that/
HELEN:             mhm/                            =mhm/
-------------------------------------------------------------------
```

First Mary checks what the question is, then she and Sally guess the answer, but with rising intonation patterns to indicate their lack of confidence. When Janet tells them the answer, Meg and Mary acknowledge it with questions, and Mary sums up the general air of amused incompetence with the statement *God I'd be hopeless at that.*

The multifunctionality of questions

Like other linguistic forms, questions can carry out several functions at once. As we've seen in the examples above, questions can ask for information at the same time as inviting another speaker to expand on a point, or they can raise a new point at the same time as protecting the addressee's face. Questions can initiate a story or introduce a topic at the same time as bringing in another speaker, or they may ask for information as a way of disclaiming expertise. They can express ignorance or astonishment or curiosity or horror, often simultaneously; they can also express the obvious (when used rhetorically) at the same time as checking the viewpoint of other speakers. This complexity is true of both questions and tag questions. The next section will look briefly at women's use of tag questions, then I'll analyse two longer extracts, to demonstrate more fully the multifunctionality of questions.

Tag questions

Tag questions get a section to themselves not just because they are formally different from other questions, but also because since the publication of Robin Lakoff's *Language and Woman's Place*, no discussion of women's talk would be complete without a discussion of tag usage. As I stated earlier, tags were treated by early commentators on language and gender as an archetypal woman's form, and as a result tag questions have received a great deal of attention from sociolinguists and discourse analysts. Lakoff claimed that tag questions that do not seek information are intrinsically weak and are typically used by women to express tentativeness and unassertiveness. In this section I'll describe some of the ways tags are used in the conversations between women friends I've recorded. In a later section I'll assess the claim that tags are 'powerless' forms.

As I've outlined above, with tag questions a statement is turned into a question by the addition of a tag at the end. The 'tag' is simply the subject and verb (or verbal component) of the main clause repeated with inversion and with the addition of *not* if the main clause is positive (and without *not* is the main clause is negative). In other words, normally the tag has contrasting polarity with the main clause: e.g. *it is, isn't it?* vs. *it isn't, is it?*. Like questions, tag questions can be used to elicit information, but this is the function of only a minority of examples in the conversations I've recorded.[2] The following is an example:

[Talking about jobs]

HELEN: you haven't been applying for jobs as well <u>háve you?</u>

Helen asks her friend whether she's been applying for jobs because she does not know: this is a true information-seeking question. The subject and the auxiliary verb in the first part of this utterance – *you haven't (been applying)* – are picked up in the tag – *have you?* – and because the verb in the main clause is negated (that is, includes *not*), there is no *not* in the tag. Note the rising intonation contour on the tag, signalling very clearly that this is an information seeking question. Tag questions with other functions tend to have falling rather than rising intonation.

In the conversations of women friends, one of the chief uses of tags is to invite other speakers to participate, to draw them into conversation. Here are three examples (tags underlined):

[Talking about the way talk changes when a man joins in]

- -

LIZ: but it does change <u>dòesn't it?</u>
ANNA: yeah/

- -

[Talking about Jen's behaviour during egg-and-spoon race at primary school]

JEN: it was dreadful <u>wàsn't it?</u>=
MARY: =appalling Jennifer/ absolutely appalling/

[Talking about doctors and youthfulness]

KAREN: I suppose if you're ill you don't care <u>dò you?</u>
PAT: I suppose not/

KAREN: there are/
PAT: but there are- um there are limits <u>àren't there?</u>

In each of these examples, the tag question results in a response (even if only a minimal response) from another participant. In the following example, the tag again results in a response, but here, because the utterance is jointly constructed by two speakers, we get the unusual phenomenon of the speaker who produces the tag also responding to it with *that's right*. This example illustrates very clearly how in a collaborative floor it is unimportant who says what: between them, these two women friends concoct a hypothesis to explain Lynn's mother's fainting bouts.

[Talking about friend's mother passing out in street]

PAT: this woman is already on . every kind of pill you can think of for

---

PAT: high blood pressure/ and if her blood pressure has naturally reduced

---

PAT: a bit/ those pills= [her pills
KAREN: =are reducing it even more <u>àren't they?</u> [that's

---

PAT: are too strong/
KAREN: right/

Tags like the ones in the last four examples are known as *facilitative tags*, and they make up the majority of examples in the conversations. But often in the talk of women friends, tags are *not* verbally responded to. Here are three examples:

[Discussion of Yorkshire Ripper case]

MEG: and they had- they had a very accurate picture of him dìdn't they? they roughly knew his age . . .

[Discussion of co-educational schools]

JANET: they are a bit under threat at the moment àren't they? there's a lot of articles about girls doing better ((in)) single sex schools/

[End of topic: Relationships]

LIZ: it's strange ìsn't it? the life some people lead/

Younger speakers often use the invariant tag *right,* as in the following examples:

[End of Becky's revelations about fancying Damien]

CLAIRE: but they're so stupid right? cos then- cos Nina said . . .

['Knicker stains' story]

BECKY: well we were in the library right? and we were in that corner where all the um- the picture books are/

In all these examples, the speaker's tag – whether it occurs at the end or in the middle of an utterance – does not produce a verbal response from other participants. Note that there is no hesitation in the speaker's talk at these points: the lack of response does not seem to perturb speakers. On the contrary, the main function of these tags is to check the taken-for-granted-ness of what is being said, to confirm the shared world of the participants. This use of tags is very similar to the use of rhetorical questions. A fuller response to these tags is not what is expected. On the rare occasion when a speaker's assumption that others are in agreement turns out to be wrong, participants have to work together to repair things. In the following example, from the topic 'Child abuse', Mary's check for her statement being a taken-for-granted is taken up by Bea, who disagrees with Mary's assumption about children's screaming:

[Discussing child abuse]

MEG: what I can't fathom out is why children who are physically battered

---

MEG: by their parents/ . there's no- there's never any suggestion that .

MEG: they contributed to it/ [and yet children who are sexually abused by
MARY: [yes there is/

MEG: their parents/ somehow that's- you know the chi- [the- the-
MARY: [well there is/ .

MARY: because there's that thing of a certain pitch of screaming

---

MARY: ìsn't there?= [oh/ =sorry=
BEA: =ah but no/ that's logical/ [genuine= =she's um-

MARY: oh/
BEA: she's talking about the emotional ((sort of)) feeling/

Mary's *oh* and *sorry* demonstrate her surprise, and also shows that speakers in collaborative talk are prepared to withdraw statements which turn out not to be acceptable to others present.

Tag questions, like full questions, as well as being facilitative and checking the shared world, also simultaneously carry out other functions, such as helping to structure conversation. The following example is taken from a point in one of the Oxton group's conversations where the topic shifts from child abuse to wives' loyalty to husbands.

BEA: and your husband has become a monster= } <END OF
MEG: =mhm/ } 'CHILD ABUSE'
SALLY: =mhm/ mhm/ } TOPIC>

MARY: I mean it's like that woman who turned in . was it . pri- Prìme?

MARY: [. . .] one of those spy cases/ it was his wife wàsn't it? who turned

---

MARY: him in= }
BEA: =yes/ } <BEGINNING OF 'LOYALTY TO MEN' TOPIC>
JEN: =oh yes/ }

Mary's tag question here serves to get agreement from the group to pursue a new (related) topic; it functions as a check on the collaborative progress of the conversation. Tags are also used in the development of topics. In the following example, Anna and Liz share in talk about a boy who has piano lessons with the same teacher as them.

They use both questions and tag questions to keep their talk tied to each other and to develop the subtopic of Dominic.

[Piano lessons]

ANNA: there's a lovely little boy who goes before me called

ANNA: Dominic= [he's got red hair/ [have you sèen him? he's just
LIZ: =Domi[nic yeah [he's gorgeous/

ANNA: [so sweet/ and he's ever so shy/ so I make a point of tal[king to him
LIZ: [yeah/ [he's just

ANNA: every week/ [that's right/
LIZ: done his grade one as well hàs[n't he?

Tags are also used to hedge utterances. In the following example, Karen and Pat have been discussing a friend's mother who keeps passing out but refuses to see a doctor; they have negotiated a joint position on what the friend ought to do about her mother, a position which Karen doesn't want to undermine by taking too firm a line.

[Topic: Friend's mother fainting in the street]

KAREN: I think if you're with someone who suddenly falls over/ if nothing else you'd get into a restaurant or somewhere where you could sit down/ wòuldn't you? wóuldn't you? . well I think Ì would/

The two tag questions use the same words, but express very different meanings. The first is a typical confirming-the-shared-world tag which expects no reply; it has falling intonation. The second is an information-seeking tag with rising intonation, which does seek a response – a response which Karen herself provides. It's as if Karen briefly doubts her assumption that she and Pat share the view that old people with blood pressure problems who pass out in the street need medical attention. But the moment passes and Karen answers her own question with the assertion *well I think I would*. (Even so, she hedges this assertion with *well* and *I think*.)

As many of these examples show, questions and tag questions often occur in close proximity. Many of their functions overlap, and speakers are able to exploit the verstility of these forms in their talk.

Two extended examples

So far I've discussed most examples as if they could be neatly labelled as meaning just one thing at any one time. In order to demonstrate the multifunctionality of questions, and to show how different kinds of questions interact in continuous text, I want now to look at two extended examples.

The first comes from a discussion of child abuse. The five friends are debating whether boy victims are viewed differently from girl victims. Meg puts forward an example of a little boy who had recently been in the news.

MEG:	you remember that little boy that was um . in Brìghton/ that

MEG:	was um . carried òff= =and sexually abùsed/ everyone was
SALLY:	yes/ yes/
MARY:	mhm/ =yes=

MEG:	outràged about [that= yes/
SALLY:	[did they ever find the people that dìd that?
BEA:	=mhm/

MEG:	they dìd/ dídn't they?
SALLY:	yeah/
MARY:	díd they? yeah/ I remember/ yes/

MEG:	yes/ they-
SALLY:	réally?
BEA:	díd they find them?
MARY:	they were in France wéren't they?

MEG:	they were part of a pornographic sèt-up/

Although phrased as a statement, Meg's opening remark *you remember that little boy that was um . in Brighton that was um . carried off and sexually abused* functions as a question: note how the other women present give answers (*mhm, yes*) to indicate that they do remember. They treat her utterance as if she had said, *do you remember . . . ?*.

One of the reasons I chose this extract was that one of the speakers here is an expert: Meg at this time was a psychologist specializing in incest cases. But Meg deliberately avoids expert status by recycling Sally's question *did they ever find the people who did that?* by adding a tag to her answer: *yes they did didn't they?*. This provokes a sequence of questions involving four of the five women present. The general effect of the interrogative forms in this passage is to blur, or share out, the roles of expert and questioner. Questions are answered with other questions, assertions are converted into questions by the addition of tags (*didn't they?*, *weren't they?*). Four of the five participants are involved before the group comes to a satisfactory conclusion. The group as a whole gets involved in both asking questions and answering them, and noone takes sole responsibility for finding answers.

The discussion continues with more general talk about child abuse.

MEG: yeah/
MARY: but I mean so much research is male-dominated/ I mean it just- .

MEG: =mhm= ((such see-through blinkered))=
BEA: =but also when you get down to it .
MARY: it's staggering isn't it?= =I mean ((xx))

BEA: [if you began to even have the faintest suspicions that your
MARY: [=that's right/

BEA: husband . was interfering with . your- . the two of you's

---

MEG: mhm/
BEA: daughter/ . how quickly- . I mean in order to accept that

---

BEA: idea/ you're having to . [completely
JEN: yes/
MARY: mhm/ . completely review your [view of

SALLY: =yes/ =yes, that's right=
BEA: change your view of your husband= =and to
MARY: your husband=

MEG: mhm/ =yes/
BEA: have him become a person who can do . the undoable=
MARY: =that's

BEA: =and how easy is it to do that?=
MARY: right= =mhm/

The chief work being done here is that of checking the shared world view of the group. Mary's tag question – *it's staggering isn't it* – draws on ideological assumptions that the group has built up over the years:

in this case, that male domination is a fact. Similarly, Bea's rhetorical questions (one incomplete – *how quickly* – and one complete – *how easy is it to do that*) draws on the assumption that changing your perceptions of your partner is difficult to do. By phrasing these assumptions as questions, women friends allow room for others to confirm that this is indeed the group's position (Meg's ratifies Mary's claim and Mary ratifies Bea's, both with the minimal response, *mhm*).

In the second example, Sue, Liz and Anna talk about a recent murder case in Oxford. As we've seen, Liz triggers the topic with the question *wasn't it terrible about that Oxford student?*. What follows is from the central section of the discussion, where they are pondering the psychology of the male student who has been arrested following the murder of a female student, his ex-girlfriend.

ANNA: ((is he)) mentally ill or whàt? oh I don't suppose they'll say
LIZ: ((oh I don't know xx))

ANNA: yet for ages wìl l they?
LIZ: but he's- he's- he's from New Zealand/ and his

LIZ: parents are flying over from New Zealand to s- . to support
SUE: oh his poor parents/ poor-

LIZ: him/
SUE: yeah but his poor- i- dg- can you imàgine? having a son

ANNA: but actually it must have been someone very close to her/
LIZ: no I can't/
SUE: that ((xx))

ANNA: because otherwise what- how would they have got into the hòuse?

[. . .]

ANNA: I wonder what your motive- what his mòtive would've
LIZ: it's very dis turbing=
SUE: =mhm/

ANNA: been?
LIZ: it's jealousy more than likely/
SUE: exactly/ what ìs his motive?

SUE: but how could you dò that to somebody?

Anna's first question – *((is he)) mentally ill or what?* – seems to be a rhetorical question, an exclamation of horror: she doesn't wait for a reply, though Liz struggles to find one. Her subsequent tag question, *oh I don't suppose they'll say yet for ages will they?*, is an example of a shared world-checking tag: she in effect asserts that it can be assumed that it will take a long time for the full facts to emerge. This tag receives no overt verbal response, implying that Sue and Liz accept her point. Liz and Sue then start to talk about the suspected student's parents; Sue asks the rhetorical question *can you imagine [having a son who is accused of murder]?*, meaning that it is impossible to imagine what parents in that position feel like, a claim which Liz ratifies (*no I can't*). Anna also uses a rhetorical question – *how would they have got into the house?* – to clinch her point that the murderer must be someone very close to the victim. She then uses an embedded question following the verb *I wonder*, asking in effect, *What would his motive have been?*. Sue picks this up and rephrases it: *what is his motive?*. When Liz suggests a motive, Sue responds with a rhetorical question – *but how could you do that to somebody?*. The overall effect of this series of questions is to express the three friends' horror and incomprehension over the murder. These questions move discussion on by stimulating new hypotheses. For example, Sue's question *what is his motive?* leads Liz to suggest that jealousy may be a factor. But overall the cumulative effect of the questions expresses the speakers' belief that there aren't any easy answers.

Women and questions

Language and gender oriented research has associated women with questions in negative ways. Several studies of mixed talk, in both public and private settings, have established that women use questions more frequently than men.[4] The inference was made that, since women are relatively powerless members of our society, and since women use questions more than men, then questions must in some way be powerless forms. This belief is historically linked to Robin Lakoff's famous claim that tag questions that do not seek information are not 'legitimate', and that such questions are typical of women speakers and are an expression of tentativeness (and of femininity).[5]

More recently, discourse analysts have suggested that questions are in fact potentially powerful linguistic forms. Various studies have established that powerful speakers, such as magistrates, doctors, teachers, and presenters of TV discussion programmes, use more questions than less powerful speakers.[6] This latter research has focused on *asymmetrical* talk – that is, talk between people who are not equals. But the talk of friends is *symmetrical* talk. The questions we find in friends' talk are not (normally) expressive of power or powerlessness. Yet questions occur frequently in the talk of women friends – more frequently than in the talk of male friends.[7] And women use questions in a wide variety of ways, though rarely as information-seeking devices. In the remainder of this chapter, I want to suggest some reasons why this might be the case.

Connection and separateness

In chapter 3, I introduced the idea that women's relationships are characterized by connection rather than separateness, an idea which originates in the work of Nancy Chodorow.[8] Language is a key means by which we negotiate connection and separateness in our interaction with others. Questions have a particularly important role here. Where they are used to demarcate roles such as those of more powerful participant and less powerful participant, or expert and non-expert, then questions reinforce the boundaries between speakers and promote separateness. But when they are used primarily to draw others into conversation, to minimize expert status, and to affirm the importance of the group rather than the individual, then questions are a powerful tool for promoting connection.

All questions can be divided into those which are primarily *speaker-oriented* and those which are primarily *other-oriented.*[9] Questions which seek information are speaker-oriented: when a speaker asks an information-seeking question, they are saying, 'I don't know and I want you to tell me'. Other-oriented questions are concerned with the addressee rather than the speaker – they invite others into talk, they check on others' views. Other-oriented questions are also concerned with conversational maintenance – they are used to initiate or develop topics, to introduce stories. Other-oriented questions essentially express solidarity and connection.

As the examples in the earlier part of this chapter have demonstrated, the questions used by women friends tend to be other-oriented rather than speaker-oriented. This arises from three underlying trends in the talk of women friends. First, the establishment and maintenance of a shared world is a crucial aspect of women's friendship. One of the things we do in conversation is check our assumptions about this shared world – questions are a good way of doing this. As earlier examples have shown, both rhetorical questions and certain types of tag are used to assert the shared value system of the group, but in a way that allows these values to be challenged if necessary. Normally, such questions are interrogative in form only: they are not answered or are answered minimally by others. Their essential function is to check the taken-for-grantedness of what is being said and to check that what is said voices the views of the whole group rather than of the individual.

Secondly, questions are used as a means to sustain the collaborative floor. Questions by their very nature acknowledge that talk involves at least two speakers: someone to ask and someone to answer (though these roles may be shared in complex ways by participants in a collaborative floor, for example by two people answering at once). Using questions is a way of staying connected to other speakers, a way of signalling awareness of others in talk. In a collaborative floor, the group takes precedence over the individual: by phrasing utterances as questions rather than statements, speakers allow for the expression of other views and for the participation of others. Questions permit constant cross-referencing across the group.

Thirdly, they are one of the ways by which we can avoid talking like an expert.[10] It is important to maintain an ethic of reciprocity in friendship and therefore in friendly talk. Questions are a useful resource for minimizing social distance and promoting equality between speakers. In the talk of women friends, they are used to communicate: 'I don't want to make out that I know all the answers, and I would like to hear what you have to say'.

Fundamentally, questions are a way of expressing solidarity and connection. These are a vital aspect of the talk of women friends. In our talk, we are not just catching up on each others' news and discussing matters of interest to us: we are through our talk constructing our friendship. (The ways in which talking is doing friendship will be the subject of chapter 11.) Far from being powerless forms, the evidence of this chapter suggests that questions are a powerful means of establishing connections between speakers. They are used very skilfully by women who exploit them at the *interactional* rather than the informational level. To describe such usage as 'not legitimate' is to misunderstand the fundamental goals of friendly talk. Such misunderstanding arises from an androcentric perspective which sees the more adversarial, information-focused pattern of men's talk as normative.

9

'I just kept drinking and drinking and drinking': Repetition and textual coherence

In this chapter, I shall look more closely at patterns of repetition in the speech of women friends. In chapter 4, I described the 'shape' of friends' talk, which consisted typically of one woman saying something, and then another woman responding with something from her own experience. When we respond to what each other says, we say something that matches or mirrors what our friend said. This matching and mirroring, which characterizes our conversations, is often realized linguistically in complex patterns of *repetition*. Repetition can involve words, grammatical structures and meaning; that is, repetition can occur at lexical, syntactic and semantic levels. For example, the sequence of mirroring turns about hot water bottles (from Jessica, Becky, Hannah and Claire's discussion of their periods) involved a great deal of repetition. Here is this (edited) sequence of turns again.

Hot water bottles

Turn 1: but hot water bottles help (Jessica)
Turn 2: hot water bottles help (Becky)
Turn 3: hot water bottles help me as well (Hannah)
Turn 4: help so much (Claire)

The phrase *hot water bottles* is repeated three times, the verb *help* is repeated four times, and all four turns repeat the same syntactic pattern – NP + VP (Noun Phrase + Verb Phrase) – though Hannah uses *help* as a transitive rather than intransitive verb and Claire omits the subject Noun Phrase. As I commented earlier, the linguistic parallelism in this sequence is designed to maximize solidarity between the four friends: the repetition of words and phrases and of sentence structure functions as a very strong form of agreement and of mutual affirmation. Repetition has several different functions, however, and in this chapter we will look at a variety of examples from the friends' conversations to try to establish what these are.

Textual coherence

When speakers repeat elements of talk – words, phrases, themes, structures, meanings – they construct text which is *coherent*.[1] The texts discussed here, conversations between close women friends, are dynamic expressions of meaning jointly negotiated by particular speakers in a particular place at a particular time. In face-to-face interaction, participants in talk will go to almost any lengths to discover coherence in utterances they hear. With or without the presence of formal textual markers, we attempt to interpret what we hear; in other words, we assume text is coherent. Our ability to discover discourse coherence is a very important part of our discourse competence.[2]

Coherence operates at many levels: thematic, syntactic (clause structure), semantic (meaning), lexical (words). And it functions in a variety of ways: in terms of production and comprehension, it binds textual elements together; at the interpersonal level, it binds speakers together. I'll begin this exploration of the way coherence operates in the talk of women friends by looking at lexical patterns in the speech of a single speaker, before moving on to the more complex patterns involving two or more speakers.

Repetition involving a single speaker

Repetition is a normal component of unplanned as opposed to planned discourse.[3] It is often interpreted as being part of the work that speakers need to do as they attempt to think out an idea, or select an appropriate word. The following three examples illustrate this relatively trivial type of repetition (repeated elements underlined).

[Discussion of general studies teaching at local comprehensive school]

I mean Simon's perfectly relaxed with Miss- . Miss Laithwaite/

[Topic: Grain trains in the docks]

I was- I was- I was stopped by a train/

[Talking about open evening at school]

well it's like Steve goes all- Steve goes all twitchy/

But often it's clear that repetition is doing more than just allowing a speaker to organize her thoughts. In the next three examples, the speaker expands her point by repeating her original words and adding to them.

[Topic: Gulf War]

ANNA: it's just too horrible/ it's just too horrible to contemplate/

[Talking about women not being able to deal with bills and mortgages]

LIZ: but it's a myth you know/I wish a lot of women would realize that it's a complete and utter myth/

[Topic: Friend who was keen Marxist]

PAT: I used to like John when he was furious/ well I like him now but I preferred him when he was furious and bitter/[. . .] I prefer him when he's all interesting and furious/ argumentative/

In these examples, the exact repetition of particular words serves to emphasize the point the speaker is making. But in every case the speaker goes on to expand her point, adding to or adapting what she says. Liz's original *it's a myth* is expanded to the more forceful *it's a complete and utter myth.* Pat's original characterization of John as *furious* develops into *furious and bitter* and then to *interesting and furious/ argumentative.* Sue does the same thing in the following example, repeating her words and adding to them:

[Discussion of obedient husband]

SUE: he's got this twi- he's got this nervous twitch/ [. . .] he's got this nervous t- [LAUGHS] he's got this real nervous twitch/

Some of the repetition here results from the work Sue has to do to continue with her story while her two friends provide a simultaneous commentary. But we see Sue's statement build up from *he's got this twitch* via *he's got this nervous twitch* to *he's got this real nervous twitch.* Here, the noun phrase is slowly extended: the speaker embroiders on her original words at the same time as emphasizing her point through repetition. In the next example, which follows on from the previous one about the husband's nervous twitch, the repeated chunks have an important rhetorical function.

SUE: but listen/ when he's not with her he hasn't got it/ he hasn't got it when he's not with her/

Through repeating what she says, Sue draws her friends' attention to this key point. Repetition here involves inversion: the structure of the utterance is (A+B) + (B+A). This means that we get the A clause – *when he's not with her* – twice and the B clause – *he hasn't got it* – twice, but in two different orders. Since in English utterances have the structure Topic + Comment or Old Information + New Information, reversing the order of the two clauses allows the speaker to give the utterance a slightly different emphasis the second time and tells the recipients of the message to process it in two slightly different ways. Sue wants to make sure her friends take in the full significance of what she is saying (that is, that this man's nervous twitch only appears when he's in the company of his wife).

Intraspeaker repetition – that is, repetition that takes place *within* the talk of a single speaker – is particularly common in narrative sections of the conversations. This isn't surprising: given that women friends tend to use a collaborative floor, it is only really in storytelling that any one speaker gets to hold the floor for any length of time. I shall look briefly now at repetition in four of the narratives.

Repetition in narrative

In the story 'Cystitis' (originally discussed in chapter 5, pages 104–5), Anna says, *So while we were waiting at the airport [. . .] I actually drank three litres of water [. . .] and I just kept drinking and drinking and drinking*. The repeated *drinking* is clearly meant to be there, that is, Anna is not wondering what to say next, but is deliberately repeating the verb in order to emphasize how much she drank. This emphatic function occurs frequently in narrative: here are the first ten lines of the 'Cystitis' story, with repeated chunks underlined.

So while we were waiting at the airport- our plane was delayed- I actually drank three litres of water.
We were there for like an hour and a quarter
and I just kept drinking and drinking and drinking
We got on the plane and of course I couldn't stop going to the loo.
5 Then it got worse and worse and worse.
I spent the whole plane journey to Ro- to Rome in the toilet.
Three quarters of the way through the plane journey I- I literally couldn't leave I was in such pain
Shirley came banging on the door.
'Are you all right? Are you all right?'
10 She was trying to get the air hostess to come and see to me.

The first bit of repetition in this extract involves repetition of part of the verb phrase – in effect, Anna is saying 'I just kept drinking' three times. The next bit of repetition involves the comparative adjective *worse* – here Anna is in effect saying 'it got worse' three times. Both these examples involve a clause in which the final element is repeated. These repeated elements are linked by the coordinator *and*. By contrast, the last example in this passage involves repetition of an entire clause: *Are you all right?* and the clause occurs twice, not three times. The effect is emphatic: the repeated question communicates Shirley's anxiety better than a single question would.

The second example has been chosen to illustrate syntactic repetition in narrative. All narrative involves a sequence of parallel narrative clauses. (A narrative clause consists of a subject – usually a pronoun – and a simple – usually past tense – verb.) This extract comes from the story 'My mother and the jogger' (originally discussed in chapter 5, pages 100–1); it illustrates clearly the pattern typical of narrative.

She took them [two Dobermans] for a walk on the beach one day,
and this was at the height of the Rottweiler scare,
and this jogger's running along the beach at Liverpool,
and Sophie, her dog that she can't control,
decided to run along after the jogger
and bit him on the bottom.
[. . .]
So she said, 'Let me have a look',
and she strode over and pulled his- <LAUGHS> pulled his tracksuit bottoms down,
and said, 'Don't be so bloody stupid man there's nothing wrong with you,
you're perfectly alright.'
At which point he was so embarrassed he just jogged away. <LAUGHTER>

Syntactic repetition here involves the repeated pattern Subject + Past Tense Verb.

The bare bones of the sequence are:

she took . . .
Sophie decided . . .
(Sophie) bit . . .
she said . . .
she strode over . . .
(she) pulled . . .
(she) said . . .
he . . . jogged away.

Such sequences of narrative clauses are intrinsic to narrative: they constitute the heart of the story and make narrative textually cohesive. The third example I shall analyse here involves more complex repetitive patterns superimposed on a sequence of narrative clauses. The extract comes from the opening section of Sue's narrative about the 'Obedient husband':

1 I told you I went round to a friend's who **had ((a)) guitar**.
[. . .]
The wife right- his wife would not let him **have a guitar**.
3 She said, 'No';
and he's so obedient.
5 She's- she said, 'You're not **having a guitar**',
so he **didn't have one**,
7 he just didn't play it ever.
And then for christmas she allowed him to **have a guitar**
9 as long as he didn't play it in front of her.

I've marked in bold all instances of the phrase *have a guitar*, which occurs four times in all, in lines 1, 2, 5, 8, plus the phrase *didn't have one* where the noun phrase 'a guitar' is replaced by the anaphoric pronoun *one*. This is not the only repetition in this short passage. The phrase *she said* occurs in line 3 and again in line 5. Lines 5, 6, 7 and 9 all involve negation: *not* in line 5; *n't* in lines 6, 7 and 9. Lines 6, 7 and 9 repeat *he didn't*, while 7 and 9 repeat the longer chunk *he didn't play it*. At the semantic level, the *'No'* of line 3 is expanded into *'You're not having a guitar'* in line 5, while *let* in line 2 is replaced by the semantically equivalent *allow* in line 8. At the grammatical level there's a repeated pattern of simple past tense verbs: *told, went, had, said, allowed*. These repetitions are marked in the passage below:

1 I told you I went round to a friend's who **had ((a)) guitar**.
[. . .]
The wife right- his wife would not let him **have a guitar**.
3 She said 'No',
and he's so obedient.
5 She's- she said 'You're not **having a guitar**',
so he didn't have one,
7 he just didn't play it ever.
And then for Christmas she allowed him to **have a guitar**
9 as long as he didn't play it in front of her.

One of the reasons repetition is such a feature of narrative is clearly the result of narrator's design. Unlike discussion sections, narrative sections often involve only one speaker, the narrator, and narrators aim to produce stories which are carefully patterned pieces of text, with a beginning, middle and end. The fact that stories typically involve sequences of simple narrative clauses means that there is bound to be syntactic coherence, and lexical and semantic coherence arise from the need for narrators to repeat material in the interest of making sure their listeners can follow the story.

Finally, if we look at the story 'Getting undressed' again (originally discussed in chapter 5, page 110), we can see that one of the reasons this story works as a coherent text is through the patterns of repetition that recur in it.

Getting undressed

it was a couple of weeks ago
I forget now which day it was
3 but I was sitting in my living room
and without meaning to I was looking out into the garden
and I was looking straight into Lever's house
6 that's the one up in Bentley Close on the corner
and I saw him get undressed in his living room
there's no reason why you shouldn't get undressed in your living room if you want to (*yeah*)
9 and I thought, 'My God' (*yeah*)
'if I can see him' *he can see you*
and I don't always just get undressed in the living room. <LAUGH>

There are many patterns of repetition here but I shall concentrate on just two of them (underlined in the example). First, the pattern *I* + *was* + *Verb* + *ing* is repeated three times, with the verb *sit* used the first time and the verb *look* repeated in the other two. These verbs all provide us with background information, and are strongly contrasted with the verb *saw* in the simple past tense, which occurs in the narrative clause at the heart of the story (line 7). The other notable repeated element in this text is the phrase *get undressed in (his/your/the) living room*. This is the key theme of this story and by repeating it word for word (apart from the minor but significant change in the word telling us *whose* living room is referred to) the narrator makes sure this theme is constantly foregrounded. At the same time, the exact lexical repetition here is in tension with the variety of structures in which it is embedded on each separate occasion. I can only begin to scratch at the surface of these here. The first time the phrase is part of a statement of an actually occurring event in the past; the second time, the phrase is part of a general (timeless) statement about normal behaviour; the third time it is part of a statement about the personal habits of the narrator. This third version – *I don't always just get undressed in the living room* – relies for its interpretation on our understanding an (unspoken) fourth recurrence of the phrase: *I (sometimes) get undressed in my living room.*

Repetition involving more than one speaker

As we've seen in previous chapters, while narrative plays a significant role in women friends' talk, talk more commonly involves all participants. We'll look now at patterns of repetition occurring *across* speaker turns in discussion sections of conversation. I shall begin by looking at examples of lexical repetition.

Lexical repetition

The first two examples involve single lexical items only: in both examples below, the second speaker repeats what the first speaker has just said. (I'm using the terms *first* and *second* very loosely here, to refer to the order in which speakers contribute in the extracts: since these examples are taken from conversation involving a collaborative floor, the terms do not mean 'first' or 'second' in any more significant sense, as all speakers are simultaneously present in a collaborative floor. I shall come back to this point in the next section.)

[Topic: Funerals and taboo]

Sally: it's obviously gonna cost him a for [tune/
Mary: [fortune/

[Topic: Local political crisis]

Jen: because they've only got to win two [seats/
Helen: [two/

This sort of repetition is relatively common in relaxed conversation between friends. The repeated material can involve longer chunks of talk, up to and including whole clauses, as the next two examples illustrate:

[Topic: Trains in Birkenhead docks]

Sally: it's the grain trains=
Mary: =it's the grain trains/

[Talking about taking pleasure in others' failures]

Mary: but I don't like feeling like that=
Meg: =no I don't like feeling

Meg: like that/

Some commentators would describe such repetition as 'redundant'.[4] The internal evidence of the texts suggests that this is not so. Let's look at fuller versions of two of these examples:

[Topic: Local political crisis]

Jen: because they've only got to win two [seats=
Helen: [two = yes I know/

[Topic: trains in Birkenhead docks]

SALLY:	it's the grain trains [I think to go to the- yes
MARY:	[it's the grain trains/ yes it was

SALLY:	yes/ yes/
MARY:	the bulk carriers/

The fuller versions of these examples demonstrate that such repetitions are interpreted by co-participants as coherent contributions to talk, and not as redundant moves. Speakers signal their acceptance of others' contributions by their use of minimal responses such as *yes*, and in these friends' conversations there are no responses signalling rejection or discomfort (such as 'I've just said that' or 'Stop repeating what I say'). This is because one of the functions of repetition is to signal agreement: repeating a chunk of talk is a much stronger way of signalling active involvement in ongoing discourse than a minimal response such as *mhm* or *yes*.

If we look at an example involving three speakers, we can see very clearly the way these cross-speaker repetitions function to signal involvement as well as to provide coherence across the text:

[Topic: Watching film in college]

SUE:	so I mean we watched the film/ the seven up film and . fourteen up

SUE:	or something/ [watched that which is
LIZ:	[oh you [watched that there/
ANNA:	oh you watched [that/ . oh that's right/

SUE:	really interesting/

Here Sue's statement that she'd watched the (series of) films called 'Seven Up' is echoed by both Anna and Liz (compare the effect of this with a version where they just said *mhm*). Sue then repeats her own statement before expanding on it to say what she thought of the series.

Sometimes in a sequence of talk it is the first speaker rather than the second who introduces repeated material. (Again, *first* and *second* are being used in an oversimplistic way just to clarify description.)

[Topic: screening trees and fear of being overlooked]

- -

KAREN: I mean OK I'm sure he's not= =peeping or anything/
PAT: =peeping=

- -

In the above example, Pat's one-word contribution is repeated by Karen and thus incorporated into the text. In the next two examples, the second speaker contributes more than one word and the whole chunk is then recapitulated by the first speaker.

[Topic: Karen's recent operation]

- -

KAREN: I went in there ek- fully expecting everything to be A1 OK/

- -

KAREN: = and it wasn't/
PAT: and it wasn't=

- -

[Topic: The kitchen as a place for women friends to talk]

- -

BEA: I think one of the reasons it used to be the kitchen was- didn't we

- -

BEA: use to try and keep the children in the sitting room where the toys

- -

BEA: were and then we would be . [away from them and hide in the kitchen=
JEN: [we escaped!

- -

BEA: ((xx)) =yes where the kettle was=
JEN: <LAUGHS> =where the kettle was=
MEG: =yeah exactly=

- -

The next example doesn't involve strict lexical repetition because the speakers have to use different words in order to keep the meaning constant.

[Topic: Novel reading]

- -

SUE: and I kind of skipped to the last chapter/ to make sure that
LIZ: yeah/ yeah/

- -

SUE: I was right= = and I was/
LIZ: =and you were=

This example can be compared with the earlier one, *I don't like feeling like that/no I don't like feeling like that*, where the lexical repetition is held constant through the use of the pronoun *I*, but where the meaning fluctuates subtly from *I (Mary) hate feeling like that* to *I (Meg) hate feeling like that*. But although such examples are superficially different, they carry the same force. In other words, repetitions involving the personal pronouns *you* and *I* are not strictly comparable with other cases of repetition, but they in fact function just like other examples in that they signal (strong) agreement.

Less commonly, lexical repetition can be subtly used to express disagreement in an acceptable way. This is sometimes referred to as the 'yes but' strategy.[5]

[Topic: Husband's saxophone playing]

LIZ: I don't think- don't think you should knock it cos I think it's really

---

LIZ: good [that he's got an interest/
SUE: [it's good but why isn't it quiet?

By repeating Liz's words (*it's good*), Sue aligns herself with the (more tolerant) point of view expressed by Liz, but then develops her position by juxtaposing the question *why isn't it quiet?*. This word *but* here signals that the second half of the utterance is going to clash with the first half in some way.

The examples we've looked at so far, whether involving one or more speakers, have focused on the repetition of *words* – that is, repetition at the lexical level. I'll now look briefly at repetition occurring at other levels.

Semantic repetition

Often when speakers repeat material, they vary the words used while preserving the meaning. In other words, repetition is total at the semantic level but not absolute at the lexical level.

[Becky and Hannah reflect on who they can talk openly to]

BECKY: I mean I've got friends that- . . . sometimes I feel

BECKY: like I have to put on a bit of a – you know say the-

BECKY: you know [say the right words and things you know
HANNAH: [say the right things . yeah/

[Topic: Child abuse]

BEA: I mean in order to accept that idea you're

BEA: having to . [completely
MARY: mhm . completely review your [view of your

BEA: change your view of your husband/
MARY: husband/

Both these examples involve very minor changes in wording. In the next example, the words are quite different but the meaning is held constant.

[Bea explains why the kitchen was the place she talked with women friends when the children were young]

BEA: I think one of the reasons it used to be the kitchen was- didn't we

---

BEA: use to try and keep the children in the sitting room where the toys

---

BEA: were and then we would be . [away from them and hide in the kitchen/
JEN: [we escaped!

In the next example, Barbara's utterance both explicitly repeats Pat's summary and also recapitulates that summary in different words:

[Topic: Amateur carpenter who is doing up his council house in bad taste]

PAT: you know normally he's so brilliant with things like that/ but .

PAT: ohhh [dear/
BARB: [brilliant with doing/ but obviously the taste is somewhat awry/

Pat's *brilliant with things like that* is repeated in Barbara's *brilliant with doing,* while Pat's *ohhh dear* is restated in Barbara's *but obviously the taste is somewhat awry.*

Here's a slightly longer example, to show how speakers use extended semantic repetition:

[Topic: Reading the Daily Mail]

SUE: Sean's mother/ the Daily Mail is her bible/

SUE: [she does- she phoned me- I know/
LIZ: [yeah/ my [friend thinks the Mail- =no/ there isn't/
ANNA: [mhm/ s- there's nothing in it=

SUE: [there isn't anything/
LIZ: [you skim [straight through it/
ANNA: [there was a copy I was looking at on the train

LIZ: [and there's nothing in it/
ANNA: tonight/ you pick through it and th[ere's nothing in it/

SUE: = yeah/
LIZ: [no/ = yeah/
ANNA: [two seconds later you've finished the paper=

The statement *there's nothing in it* is repeated over and over, both word for word and also in a series of paraphrases: *there isn't anything* (Sue); *you skim straight through it* (Liz); *you pick through it and . . . two seconds later you've finished the paper* (Anna). Working collaboratively, these friends use semantic and lexical repetition to emphasize their low opinion of the Daily Mail.

Syntactic repetition

Repetition at the syntactic level has already been illustrated in the opening example (hot water bottles), where clause structure was repeated (with variations). We've also seen how syntactic repetition is a regular feature of narrative. In the following example, repetition involves a larger unit of structure – a clause followed by reported speech.

[Topic: Yorkshire Ripper murders]

MEG: I remember at the time thi- you know really thinking 'now could this

MEG: be M-' I think it was Mike/ [. . .] and I actually made a special point

MEG: of thinking 'could it be him'/ and I wondered if other women

MEG: at the time . thought-
SALLY: oh god yes/ well I mean we were living in Yorkshire

SALLY: at the time/ and I . I mean I . I mean I did/ I sort of thought well

SALLY: 'could it be John?'/

Sally repeats the pattern *I + think + 'could it be [male name]?'*. This makes these two contributions highly coherent. Given the controversial nature of the disclosure here, it is probably very functional for Sally to tie her utterance so closely to Meg's, to emphasize the similarity of their positions, and thus to have solidarity.

A more complex example of syntactic repetition comes from the discussion section of the child abuse topic.

[Topic: Child abuse]

MEG: but this business about mothers not protecting their daughters/

MEG: if you carry that through logically/ it's actually basically saying-

MEG: and men put that out= =but it's basically saying you must watch
MARY: =mhm=
BEA: =mhm=

MEG: your child twenty-four hours a day/ you shouldn't go to bingo/

MEG: you shouldn't have a job/ you shouldn't wash up in the kitchen
MARY: mhm/

MEG: while he's putting the kids [to bed/
BEA: [and you can't trust your husband

MEG: that's right/
MARY: right/ yeah/
BEA: because he's a man whose brute forces will overwhelm him=

MEG: =yeah/ [and so you must watch your child ALL the time/
BEA: [((xxx))

Repetition here involves two interweaving patterns, one a negated version of the other:

you + Modal + Proposition
you + Modal + not + Proposition

(Modals are auxiliary verbs such as *must, should, can, will.*)

The sequence of repetition proceeds in six chunks, as follows:

1 you must watch your child twenty-four hours a day
2 you shouldn't go to bingo
3 you shouldn't have a job
4 you shouldn't wash up in the kitchen while he's putting the kids to bed
5 you can't trust your husband because he's a man whose brute force will overwhelm him
6 you must watch your child ALL the time

Most of this sequence is produced by one speaker, Meg, with Bea joining in near the end. Note how the first and final clauses are identical apart from the time adverbial, and how these frame the other four lines, which all involve negation. These four lines form a kind of litany, listing proscribed activities, with the pattern *you shouldn't x* recurring three times, changing to a more complex chunk which introduces *can't* in place of *shouldn't.* So the pattern is: A + B + B + B + C + A. The patterns of repetition are very powerful here, involving words and meaning as well as syntax.

Thematic repetition

Conversations between friends often establish themes which recur throughout the talk. For example, as I've already discussed in chapter 4 (page 69), one of Pat and Karen's conversations has a christmas theme, with this theme recurring in four of the six topics discussed: 'Christmas cards', 'Christmas trees', 'Christmas lights', 'End-of-term (christmas) school plays'.

More striking is the rabbit theme which develops in one of the conversations between Sue, Liz and Anna. One of the topics in this conversation is 'Rabbits', a topic which arises because Sue has brought the school rabbit home for the weekend. (This topic was also discussed in chapter 4, particularly in the final section.) Here is a brief extract from the early part of this topic, where the theme is established:

[Topic: Rabbits]

ANNA: oh how's the bunny rabbit?= [ooh it's lovely=
LIZ: [have you seen it?
SUE: =a [ah/ [it's-

LIZ: =you see I've not seen it [yet/
SUE: [it's so adorable/ [. . .]

SUE: well she runs around the kitchen but I actually got a ((run))

LIZ: [what/ with
SUE: as well for her to go out in the garden tomorrow/ [((well I)) –

LIZ: netting?= =yeah/
SUE: =yeah=

The conversation moves on through other topics to the topic of 'Relationships'. Towards the end of their discussion of the obedient husband, Sue reintroduces the rabbit theme. (Underlined chunks repeat words and ideas raised in the 'Rabbits' topic.)

[End of topic: Relationships]

ANNA: = yeah =((he
LIZ: oh [bless him= [he does]n't have much of a life=
SUE: [he's- [((he's just))] =he

ANNA: doesn't [by the sounds [of it/
SUE: doesn't real [ly/ [((it's a)) bit like a RAbbit/

LIZ: [he is, really isn't he/ [she should
SUE: ((yeah)) <GIGGLE> I think [I should bring him- [I think I should

---

ANNA: [introduce them/
LIZ: get him- <GIGGLING> [I wonder why she doesn't [get him a RUN in
SUE: bring him home for [weekends/<LAUGHS>

ANNA: introduce them=
LIZ: the GARden <GIGGLING-------------------------------------
SUE: =((and then you'll be able to bring

ANNA:
LIZ: ------------------>
SUE: him home at)) weekends and let him go out in a run/

The repetition of the rabbit theme makes these friends' talk highly coherent: they repeat the word *rabbit*, and the idea of bringing a rabbit home for the weekend, and of letting it go out in a run in the garden, is reintroduced as a metaphor for the husband. At the same time, returning to this theme allows the friends, under the guise of joking, to say some pretty devastating things about the obedient husband. (I will discuss the ideas introduced here at greater length in the next chapter.)

Repetition and the collaborative floor

Repetition then is a regular feature of the talk of women friends, and operates at many different levels. In this section I want to argue that repetition occurs so frequently in these conversations because the women friends adopt a collaborative floor. Collaborative floors typically involve more repetition than single floors, as well as shorter turns, more overlapping speech, and more joking and teasing. As I've said before, the collaborative floor is a shared space, and therefore what is said is construed as being the voice of the group rather than of the individual. Repetition is a powerful way of affirming the group voice, since it means that two or more speakers explicitly *say the same thing* in some form or another. Let's look at a short example to see how this works.

[Mother and funeral]

ANNA:	bet the milkman couldn't believe it/
LIZ:	[yeah/
SUE:	[did he know she was going

ANNA:	= well she probably told them/
LIZ:	probably told [him=
SUE:	to the funeral? [probably/ yeah/

Repetition of the single word *probably* ties the three speakers' utterances together and signals that what each of them says is the jointly achieved viewpoint. The next example involves just two speakers, but demonstrates clearly how through repetition the individual voices merge into a larger whole.

[Topic: Colour of newly painted front door]

PAT:	so which bus did you get on then/ oh yeah/ yeah/.
BARB:	the 733/

PAT:	did you see they've painted our old front door green/
BARB:	yes/

PAT:	[bright . green/ [London Country Buses green/
BARB:	we noticed [that/ very [bright green/

PAT:	it looks ludicrous [doesn't it?
BARB:	[we were unimpressed/

Although Pat introduces the topic of the colour of their old front door, the two friends together make fun of this colour through repeating the word *green* and elaborating on it. Once they've established what sort of green it is, using lexical repetition, they evaluate the effect of this colour, using semantic repetition: Barbara's *we were unimpressed* repeats Pat's *it looks ludicrous doesn't it* but in different words. This bit of text is a joint production, and it makes no sense to look at the two speakers' contributions separately.

Finally, let's look at an example which involves longer repeated chunks:

[Topic: Relationships]

LIZ: what IS it with these men though that they- they have to do that/

LIZ: I mean [they don't- they- they particularly- [they don't
ANNA: [it's a typically male thing though that they- [they-

LIZ: particularly want you any more/ they've done- [I mean they've
ANNA: [no but they don't

LIZ: decided- [no they don't want anybody else
ANNA: want anybody else to have you [either/

LIZ: to have you/ but they also want to still own you=
ANNA: =yeah/

Anna and Liz work together here to explore their feeling about men's behaviour after the breakup of a relationship. They repeat the phrase *they don't want* (with the variation *they want*), and also repeat the idea of ownership through a range of words: *want, have, own*. This piece of collaborative text is jointly produced by the two friends, and expresses their joint view. It would make no sense to call one of these friends 'first speaker' and the other 'second': they are both participating in a collaborative floor and repetition is one of the ways they signal their commitment to the shared production of talk.

As all three examples demonstrate, repetition is very often associated with overlap in a collaborative floor. As we've already seen in chapter 6, overlap can be carried to the extreme where lexical repetition occurs as simultaneous speech. Here's just one of the examples again.

[Helen and Jen discuss local political crisis]

JEN: [she had this grammar school meeting/
HELEN: did you hear [she had this grammar school- yes/

It isn't surprising that we find repetition and overlap in combination. After all, where overlap involves repetition, especially lexical repetition, then it is clearly marked as supportive.[6] Moreover, the development of a group voice will inevitably lead to the simultaneous expression of material that is parallel, either lexically, semantically, syntactically or thematically. This is precisely what we would expect in talk that works as a kind of jam session. The heart of good conversation for women friends is group talk, with speakers combining in various ways to produce text. Repetition is one of the ways that the 'melding in together' valued by women friends is achieved.

Some extended examples

My aim in this section is to show how repetition functions over longer stretches of talk. But I'll begin with just four lines from the end of Val's story about her conflict with her friend Cathy.

it was horrid
it WAS horrid
but she has forgiven me now
but she hasn't forgotten it.

These four lines are carefully patterned. The first two involve exact lexical repetition, but Val's use of a different, contrastive stress pattern in the repeated version alters the emphasis: the first time – *it was horrid* – we focus on the unpleasantness of the misunderstanding between the two friends; the second time – *it WAS horrid* – we are reminded that this happened in the past. The last two lines both begin *but she. . . .* The first is positive – *but she has forgiven me now* – and brings us back to the present with the final adverb *now*. The second, by contrast, is negative – *but she hasn't forgotten it* and the final *it* picks up the subject of the earlier *it was horrid*. The words *forgiven* and *forgotten* repeat a similar *sound pattern*, a form of repetition which happens more rarely in everyday talk.

The second extract I shall examine in detail is the story 'Grain trains in the docks', which has already been discussed in chapter 5 (pages 113–15) and which is told by Mary and Sally, with occasional minimal responses added by other speakers. As we've already noted, this story opens with four staves which involve repetition of all kinds: lexical, syntactic and semantic.

Grain trains in the docks

---

1 Mary: I was- I was- I was stopped by a train/

Mary: have you ever been stopped by a train in the docks?

---

3 Mary: [I got stopped by a train in the docks yesterday/
Sally: [yes/ oh yes/ frequently/

Mary: I've never been stopped by a train before/
Sally: yeah/

---

5 Mary: it was lovely/
Jen: oh I-

Mary: cos it was- it was going across um Duke- Duke Street [bridge/
Jen: oh it's super/ [yes/

---

7 Mary: the [middle one/
Sally: [that's right/ yeah/

Sally: and the guy just gets off/

---

9 Mary: [that's right/ [and walks/
Sally: [((xx)) [and ((sort of stops))/

Mary: and there's this bloke walking in front of the train/
Sally: yeah/ that's-

---

11 Mary: and you can hear this clanging noise/
Sally: yeah/

Mary: [cos one of the chains is clanging on-
Sally: [yeah/

---

13 Mary: and it sounds very romantic/
Sally: yes/
Meg: yes/

Mary: like it's like the far- the West/

---

15 Mary: you know this clanking noise/

Mary: and all it is- is- is this bit of metal that's clanking along the ground <LAUGHS>

17	MARY:	but I didn't realize-
	SALLY:	oh it's LOVEl-

	MARY:	but I've seen all these train tracks/
	SALLY:	((xxx))

19	MARY:	[it's the grain trains/ yes/
	SALLY:	it's the grain trains [I think/ to go to the-

	MARY:	[it was the bulk carriers/
	SALLY:	[yes/ yes/ yes/

As I said in chapter 5, the first four staves are variations on the opening statement *I was stopped by a train*. Every one of these four staves uses the same verb: *was/got stopped* followed by the same phrase *by a train*. Three of the four staves have *I* as their (grammatical) subject. The fifth stave – *it was lovely* – breaks the pattern. This evaluative phrase is echoed twice in the rest of the passage: *oh it's super* (Jen) in stave 6 and *oh it's LOVEl-* (Sally) in stave 17.

In the central section of this passage (staves 8–16), verbs are all in the timeless present: *gets off, walks, sounds, is*. We find repetition and contrast simultaneously when Mary expands her statement *and walks* (stave 9) to *there's this bloke walking*: the verb *walk* is repeated. But the first time it is a third person present tense verb, the second time a present participle modifying the noun phrase *this bloke*. Textual cohesion is also created in this central section through the (lexical and phonetic) repetition of *clanging/clanking* and through the (semantic) repetition of *one of the chains/this bit of metal*.

The last two staves of this passage, like the opening, show strong parallelism, with exact repetition of the statement *it's the grain trains* by two speakers in stave 19. The final stave repeats the structure of this statement: *it is the Noun Premodifier + Noun*. *Bulk carriers* substitutes for *grain trains*, and the tense of the copula (verb *to be*) alters from present to past: *it was the Noun Premodifier + Noun*. The switch to *was* reorients us to the past of Mary's original story.

One of the striking things about this passage is the absence of agentive verbs – that is, verbs which co-occur with a subject which is also an agent (verbs like *take, shout, sing, jump*). The narrator/observer is presented as a passive (but delighted) audience to the spectacle of the trains in the docks. The verbs *hear* and *see* (staves 11 and 18) seem to describe a receptive rather than an active state (compare *listen, look*). The only agent in the entire passage is *the guy/this bloke* who *gets off* and *walks*. Even this activity seems very distant, since the agent is so general: *this bloke* could be any man – or everyman. Even the verb *clanging/clanking* (in staves 12 and 16) is non-agentive here, since chains are inanimate objects that only clang or clank because something is dragging them along.

'Grain trains' is an example of collaboratively produced narrative. Repetition here involves two speakers. Now let's turn to an extract from conversation involving three women friends, to look at the way repetition works across an extended piece of multi-party text. This extract comes from the topic 'Relationships' and shows very clearly how the balance and mirroring typical of women's friends' talk is closely inked with the patterns of repetition we find in such talk. The subtopic of 'coupledom' is introduced by Anna in a general way.

ANNA: I wonder if anybody's ever done a study of sort of coupledom/ and what it is that makes one couple such ((xx))

Anna and Liz then develop this subject and begin to focus on the idea of change – on the way being in a (heterosexual) couple can change the behaviour of the woman.

LIZ: I think you're much more aware of it when you're on your own/ I'm much

---

ANNA: yes/ [and
LIZ: more aware of it now than . I was when I was married/ [I can

---

ANNA: probably more aware of the situation that you yourself have been
LIZ: actually-

ANNA: in/ [and how much somebody changed you when you were with them/
LIZ: [yes/ I mean it's very easy to sit back/
SUE: mhm/

The idea of change is taken up by Liz who tells a brief anecdote to illustrate the way women change in the presence of a (male) partner:

LIZ: when I was at the Health Club the other night/ and this girl I went with her husband turned up to have a drink with us in the bar/ . and like the whole atmosphere changed when he arrived/ <LAUGHS>

Anna herself then makes a mirroring comment about a friend of hers:

ANNA: with Karen for instance and her new fiancé/ I just feel like I can't
SUE: mhm/

ANNA: talk when they're together as a couple/
LIZ: yeah/ but it does change
SUE: yeah/ mhm/

ANNA: yeah/
LIZ: doesn't it/

Liz then elaborates a little further on her example:

LIZ: and she changed/ she changed/ she- she- she suddenly went tense/ you know/ and he was a pig/ he was an absolute pig/

She underscores the theme of change by repeating the clause *she changed,* then explains how the woman changed: *she suddenly went tense*. Her explanation of what was pig-like about the husband's behaviour touches a chord in Sue:

LIZ: but he was an absolute- he sort of . sat and read the newspaper/ and

---

LIZ: then moaned/ cos we were taking a long time drinking our [glass of
SUE: ooooh/ [I hate

LIZ: wine/ we were supposed to be having a nice evening/ relaxing
SUE: that/

LIZ: evening/ you know/

Sue then comes in with an anecdote of her own, picking up her phrase *I hate,* and repeating the theme of sitting and reading the newspaper:

SUE: that's what I hate about Beverley's husband/ I mean I really like him/ and he's gr- he's a good laugh/ but when you go there he sits and watches the telly sometimes/ he puts the cricket on/ or he sits and reads the- the newspaper/

This leads into general agreement about men's rudeness, with the word *rude* repeated three times:

SUE: but when you go there he sits and watches the telly sometimes/

LIZ: he's so rude=
SUE: he puts the cricket on/ =or he sits and reads the- the

ANNA: yeah/
SUE: newspaper/ and I think well we've driven here to see you/ I wouldn't

ANNA: it's rude isn't it/
LIZ: yeah it is rude/ and in fact- and it's
SUE: do that/

LIZ: always men that seem to do it/ not women/
SUE: yeah/

So far, the shape of the passage is:

General statement on couples (Anna, with Liz)
Anecdote about married couple at the Health Club (Liz)
Anecdote about Karen and her fiancé (Anna)
Anecdote about Beverley's husband (Sue)
Discussion about rudeness

The three anecdotes mirror each other: each one takes up the general theme introduced by Anna and illustrates it, and each one brings in a slightly new focus. The three anecdotes are very coherent, with a lot of repetition of words and phrases (underlined in the examples), as well as repetition of particular themes (marriage, for example, is a theme, with words from the lexical set associated with marriage – *husband, fiancé, couple, married* – recurring throughout the text). Contrastive patterns are also set up – the idea of being in a couple is set against the idea of being *on your own; like* and *love* contrast with *hate;* Liz's friend is described as *tense* and this is in contrast with *relaxing* – the word chosen to describe how their evening might have been without the husband's presence. Moreover, the entire passage depends on a framework which assumes a general contrast between women (good) and men (bad).

The final part of this extract continues with more discussion about the issues that have been raised.

LIZ: and he ruined- he ruined the whole thing of the eve-

Liz: and I . actually drove home from there/ and I thought . I'd

---

Liz: rather be on my own than in that [situation/
Sue: yeah/ [((don't agree with it))

Anna: yes/ . well I think you do think like that/ when you've been in
Liz: yeah/
Sue: sometimes/

Anna: that situation and then you're free [of it/
Liz: [and you think I'm glad I'm not

Anna: [and you're more independent = = and you think- yes/
Liz: [in that any more/ =yeah=

[. . .]

Anna: I just sometimes think I probably never will get married again/or

---

Anna: never be with anybody again/ 'cos I just love my life on my own/
Liz: yeah

Anna: [makes you really selfish/
Liz: this is it/ I think you [just- cos you tend to get terribly selfish/

Liz: you do get selfish/

The discussion section is not only coherent in its own terms, but also in relation to the preceding anecdotes. The three friends use each other's words and phrases to bind the text together thematically. The theme of independence becomes primary, involving repetition of words and phrases such as *free, independent, on my own,* and finally *selfish,* which contrast with *in that situation* and *married*. There is also a great deal of repetition involving the verb *think,* with the friends disclosing their thoughts and feelings. There are also many hedges, particularly *I think, I mean, just* and *probably* (these hedges' chief function is to promote open discussion and to protect face, given the three friends' differing life experience). The pronouns *I* and *you* are repeated over and over again as these friends share their personal experience. Both *I* and *you* are gendered in this extract – they refer only to women – and together with *she* these female-referring pronouns have positive connotations. This is in contrast with *he* which occurs much less frequently and always with negative overtones, because it refers to the husbands and fiancés who behave badly and / or cause the women to change.

It is impossible to do full justice to the patterns of repetition in this extract. But what this extract from an extended chunk of multiparty talk demonstrates is the richness and complexity of repetition in the talk of women friends.

Women's talk as poetic

In this chapter I've shown the different patterns of repetition that occur in women friends' talk. These serve a variety of functions. Most importantly, perhaps, they signal solidarity between women friends and communicate the active involvement of speakers in ongoing talk. They express the group rather than the individual voice, and, in this sense, they are a key component of the collaborative floor.

They also play a vital part in the construction of coherent text. Some commentators have suggested that we should apply the tools of literary criticism to everyday talk.[7] At first glance, this seems nonsensical – after all, when we talk, especially when we let our hair down and have a good chat with our friends, our language is all over the place, it's not a polished work of art like a poem. But how accurate is our sense that our talk is all over the place, that it's messy? Can we rely on our perceptions, which are probably heavily influenced by our culture's emphasis on the high status of literacy? This cultural prejudice ignores the fact that most languages in the world have no written form, and that most poetry and most narrative in existence are oral rather than written.[8] Because English is one of the world's major written languages, and therefore intimately linked to print culture, we, as English speakers, tend to ignore or devalue the spoken word.

On top of this, we tend to ignore or devalue *women's* speech. But the evidence of this chapter (and of previous chapters) is that women's talk is far from all over the place, far from messy. On the contrary, our conversations display not only orderliness but patterns that *could* be called 'poetic' without too much stretching of the word.[9] This should not surprise us. After all, it is vital for human survival that talk works, and in order to work, talk has to be coherent. Repetition is just the most marked phenomenon of the textual coherence that typifies successful communication. But what seems to be particularly marked about the women's conversations we've examined is the extent to which repetition occurs *across* speakers. This, I've argued, is because women treat talk with friends as a kind of jam session. By choosing to operate in a collaborative floor, women friends share in the construction of text. Repetition – saying the same things as each other and using the same linguistic patterns as our friends – is a powerful symbol of the connection women feel with each other.[10]

10

'Thank god I'm a woman': The construction of differing femininities

The last five chapters have concentrated on *how* women friends talk, but now I want to turn to the important issue of what is being *done* in this talk. The two most important things being accomplished in the talk of women friends are *friendship* and *femininity*. Friendship will be the subject of the next chapter. Here I want to focus on femininity and on the role of talk in constructing us as gendered beings, as women. (*Femininity* is a problematic word, because of the everyday connotations of the adjective *feminine*. By *femininity* I mean the abstract quality of being feminine (just as masculinity is the abstract quality associated with being masculine): *doing femininity* can be paraphrased as 'doing being a woman'. The latter is a much clearer and less ambiguous way of saying what I mean, but far too clumsy to use repeatedly.)

Most of us spend very little, if any, time thinking about gender, and we are rarely aware of 'doing' (or 'performing') gender. (By 'doing'/'performing' gender, I mean presenting ourselves to others as a gendered being.) We just take for granted that we are women. But we assume that 'being a woman' is a unitary and unified experience – in other words, we think of ourselves as 'I'/'me'; that is, as singular. However, the woman we perform is not the same woman in all circumstances: we have all had the experience of feeling like a different person when we are in a different situation. For example, the 'me' that changes a baby's nappy or mashes a banana for a toddler is a different 'me' from the one who participates in a committee meeting or who poses as a life model at the local art school. Even in the same context we can change if something alters in that context. Liz's anecdote (given at the end of the last chapter) about her friend changing when her husband joined them for a drink is a good illustration of this:

LIZ: when I was at the Health Club the other night/ and this girl I went with her husband turned up to have a drink with us in the bar/ . and like the whole atmosphere changed when he arrived/ <LAUGHS> [. . .] and she changed/ she changed/ she- she- she suddenly went tense/ you know/

We change because different audiences require different performances – and also because we sometimes feel like playing a different role. All kinds of different 'self' are possible, because our culture offers us a wide range of ways of being – but all these ways of being are *gendered*. These possible selves are not different kinds of person, but different kinds of *woman*. Moreover, the alternative versions of femininity available to the women in my recordings are specific to the so-called 'developed' world at the end of the twentieth century.

A range of femininities

In this section I shall look at a few examples from the conversations to show what I mean by 'doing' or 'performing' femininity, and to give a sense of the range of femininities available to girls and women in Britain today.

The first example comes from a conversation where three sixteen-year-old girls are commenting on the appearance of the fourth, Sarah, who is trying on Gwen's make-up.

[Sarah tries on some of Gwen's make-up]

GWEN:	doesn't she look really nice?	
KATE:		yes/
EMILY:		she DOES look nice/

GWEN:		[I think with the lipstick
KATE:	you should wear make-up	[more often . Sarah/

GWEN:	it looks good/	[Sarah your lips . s- suit lipstick/
KATE:		
EMILY:	yeah looks	[nice/

GWEN:	((I'm saying)) what you said- big lips suit	[lipstick/
KATE:	oohh yes/	
EMILY:		[you should be

GWEN: yeah/ looks good to me/
KATE: [share it/ yeah/
EMILY: [a model/ models have big lips/

GWEN: Sarah you look really nice/
KATE:
EMILY:

In this talk, the girls are overtly complimenting Sarah. This is part of the routine support work that girls and women do with each other as friends. At the same time they are co-constructing a world in which the putting on and wearing of make-up is a normal part of doing femininity, and looking nice/looking good is an important goal. In this world, the size of your features – your eyes, your lips – is highly salient, and the fashion model is a significant figure, with high status.

The next example also comes from the talk of younger speakers, girls of fifteen. But they are doing a different sort of femininity. Jessica, Becky and Hannah are talking about a crisis which occurred on the school trip (a trip which Ruth and Claire didn't go on).

[Talking about disastrous time on school trip]

JESS: I can't believe that night/ I mean I can't believe ((xx))-

---

BECKY: I can't- no I can't believe it either/ we were all crying/ <AMAZED>

---

3 BECKY: I couldn't be[lieve it/ everybody [was/
RUTH: [who was crying?
HANNAH: [everybody/
JESS: apart from me/

BECKY: yeah/ <LAUGHING>
RUTH: ((no but)) what were you crying about?
JESS: I was in bed/ <LAUGHTER>

BECKY: because- ((well)) I was crying because Hannah was crying/

---

6 BECKY: Hannah was crying because Ben was um a sexist bastard/ <LAUGHS>
HANNAH: <GIGGLES>

BECKY: [and Vicky was crying because Susan was going to be sent home/
HANNAH: [%oh he was REALly horrible to me/%

BECKY: and I was crying because [she never cries/
CLAIRE: [did she get sent home?

---

9 BECKY: no/
HANNAH: and I was crying because Vicky [was crying/ no/
CLAIRE: [did she get sent home?

The three friends who are describing what happened agree on the significance of crying. They recount this episode in a tone of amusement, even pride: they seem to be saying 'we're real girls'. The phrase *was/were crying* occurs ten times in all (twelve times if we include those utterances with an ellipted verb, such as *everybody was*, stave 3). The repetition of this phrase functions to emphasize that crying was the key feature of this particular night, and to underline the fact that everyone was involved. Both Becky and Hannah say that they were crying, and they both claim that Vicky was crying. (Jessica, the only one who was not crying, explains, *I was in bed*.) Their reasons for their crying focus on friendship: Becky cried because Hannah was upset; Vicky cried because she thought her friend was being sent home. The only boy mentioned – Ben – was *not* crying: he is one of the reasons that Hannah was crying. Crying is constructed here as a gendered behaviour, something girls do at times of emotional crisis.

Crying is a stereotypical way of performing femininity. This version of femininity continues into adulthood, though, as the next example shows, adult women have some reservations about expressing their feelings in this way.

[Anna arrives from work late and explains why she is upset]

ANNA: I just had such a bad week/ and then my boss just stood in the office

---

ANNA: tonight and told me and his deputy that we're both crap managers

---

ANNA: basically/
SUE: oh/
LIZ: oh god/

[. . .]

ANNA: I get so angry at myself for crying/ but . I wish I could just . ooh!

ANNA: punch him on the nose or something/
SUE: you shouldn't let it get to you/

ANNA: [I know/ but-
LIZ: [at least you CAN cry/ because I think you should let it out/

ANNA: [but it's bad/ because it makes [them think
SUE: [I know/
[<GROANS>
LIZ: it's when you don't [cry/

ANNA: you're a wimp/
SUE: yeah/
LIZ: yeah/

Anna, like Becky and Hannah, talks about an episode that is characterized by strong emotion, which she responded to by crying. Her use of the powerful phrase *crap manager* to describe herself reveals how negatively she has interpreted what her boss said to her. (Later she says glumly, *maybe he's right, maybe I am a crap manager*.) The three friends demonstrate that they share the assumption that if someone significant, such as your boss, is displeased with you, then crying is a 'normal' reaction. But they talk about this reaction with more ambivalence than Becky and her friends. Anna wonders if crying was the appropriate response to her boss. She wonders if she should have punched him on the nose (thus revealing an awareness that anger rather than sadness might have been her chief emotion). Liz supports her in her account of herself, taking the position that it's better to let it out, but Sue's advice is to stay calm (*you shouldn't let it get to you*). Liz implicitly alludes to the gendered nature of crying when she says, *at least you CAN cry*, implying that there are those who can't – men. Anna herself worries that crying is a weak move: it may perform femininity but it also performs powerlessness (*it makes them think you're a wimp*), which is not the impression Anna wants to give to her male boss.

In the next example these same three friends talk about assertiveness training.

[Topic: Assertiveness courses]

ANNA: Linda's going on an assertiveness training course at work/

ANNA: [I ought to go with her/
SUE: [J o h n' s m u m went on one/
LIZ: I'd love to go on one/

ANNA:	assertiveness?=
SUE:	=assertiveness/ and she said 'I only- I'm only doing it
LIZ:	I really would/

SUE:	so that I can be like you Susan'/ I said 'But I'm not assertive'/

SUE:	I mean she's more assertive than anyone I know/

There seems to be an underlying assumption here that assertiveness training is for women: both the people mentioned in association with it are female – Linda from Anna's office and John's mum (Sue's mother-in-law). (However, Sue's claim that her mother-in-law is *more assertive than anyone I know* is ambiguous: does *anyone* refer to all Sue's acquaintances, or just to women she knows?) Both Anna and Liz express positive attitudes to the idea of assertiveness training: they both say they would like to go on a course. Sue is more sceptical. Her statement *John's mum went on one* communicates 'everyone's doing it these days', and her brief story about what John's mother said to her reveals a profound gap between John's mother's reading of Sue as assertive and her own sense of herself as unassertive, with a parallel discrepancy in her sense of her mother-in-law as very assertive and not in need of any training. As women move into more prominent positions in the workplace, we have to juggle with our self-presentation to find ways to perform ourselves as both competent and at the same time feminine. Whether assertiveness is the answer is unclear; certainly the rhetoric that women need some kind of training perpetuates the idea that it is women who don't fit in the public sphere and therefore women who have to change.

The final example is an instance of a woman sharing her sense of achievement with her friends. Janet has been for interview; the following extract shows her responding to her friend's request to 'tell us about it'.

[Janet's job interview]

MEG:	did you get your job?
MARY:	oh did you go for a job? <HIGH, SURPRISED>

MEG:	((xxxx))
JANET:	((xxxx))
JEN:	what job?
MARY:	tell us about it/

JANET: I was- four people got interviewed the same day as I did/
MARY: ((four

ANN: hello Bea/
JANET: and they rang me up- that was on the . Tuesday/
MARY: other people/))

<GENERAL NOISE INVOLVING BEA'S ARRIVAL>

JANET: they've still got one more person to interview/ [somebody got
MARY: [what job is it?

JANET: mugged on the day of the inter [view/ and so they said they were
HELEN: [oh hell/

JANET: interviewing her at the end of last week/ cos they couldn't not

---

JANET: interview her just 'cos she'd got mugged=
MEG: [so
BEA: =no that would be [((very

JANET: =they told me that there was
MEG: anyway they told you that apart from that=
BEA: unfair/))

JANET: only me and her= =it's external affairs officer for the
MARY: =what job is it?=

JANET: Regional Health Authority=
MARY: =oh I remember/ I remember you were- yes/

JANET: it's quite a good job= =I was really good in this interview
MARY: =yes/
HELEN: yes=

JANET: because I was so unbothered about whether I got the job/ I think

---

JANET: that's the actual [crunch of [the thing= =it takes the pressure
HELEN: [mhm/ =mhm= mhm/
JEN: [Meg's told me that/

JANET: off you enTIREly if you- if you know it's not all or nothing/
HELEN: yes/

Although the five other women present all contribute in various ways to this stretch of talk, Janet's story is the focus of attention. It's important to note that women friends allow each other space not just to complain or talk about problems, but also to talk about successes and feelings of achievement. In this example, Janet asserts that the job is *quite a good job* and that she was *really good* in the interview. This is a much more forceful version of femininity, and the interest that Janet's friends display in the details of her story shows that this story has resonance for them all as potential job-seekers, women who want to succeed in the public world outside the home. At the same time, Janet explains her good self-presentation in terms of not caring about the outcome (because she already has a job). The modesty of this claim balances her description of herself as 'really good'. (Compare this with Sue's denial of herself as being assertive.) The balancing act that Janet carries out here shows that even with close friends, presenting oneself as competent rather than weak or vulnerable has to be done with care; women have to avoid the accusation of 'showing off'.

All these examples, as well as showing female speakers talking *about* issues connected with femininity and self-presentation, also show girls and women *doing* femininity. They present themselves as different kinds of woman, concerned both about their external appearance and about social performance, sometimes more emotional, sometimes more hard-nosed. The talk we do in our daily lives gives us access to these different modes of being, these different versions of femininity. This is because language plays a crucial part in structuring our experience.

Language and the construction of different 'selves'

It would be more accurate to say that *discourse*,[1] rather than language, plays a crucial part in structuring our experience. The whole idea of 'language' is something of a fiction: what we normally refer to as 'language' can more realistically be seen as a heterogeneous collection of discourses.[2] Each of us has access to a range of discourses, and it is these different discourses which give us access to, or enable us to perform, different 'selves'. A discourse can be conceptualized as a 'system of statements which cohere around common meanings and values'.[3] So, for example, in contemporary Britain there are discourses which can be labelled 'conservative' – that is, discourses which emphasize values and meanings where the status quo is cherished; and there are discourses which can be labelled 'patriarchal' – that is, discourses which emphasize meanings and values which assume the superiority of males. Dominant discourses such as these appear 'natural': they are powerful precisely because they are able to make invisible the fact that they are just one among many different discourses.

Theorizing language in this way is still new in linguistics (to the extent that many linguists would not regard analysis in terms of discourses as being part of linguistics).[4] One of the advantages of talking about discourses rather than about language is that the concept 'discourse' acknowledges the value-laden nature of language. There is no neutral discourse: whenever we speak we have to choose between different systems of meaning, different sets of values. This approach allows me to show how language is implicated in our construction of different 'selves': different discourses position us in different ways in relation to the world.

Using the phrase *discourses position us* gives the impression that speakers are passive, are at the mercy of different discourses. But language use is dynamic: we make choices when we speak; we can resist and subvert. Social and cultural change are possible precisely because we do not use the discourses available to us uncritically, but participate actively in the construction of meaning. Talk is particularly significant in our construction and reconstruction of ourselves as women, as gendered subjects. As Simone de Beauvoir said, 'One is not born a woman, one becomes one',[5] and we go on 'becoming' all through life. This is done in many different ways, through all aspects of behaviour, through the way we dress, the way we move, but particularly through the way we talk. Each time we speak, we are saying, 'This is (a version of) me', and, as I've argued, we are also saying, 'I am a woman', because the 'I'/'me' is always gendered. How this is done has been illustrated briefly in the opening section of the chapter. In the rest of the chapter I propose to re-examine the conversations of these women friends to explore some of the tensions arising from competing versions of what it is to be a woman, and to pinpoint the resistant discourses available to women today. Some of the issues to be explored have already been touched on in chapter 5, in the discussion of women's use of narrative. Here I shall draw on the whole range of conversational material that I've collected.

Competing discourses

To clarify what I mean by discourse, and to demonstrate how discourses can position us differently in relation to the world, I'll begin by looking at a few brief examples. The first two both come from conversations about mothers. In the first, Meg is talking about the function of funerals:

MEG: I would see it [the funeral] as honouring her memory in some way/

The second comes at a point in conversation when Sue has stated that she phones her mother but her mother never phones her.

SUE: [((xx)) I'm not very close to my mother really/
LIZ: [cos most mothers are a pain in the bum/

In the first example, Meg positions herself as a loving and dutiful daughter. She and her friends discuss whether it would be taboo to miss your mother's funeral. They draw on a dominant discourse where the family is revered and parents are to be honoured, a discourse which upholds the taboo against missing your mother's funeral. The second example represents mothers in a very different way. Here Sue and Liz resist dominant discourses of the family and express feelings which reveal a different picture of mother–daughter relations. This discourse challenges the hegemonic idea that all families are happy and all parents benevolent. We have all probably experienced both positions, and may even hold both views simultaneously. This is possible because of the existence of alternative discourses, alternative ways of thinking about the world.

The next two examples also draw on discourses relating to the family; they both come from conversations about children. In the first, Pat tells Karen about the end-of-term plays at her children's primary school.

[Topic: End-of-term school plays]

KAREN:	did Peter do his song?		was he good?	
PAT:		yes/		he was marvellous/

KAREN:		oh the-
PAT:	he was marvellous/ every kid in it was marvellous/	

KAREN:	I think they always are/

The second example comes at a moment in a conversation between Anna, Liz and Sue where they have been talking about a family they all know with difficult children. Their expression of negative feelings about these particular children (*they were ghastly children*) leads them to consider their attitude to children in general.

LIZ:	I think it's a- . a fallacy as well that you like every child/

ANNA:		no/ . that's right/	
SUE:	mhm/		I still quite often don't like
LIZ:	cos you don't/		

ANNA:		<LAUGHS>	
SUE:	children/	<LAUGHS>	
LIZ:			actually I think you particularly dislike your own/

Again, we can see the clash between the dominant discourse, which says that children are 'marvellous', and where all mothers take pride in their child's achievements, and an alternative discourse which asserts that not all children are likeable (in fact, some are *ghastly*) and that it is not compulsory for adults to like all children. For women speakers, particularly women who are themselves mothers (Sue and Liz), this is a very subversive discourse. Dominant ideas of femininity (and of motherhood) do not allow for the expression of negative feelings about children. Anna, Sue and Liz support each other in sustaining a radically different view, one which starts with the proposition 'you don't like every child' (Liz, supported by Anna), which moves on to 'I quite often don't like children' (Sue),[6] and then to 'I think you particularly dislike your own' (Liz), a very strong position which directly challenges the idea of women as loving, caring, nurturing beings for whom having children is the ultimate experience of their lives.

Finally, here are two examples drawn from talk about the body and appearance. The first arises in a conversation where Pat shows Karen her new sundress and they discuss the new style and whether it makes you look fat.

[Topic: New sundress]

KAREN: you'll look at yourself in the mirror and you'll think 'God I look fat' /

The second example comes in a conversation where Hannah has called Jessica's thighs fat, Jessica has protested at this and Becky (in the role of peace-maker) has insisted that hers are unpleasantly thin (*mine are skinny as a pencil – ugh!*). Hannah then suggests that they would both be happier if Jessica gave some of her fat to Becky.

[Topic: Size of Jessica and Becky's thighs]

HANNAH: well if you think your thighs are fat and you think your thighs are thin/ you just scrape off a bit of fat and plaster it on/

Both these examples draw on an ideology which insists that women should maintain their bodies at a size which accords with current fashion (these days, this means slim). Hannah takes up a resistant position in relation to that view, by making fun of Jessica and Becky. Karen and Pat by contrast adopt a discourse which positions them as accepting the dominant ideology. Their conversation is full of references to size and appearance – Karen says later in the same conversation (with reference to some dresses she's seen in the market) *the thing is with them you've got to be ever so skinny I think to wear them.* Moreover, where the ideology imposed by this dominant discourse clashes with reality – in other words, when the perfect body constructed by the dominant discourse doesn't match our actual bodies – we tend to assume that it is we who are at fault. Note how Pat and Karen use laughter to help them deal with the tension produced by the clash between the ideal and the real:

KAREN: I've only got about four inches between my bust and my waist/
PAT: yeah/

KAREN: <LAUGHS>
PAT: <LAUGHS> you sound quite deformed <LAUGHS>

These examples give some idea of the conflicts surrounding contemporary ideas of femininity. The dominant discourse constitutes women as loving, dutiful (in relation to parents), uncritical (in relation to children), and caring about our appearance, in particular by trying to stay slim. But as some of the examples illustrate, women are not passive in the face of this dominant ideology: we can resist by drawing on alternative discourses where we assert the right to say that sometimes we can't stand our mothers or sometimes our kids drive us mad, or where we mock the dominant view of ideal thigh size.

Competing views of men

The dominant discourses in our society teach us to see ourselves in relation to men. In so far as dominant discourses place men at the centre of the universe, then women are always marginal and only have meaning when fulfilling roles that are significant for men, as mother, as partner, as daughter. In this section I shall look at some of the ways in which women (and girls) talk about men. (Women friends' interest in competing versions of masculinity have already been demonstrated in texts such as those about the obedient husband, and men's involvement in child abuse.) Our talk about men does powerful work in our construction of ourselves as (certain kinds of) feminine subject.[7] It is certainly noticeable that girls in their early teens start talking compulsively about boys, as part of the negotiation of identity involved in the transition from girlhood to womanhood. I'll begin with two examples from girls in my sample (Emily is sixteen years old, Becky fourteen):

[Talking about poster of pop star]

EMILY: what a hunk!

[Talking about boy at school]

BECKY:	did you really know?	that I still fancied Damien?	
CLAIRE:	what?		
JESS:			yeah/

BECKY: I was too embarrassed to admit it though/

Adolescent girls relate both to male fantasy figures such as singers and film stars, and to real boys (boys such as Damien, who they go to school with). Emily, in the first of these examples, is more outspoken in her admiration for the man pictured in the poster on Gwen's wall than Becky is about Damien in the second. Where the male in question is known, then there is embarrassment as well as more positive feelings. But both examples draw on vocabulary – *hunk, fancy* – that was not present in the girls' talk a few years earlier,[8] vocabulary which constitutes them as heterosexual feminine subjects.

When the adult women in my sample talk about men in their lives, we find the whole gamut of emotions from love through amused tolerance to anger and contempt. The first two examples both come from the interviews.[9]

[Talking about husband]

JILL: in a funny way I suppose Roger's my best friend/

[Talking about husband]

MARY: well my partner's my friend you see/ [. . .] if you like Dave's my best friend/ so- so I feel totally relaxed with him/ and [. . .] I look forward to doing more things together/

While Jill and Mary express very positive feelings about their partners, Pat's story about her partner in the next example is more critical. But despite her evaluation of his characteristic behaviour as *dreadful*, her feelings are clearly affectionate rather than hostile.

[Talking about husband]

PAT: he gives me these little um . notes when he sends me shopping/ you

PAT: ought to see the notes I get with anything that I don't actually .

PAT: deal with myself/ like framing bits or anything like that/ you get

PAT: this long sort of paragraph/ which more or less starts with 'Go out

PAT: of the house/ proceed down the road' <LAUGHS> you know/
KAREN: I know/

PAT: sometimes there's a map of where the shop is/ and sometimes there's

PAT: a little drawing of what the thing ought to look like/ and I always

PAT: play to the gallery by going into the shop and showing them the

---

PAT: note/ <LAUGHS> [and they fall [about/
KAREN: absolutely/ [why not/ [about/ that's right/

PAT: dreadful/

Sue's criticism of her husband in the next example cannot be described as affectionate. But her complaints about the noisiness of his music-making (which is a recurrent feature of her conversations with Anna and Liz) occur against a background where John is seen by all three women as a good bloke, in comparison with men in Anna and Liz's lives. (For example, Anna comments at one point in the discussion of coupledom and relationships: *there's always a voice of reason I think with John, he's- he's very mature like that.*)

[Sue's husband's music gets louder]

SUE: I mean how can you live with this/
LIZ: well I know it's difficult when

SUE: [oh it drives you insane/
LIZ: you've got a man around [but-

The four examples I've given so far are all from speakers who are married. But among the women I've recorded are several who are divorced or separated. The next two examples come from moments in conversation where an estranged or ex-husband is the subject of conversation. (The first of these I'm including deliberately as a warning of the penalties which can be incurred by anyone unwise or unethical enough to record their friends surreptitiously.)[10]

[Discussing Jen's arrangements to get her ex-husband to help with her move to London]

MEG: I mean I wouldn't um rely on him for something as vital as

---

MEG: that/

[. . .] <JEN LEAVES ROOM TO ANSWER PHONE>

SALLY: your faces when <u>Jennifer said that- that Paul was going to do</u>
MEG: <LAUGHS--

- -

SALLY: the move/ .hh I wish I'd got a camera / <LAUGHING> ((it)) was
MEG: ---->   <LAUGHS----

- -

SALLY: sort of- ((xx)) in total disbelief/   I think the most difficult
MEG: ------>   mhm/

- -

SALLY: is- is that when you've loved someone/ you- you half the time you

- -

SALLY: forget their faults [don't you? and still maybe love them/ . . .
MEG: [yeah/

- -

Note the way Meg hedges her critical comments at the beginning of this example, prefacing what she says with *I mean* and then phrasing her utterance in a hypothetical way with *would*. Hedges are necessary as this is a very face-threatening subject. It's also noticeable how protective this group of friends are of one of their number: they clearly think that I (Jen) am acting foolishly in trusting my ex-husband. But Sally avoids outright criticism of me by positioning herself in a discourse where women are viewed as making bad decisions or acting stupidly because their judgement is clouded by emotion. While this discourse provides women with an excuse for bad decisions or stupid behaviour, it positions us as emotional, as nonrational (in contrast with men, who are positioned as rational).

The second of these examples focuses more explicitly on the male: Liz and Sue together describe Liz's husband's behaviour after he left Liz and the two children.

[Vindictiveness of estranged husbands]

- -

LIZ: I was like terrified/ I thought I was

- -

LIZ: going to ((be)) on the [streets/
SUE: [I think he was so horrible as well/

- -

LIZ: [he was not supportive at all/
SUE: [I mean he was really nasty/ but he wasn't even not supportive/

- -

LIZ: [oh he was vindictive/ he really wanted me to suffer/
SUE: he was . vindic [tive/   yeah/

- -

LIZ: [he really wanted-   yeah/
SUE: [and his children/ that was the thing/   his children to go with

- -

SUE: it/ oh . horrible/

Here, Sue and Liz explicitly label the man as bad, using words like *horrible, nasty, vindictive*. But at the same time, the man is portrayed as active, the women as more passive: *I was like terrified, he really wanted me to suffer*. And it is only because of Sue's intervention that Liz amends the weaker *not supportive* to the stronger *vindictive*. (Similarly, Becky's words in the example we looked at earlier, *Hannah was crying because Ben was a sexist bastard*, label the boy Ben as bad, drawing on a feminist antisexist discourse, but present Hannah's response as weak.)

The final example comes from the discussion of coupledom analysed in some detail at the end of the last chapter. During the course of this talk, Sue, Liz and Anna ponder whether it is better to be in a couple or independent. Anna comes down on the side of independence:

[Discussing the relative merits of coupledom and independence]

ANNA: I just sometimes think I probably never will get married again/ or never be with anybody again/ cos I just love my life on my own/

While the women in these examples are positioned in a variety of ways – as women who love men, as women who are critical of men, as women who prefer to live alone – they all share the dominant world view in which heterosocial relations are seen as the norm. In other words, for all these women (and for the girls in my sample) the construction of themselves as feminine involves simultaneously the construction of themselves as heterosocial. As is typical of dominant discourses, this process is virtually invisible: this means that criticism or resistance becomes very difficult. And because my sample contains no women who were lesbian at the time these recordings were made, then a non-heterosocial discourse is not voiced.

Resistant discourses

However, resistance to the androcentric norms of the dominant culture does occur. There is evidence in the conversations that the women in my sample have access not only to dominant (androcentric) discourses but also to resistant discourses, particularly feminist discourses, which offer alternative positions, alternative ways of being a woman. In the final example above, we heard Anna resisting the normative pressures to live as part of a (heterosexual) couple. Here are four more examples of women using resistant discourses.

The first draws on a psychotherapeutic discourse which challenges the construct 'the happy family'.

[Topic: Anna's mother and her sister Diana]

ANNA:	but now looking back on it she [A's mother] was really bad to her/
SUE:	mhm/
LIZ:	why?

ANNA:	and [Diana says that-
SUE:	[it's funny because your mum holds up the thing
LIZ:	I wonder why/

ANNA:	yeah/ [that's right/ well that's-
SUE:	of the happy family quite a lot doesn't [she?

ANNA:	you have to don't you? that's the [conspiracy/
SUE:	yeah/ [that's it/

Anna resists the normative pressures to speak of her family and of relationships between her mother and her siblings in glowing terms. In the conversation preceding this extract she self-discloses to her friends about some of the problems in her family; then, with Sue's support, she goes on to challenge the idea of the happy family and names the discourse that promotes it a 'conspiracy'.

The next example shows how women friends help each other to struggle against prevailing discourses. Helen challenges me – and the discourse I adopt – by refusing to accept my description of recent events in my life.

[Talking about jobs]

HELEN:	you haven't been applying for jobs as well have you?
JEN:	yes/

HELEN:	oh have you? that's right/ so-
JEN:	there's one at Cambridge/ <LAUGHS>

HELEN: so have you applied [for it? [oh no but
JEN: Cambridge! <LAUGHING> [oh what hubris/ [%honestly%

HELEN: that's TERRIBLE though isn't it? <HIGH, APPALLED> I mean
JEN:

HELEN: [you can't imagine any men sitting round/ . saying about their
JEN: [oh you mean I'm being ((xx))-

HELEN: applications that it's hubris/
JEN: oh all right/ <MOCK GRUMPY>

HELEN: you're conditioned to think that/
JEN:

Helen draws on a liberal feminist discourse which resists the idea that women and men do things differently or have different abilities. She also draws on the feminist idea that socialization rather than biology determines our sense of ourselves as inferior, arguing that we are socialized to internalize such views – *you're conditioned to think that*. In this brief dialogue we see how friends can challenge each other's views and resist each other's discourses at the same time as supporting each other, since in effect Helen is saying, 'You have as good a right as any man to apply for a job at Cambridge University'. We can accept each other's challenges – and can therefore adopt more radical positions – because we feel supported and validated by each other.

The next example comes from the Oxton group's discussion of child abuse. This discussion, like the one between Anna, Sue and Liz above, focuses on the family, but this time the emphasis is on the tendency to blame the mother when families malfunction.

[Discussion of child abuse]

MEG: one of the things often said about the incestuous family is that um it's really the mother's fault one way or another/ [. . .] I mean I'm so terrified of joining in the blaming of mothers/

[. . .]

MARY: but I mean so much research is male-dominated/ I mean it's just- it's staggering isn't it?

Here we find a group of women discussing a topic which forces them to consider the nature of patriarchy. They struggle to avoid adopting a more conventional discourse on the family and on sexuality, and draw on a feminist discourse to challenge conventional views, explicitly naming *the blaming of mothers* as the construction of a more patriarchal discourse, and using the phrase *male-dominated*, which allies them all with a feminist position which sees male–female relations in terms of dominance and oppression. (But it's interesting to note the presence of the phrase *the incestuous family*, a phrase which does the work of concealing *who* in the family abuses other members of that family, and thus a phrase which clearly serves patriarchal, not feminist, interests.)[11]

The last example comes in a stretch of conversation where Liz and Anna have been telling anecdotes about men in their lives (brothers, ex-husbands) who have let them down or behaved badly.

[Talking about the inadequacy of some men]

ANNA:	women are just vastly superior/		[thank god I'm
LIZ:		they ARE/ VASTly	[a superior/
SUE:		<LAUGHS-	----------------------

ANNA:	a woman/ and not like that/	
LIZ:		yeah/
SUE:	------------------------------	->

Anna's statement draws on a radical feminist discourse which claims that, far from being inferior, women are in fact superior. This is a very powerful discourse, since it positions women as being positive about themselves, it allows us to like ourselves and to say things like *thank god I'm a woman*. But Sue's laughter indicates that these three friends make these remarks fully aware of the discrepancy between what they are saying and dominant ideas about women and men. The laughter signals that they can amuse themselves by expressing this view to each other, but suggests that they maybe have doubts about its relevance to their lives in the outside world.

Tensions and contradictions

Given the range of discursive positions available to us, it is not surprising that we present ourselves in talk as different kinds of woman, sometimes more forceful and assertive, sometimes more passive and ineffectual. The clash between different positions produces tensions and contradictions in our talk, where competing discourses came into contact with each other. Earlier brief examples have illustrated that we draw on a range of discourses, but in this section I want to look at a few longer examples to show how different discourses coexist in a single conversation.

First, here's an extract from a conversation between Hannah, Becky, Claire and Jessica when they are fourteen years old. The topic is periods, and at this point they are talking about mood swings.

HANNAH: everything seemed to be going wrong and everything/

HANNAH: it was horrible/ [. . .] it was really horrible

HANNAH: [that day/
JESS: [but you know when I [had that really bad . um
CLAIRE: [do you get PMT ((xxx))

HANNAH: <LAUGHS>
BECKY: yeah/ I'm a bitch/ <LAUGHS> I'm
JESS: premenstrual tension/

HANNAH: so I've noticed/ no- no but [some-
BECKY: REally HORrible/ no but- [so whenever

HANNAH: ='Right I might be horrible
BECKY: I'm on my period I say to Hannah um=

HANNAH: to you but=
BECKY: ='Don't take any notice'/

This passage is part of a more lengthy chain of mutual self-disclosure on the subject of mood swings. The girls in turn tell anecdotes to illustrate how premenstrual tension affects them. Throughout this section of the conversation at least three discourses are simultaneously present: a medical discourse, a repressive discourse, and a more resistant feminist discourse. The friends choose words such as *premenstrual tension* in their talk about their periods; these words are part of a medical discourse. A feminist discourse expressing solidarity and sisterhood is realized through overlapping turns, expressions of agreement, and through the joint construction of text (Becky and Hannah share in constructing the utterance *so whenever I'm on my period I say to Hannah um 'Right I might be horrible to you but don't take any notice'*). The sequence of self-disclosing anecdotes (here we have the end of Hannah's and the beginning of Becky's) involving mirroring and exchange is another feature of this discourse. The third discourse present is a discourse of repression: the girls jointly represent themselves as beings who are *affected*, at the mercy of larger forces, rather than as *agents*, in control of their lives. This is realized through their choice of stative verbs: *was, had, got*, and through the use of negative words such as *horrible* and *bitch*. Through the use of these discourses the girls are simultaneously positioned as having solidarity with each other and as oppressed.

Contradictions are also apparent if we look at a longer extract from the conversation where Anna says, *women are just vastly superior*. The subject of men's inadequacy is part of the larger topic 'Relationships', and follows on from the discussion of the obedient husband and of coupledom. Anna tells a story about the break-up of her last relationship, and complains that men seem to find it hard to understand when a relationship is over. Liz responds with a story about her ex-husband who had come round the previous weekend to help her clear out her loft. She describes wryly how she had 'made a point of it being my loft and my rubbish', so she ends up doing most of the work, and as she leaves for her last trip to the dump she recounts how her ex-husband, now sitting watching football on television, got out a five pound note and asked her to buy him some fish and chips. Her point is that she considers such behaviour appalling (though she does in fact buy his fish and chips). Anna then tells a matching story about her brother (Mark) who had recently come and leaned against the kitchen door, complaining of depression, while she was 'humping twenty-five kilos of cement across the kitchen'. It is at this point that Anna says that women are superior:

- -

ANNA: I mean in a way it doesn't upset me things like that any more/

- -

ANNA: [cos I just laugh/ cos I think well . women are just
LIZ: [no they don't upset you/ you laugh about it/ yes/

- -

ANNA: vastly superior/ [thank god I'm a woman/ and
LIZ: they ARE/ VASTly [superior/
SUE: <LAUGHS-------------------------------------

- -

ANNA: not like that/
LIZ: yeah/
SUE: ------------------>

- -

This leads into a long discussion between the three friends about men and the reasons for some of them being so inadequate. It is this last section that I want to examine in some detail. The three friends move from a radical discourse which is self-affirming, which asserts the value of women, to an oppressive, woman-blaming discourse:

ANNA: why though why are boys like that? [why are they?
SUE: [it must be ((about having the
LIZ: boys ARE

ANNA: I mean my mother- my mother and my youngest sister both ring
SUE: xxx too x apart))
LIZ: like that/

ANNA: Mark up regularly/ and my- my younger sister Felicity writes

---

ANNA: to him/ and she says . um 'We- Mummy and I are really worried

---

ANNA: about you cos you're so depressed/ and you know if there's anything

---

ANNA: we can do just give us a ring'/ and I said to her 'But it makes

---

ANNA: him worse'= [he's been like it since my father died/
LIZ: =yeah/ [it feeds it/ yeah/
SUE: =yeah/

ANNA: and that's over a year now/ and it all affected us very badly/
LIZ: yeah/ yeah/

ANNA: but you know life is to get on with= =and the more you
LIZ: yeah/ =yeah=

ANNA: pander to him being depressed/ and telling him 'Oh poor thing

---

ANNA: never mind'= [he's going to get worse/
LIZ: =[the more he'll [revel in it/ yes/
SUE: =[no he loves it/

ANNA: [it makes me so cross/
LIZ: [that's right/

- -

→ ANNA: and I think in a- in a w- in a way it's women who perpetuate that/

- -

ANNA: it's women who . despise weak men and then just produce more
SUE: oh yeah/

- -

ANNA: of them/ and say to them you know 'Don't worry darling/ it'll all

- -

ANNA: be all right/ and you don't have to-'
SUE: 'I'll look after you'/ <LAUGHS>

- -

Anna, focusing on the particular case of her brother, argues that it is her mother who is to blame, and generalizes from this that women are to blame for producing weak men. Liz and Sue go along with this argument. They add minimal responses as well as more substantive forms of agreement; they also jointly construct utterances with Anna: Anna's *the more you pander to him* . . . is completed by Liz with *the more he'll revel in it*, and Anna's *it's women who . . . say to them . . . 'Don't worry darling it'll be all right'* is completed by Sue with *'I'll look after you'*. Liz then develops this woman-blaming theme as follows, introducing the notion of the 'strong' woman.

- -

LIZ: it's probably because everybody's- if he's had strong women in the

- -

ANNA: it probably is/ [it probably-
SUE: oh god/ yes/ [that's right/
LIZ: house/ and other people- and other people have made [decisions

- -

ANNA: [yes/ it's awful I know/ I do appreciate that/ I mean
LIZ: FOR him [you see/

- -

ANNA: I'm quite bombastic/ <SUE EXITS TO GO TO LOO>

- -

At this point, Anna starts to blame herself rather than her mother for her brother's weakness. She includes herself in the category 'strong women' with her apologetic statement *I'm quite bombastic*. This switch from mothers to themselves is continued by Liz, who starts to talk about her worries about her own son, who is away at boarding school.

LIZ: I worry that I'm too strong/ that's the rea- one of the reasons I

ANNA: [yes/
LIZ: sent Dean away/ [. . .] because um I'm strong/ and he [leans on me

---

ANNA: Mark does it/ I mean [I- I pay all the bills/
LIZ: for decisions/ [yeah/

ANNA: I [do the mortgage/ I do the insurance/ [I- .hh I ring up the bank
LIZ: [yeah/ [yeah/

ANNA: when they won't give us an overdraft/ I negotiate the building

---

ANNA: society when they won't [lend us m- the amount-
LIZ: [well that starts from being

ANNA: =it does/ it does/ yeah/ but at the same time . I just
LIZ: very young=

ANNA: think if I don't do it/ HE's not going to do it/ and then that's

---

ANNA: [more worry back on me because it's not being done/
LIZ: [but you- yeah/ and you- you- you'd have to

ANNA: yeah/ it's easier to
LIZ: do it for yourself anyway/ so you do it/

ANNA: do it for both of you/

In the above passage, Anna and Liz collude in a view of themselves as strong and therefore potentially dangerous to males who live with them. They then collaborate in arguing that they are forced to be active and competent because if they weren't, things wouldn't get done and they would be the ones to suffer. Having worked themselves into a position where they feel they have a good reason for taking responsibility for the bills and the mortgage, Liz initiates a more positive move by asserting that women are normally prevented from realizing how easy it is to run your own life – to deal with the *bills and mortgages and everything else.*

LIZ: but it's a myth you know/ I wish a lot of women would

LIZ: realize that it's a complete and utter myth/ . this- this being on

---

LIZ: your ow- I mean . when I was first- when I was first thrown out

---

LIZ: there on my own if you like/ I was bloody terrified/ bills and

---

ANNA: yeah/ but how much have you learnt since you
LIZ: mortgages and everything else/ but- but yeah

ANNA: first ((xx))
LIZ: but once you get on with it there's nothing- there's- .

ANNA: there's nothing [to it really/
LIZ: [there's nothing to it/

This last section of their talk about women's competence and men's incompetence represents a dramatic shift of position. Here, rather than bewailing her competence, Liz is celebrating it. And rather than claiming that women as a group are powerful and dangerous and produce weak and damaged men, she argues that women are prevented from understanding how easy it is to be independent (though she doesn't name *who* is responsible for preventing this). She feels strongly that women should be given the information they need – and thus, she implies, should have the right to be competent autonomous people in their own right. This bit of talk ends with the triumphant repetition of the phrase *there's nothing to it* by both Liz and Anna. So we see Liz and Anna (with Sue in the earlier part) holding the contradictory positions that (i) boys and men are inadequate; (ii) women are superior to men; (iii) it's good to be a woman; (iv) women are too strong; (v) women are to blame for men's inadequacy; (vi) women have to be strong/competent because otherwise nothing would get done; (vii) running a house is easy; (viii) women are misled into thinking it's difficult.

At the heart of these contradictions is ambivalence about being 'strong'. These women friends are positioned by a patriarchal discourse to see strength as incompatible with femininity and somehow bad, even dangerous. Simultaneously, their exposure to resistant feminist discourses means they also have a sense of strength as good, as part of a different type of femininity, a femininity which is distinct from masculinity but not inferior to it. The problem seems to be that they find it hard to sustain the latter, feminist position: their assertions that they are strong trigger anxiety about weakness in men. In other words, they fall back onto a world view that sees all relationships in hierarchical terms, so if one group is strong, the other group must be weak (or less strong), and if men are weak, that is somehow women's responsibility.

Women's anxiety about our strength is closely related to our ambivalence about power. I've chosen the final extract to show a woman using a more powerful discourse. Meg, in the next example, starts to talk about her experience on an interview panel. This follows on from Janet's story about her recent interview for a job. But where Janet was telling a story where she, the protagonist, was an interviewee, Meg chooses to tell a story where she is in the powerful position of being one of the interviewers. There are several discourses present in the extract, but I want to focus on two: a powerful professional discourse, and a sexist patriarchal discourse.

[Topic: Interviews]

MEG: we did the interviews for the- [. . .] you know I'd been shortlisting/

MEG: and there were twenty-four/ and um inCREDibly well-qualified/ and

MEG: the twenty-four that applied for er nine places . all had um good

MEG: degrees in psychology/ I mean and some of them had . M- MPhils

MEG: and DPhils and um .hh PhDs/ you know they were very well qualified/

MEG: and . all- virtually all of them had done some . proper ongoing

MEG: research into child abuse or-

MEG: the M- it's called the MClinPsychol/
MARY: what's the course?

MEG: it's the qualification I did/ [masters in clinical [psychology/
MARY: [yes/ [mhm/

MEG: um . anyway we interviewed them on two days running/ Thursday

MEG: and Friday/ and ((something)) really funny thing happened/ .

MEG: one was an extremely pretty girl that's doing . um er er-

MEG: what's the diploma? a- a- a Master's in Child Development at

MEG: Newcastle with Professor Newton/ and she got a SPLENdid

MEG: reference from Professor Newton/
JEN: you used to have Professor

MEG: [yeah/ yeah/ but s- and saying things
JEN: Newton [didn't you?
HELEN: did you? mhm/

MEG: like- can't remember the girl's name/ Nicola I think/ saying um you

MEG: know 'She's academically u- u- unimpeachable/ she's absolutely

MEG: superb/ she's also an extremely nice girl/ and she's . the sort that

MEG: joins in well at the party/ and is always- has al- always there- er

MEG: also there for the washing up'/

<LAUGHTER>

MEG: that was a nice little domestic note/ anyway um-
HELEN: they wouldn't

MEG: [well there WAS
HELEN: have said that about a bloke [((xx))/
SALLY: [I was going to [say/

MEG: that/ um . anyway during the interview um . it went okay/ .

MEG: um she's- she's the sort of- she has a very pleasant manner/

MEG: and she answered quite competently/ and at the end/ um David

MEG: Blair said to her . um 'You've been working with autistic

MEG: children'/ she's done two special projects with autistic

MEG: children/ [. . .] he said to her . um 'Do you believe um

MEG: there's any relationship between dyslexia and autism'?/ and she

MEG:	absolutely panicked /	<AGHAST> and it was TERRible for us	
BEA:		heavens /	
HELEN:			mhm /

MEG:	to watch /

Meg presents herself here as a competent professional. This is done in part through the use of specialized vocabulary such as: *short-listing, clinical psychology, reference, dyslexia, autism,* and abbreviated terms: *MPhil, DPhil, MClinPsychol,* which assume in-group knowledge. It's also done prosodically, with the rhythm and stress patterns of phrases like *she got a SPLENdid reference from Professor Newton* carrying powerful signals about social class and educational level which are readily understood by British English speakers. Meg also accomplishes professionalism through her presentation of herself as someone with agency, a doer, not a person who is done to: *I'd been short-listing; it's the qualification I did; we interviewed them* . . . which is implicitly contrasted with the young woman interviewee who is presented as *an extremely pretty girl* who has a *very pleasant manner* and who *answered quite competently*. The presentation of the young interviewee is derogatory: Meg's description of her doesn't just accomplish power; it also accomplishes the oppression of women. Not only is the young woman called a 'girl' (thus reducing her to non-adult status), but she is described in terms of her appearance, which is clearly irrelevant to the situation. Later, Meg repeats Professor Newton's reference with approval, though its allusion to the young woman's willingness to wash up after parties is blatantly sexist. Meg initially describes this as *a nice little domestic note,* and it is only when Helen challenges this position with the comment *they wouldn't have said that about a bloke* that she concedes there might be a problem with this aspect of the reference.

It seems as though women like Meg – women who were among the first to take on more senior positions in professions like law and medicine and psychology – can only adopt a powerful role if they also take on the patriarchal values that normally accompany such power. So Meg's self-presentation here illustrates the tensions associated with doing femininity and power at the same time: Meg succeeds in doing power, but at the same time she presents herself as colluding in an ideology that denigrates and trivializes women. The crux of her story to her friends is that a very talented young woman panicked in her interview – in other words, the younger woman lost all claim to competence by contrast with the calm professionals on the panel. Meg's self-presentation works in part because of the contrast between herself – calm, competent, professional – and the young woman who panics.

On the other hand, there are features of her talk which undermine the discourse of power. She hesitates or says *um* and *er* frequently, as well as stammering and repeating her words. She has brief lapses of memory when she appeals for help to her friends – *what's the diploma?*. She also includes hedges in her account – *you know, I mean, sort of*. In part, these 'lapses' are designed to reduce distance between herself and her addressees: as I've said in earlier chapters, women friends avoid playing the expert where possible. But these features of Meg's talk also accomplish a femininity that is not powerful, that needs help and support. This latter aspect of her talk demonstrates how problematic it is for us as women to claim power for ourselves.

Conclusion

As the examples in this chapter have illustrated, there is no single unified way of doing femininity, of being a woman. In the contemporary developed world, many different versions of femininity are available to us. Different discourses give us access to different femininities. More mainstream discourses position us in more conventional ways, while more radical or subversive discourses offer us alternative ways of being, alternative ways of doing femininity. We are unwittingly involved in the ceaseless struggle to define gender: as Chris Weedon puts it, 'The nature of femininity and masculinity is one of the key sites of discursive struggle for the individual'.[12]

The meaning of 'Woman' has changed through time, and at any given time it will vary – between, for example, meanings associated with more madonna-like images of femininity and meanings associated with more whore-like images. There is no such thing as a 'woman'; the meaning of 'woman' will depend on which discourse the word occurs in. 'Discourses do not just reflect or represent social entities and relations, they construct or "constitute" them; different discourses constitute key entities [such as 'woman'] . . . in different ways.'[13] What 'being a woman' means at this moment in late twentieth-century Britain is a site of struggle, with dominant ideologies being challenged by more feminist ones.

It seems to me that the talk we do with our women friends is particularly important in terms of our sense of ourselves as women, because in our talk we collaborate in constructing a shared view of what constitutes womanhood. We also support each other in resisting particular versions of femininity and in preferring others, and we help each other (consciously or unconsciously) to reconcile conflicting or contradictory femininities. We do this as part of the ongoing work of doing friendship. Doing friendship is the subject of the last chapter.

11

'Talk's absolutely fundamental': Being a friend

Having friends is something most of us take for granted. This means that the things we do in order to make friends and to sustain friendship are so much part of our everyday social practice that they are pretty much invisible to us. But doing friendship is a significant accomplishment: some people find it difficult, or get it wrong; others never grasp what it means, to be 'a friend'. And friendship is a serious undertaking: as Mary said, 'It is time-consuming, you see, so when you think about the amount of time that you have to spend working on your friends . . . I mean you have to make a conscious decision to be friends, don't you'. Talking with our friends is an important part of that work. The talk that we do isn't just incidental to friendship: without talk, we couldn't sustain friendship. Talking with friends is constitutive of friendship; through talking, we do 'being friends'.

In this final chapter, I want to pull together the various strands of the book and to reassert the value of women's ways of talking. The chapter will suggest some new ways of thinking about friendship, emphasizing the links between talk and friendship. I shall also look at some of the ways that we can 'get it wrong'.

Linguistic strategies

In this section I will recapitulate the linguistic strategies women use in talk with friends, to answer the question, How do these strategies 'do' friendship? The linguistic forms which are characteristic of women's talk are not arbitrary, but highly functional in terms of the goals of women's friendship. The primary goal of talk between women friends is the construction and maintenance of close and equal social relationships. Friendship depends on an ethic of reciprocity and on the maintenance of equality. And while we may have other relationships which are relationships of equals (e.g. with colleagues, workmates), such relationships are not characterized by intimacy: friendship depends on minimizing social distance. The linguistic strategies deployed by women friends all fulfil one or both of these goals.

Telling stories

Stories are an intrinsic part of the talk of women friends. Telling stories fulfils women friends' need to keep in touch with each other's lives; moreover, hearing about others' experience helps to place our own experience in an explanatory framework. The exchange of stories carries out some of the work of mirroring; in particular, the anecdotes which are told as part of reciprocal self-disclosure are a key way of 'doing' friendship. Stories also serve to introduce new topics or to develop topics. With their emphasis on people and places, women's stories function to ground us in the everyday world and allow us to reflect on our everyday experiences. They allow us to explore themes of connection, of the importance of acting in conjunction with others and of the foolhardiness of acting alone: they remind us that heroism is rarely an option for us. Through story-telling we can draw on humour to talk about problematic issues. Story-telling plays a very important part in our construction of ourselves as women and as friends.

Hedging

Hedges have multiple functions: they can express shades of doubt and confidence; they allow us to be sensitive to others' feelings; they help us in the search for the right words to express what we mean; they help us to avoid playing the expert. The first of these functions – to express doubt and confidence – is basic, but less significant in terms of women's friendships. The other three functions all have an important role in the maintenance of friendship. If friendship is the arena in which we can most completely 'be ourselves', as the women I interviewed claimed, then obviously we need to be able to draw on resources to protect ourselves when we make ourselves vulnerable. But we also need to be sensitive to our friends' feelings. Because we often discuss sensitive topics with our closest friends, and because mutual self-disclosure is criterial for female friendship, then linguistic forms which allow us to pay attention to the face-needs of all participants are a vital part of our repertoire.

Being able to search for the right words to say what we mean is also important in establishing a close relationship. Women friends allow each other time to 'struggle with words', as Rachel put it in her interview: 'Talking with women I'm- I'm much happier about struggling around how to say things . . . and also women give you time to struggle with it'. In so far as talking with others gives us the opportunity to explore possible selves, different versions of 'I', then feeling accepted, feeling confident that we can say anything and be judged, allows us space to grow. It also allows us space to rehearse existing knowledge and to explore new knowledges. These are important claims which I shall come back to later in the chapter.

Hedging also allows us to avoid expert status. In order to 'do' friendship, we want to avoid anything that will increase social distance between us and our friends. Talking about a subject where we have some expertise can potentially open up distance, but the evidence is that women friends use hedges judiciously to downplay their expert status. In terms of the goals of friendship, it is more important to preserve equality with friends than to gain status as individuals.

Hedges also play an important role in the maintenance of the collaborative floor (see below). They help to preserve openness and to avoid closure and conflict. In a collaborative floor, the group voice takes precedence, which means that speakers need to avail themselves of linguistic forms like hedges which enable them to say what they mean without blocking others from making their own personal statements.

Questions

Questions, like hedges, are multifunctional. Many of these functions construct and sustain friendship. For example, both questions and tag questions function to draw speakers into conversation and to keep conversations going. They help us to check that we are still 'in tune' with each other, and allow us to ask for help when we're stuck for a word. Questions are also used to invite friends to tell stories. Moreover, they are a useful resource for speakers who are trying to protect their own face and that of their addressees – asking a question is much less threatening than making an assertion. We also use questions in the discussion of controversial topics to introduce a different point of view without overtly disagreeing with another speaker. In this way we maintain the collaborative floor (see below).

Rhetorical questions are used frequently in the talk of women friends. They are a way of expressing general truths, which assert the group's world view and check that consensus still exists. Tag questions are also used to check the taken-for-granted-ness of what is being said, to confirm the shared world of the participants. In terms of avoiding playing the expert, questions are a valuable resource, emphasizing the shared quest for answers rather than individual knowledge. Even information-seeking questions have a role in sustaining friendship: in the talk of younger female speakers information-exchange is important, especially information about boys and about adolescent problems in general.

Fundamentally, questions are a way of expressing solidarity and connection. They are used with great skill by women who exploit them at the interactional rather than the informational level, as part of 'doing' friendship.

Repetition

Repetition is a regular feature of the talk of women friends. It is a powerful way of affirming the group voice, since it means that two or more speakers say the same thing in some form or another. Repetition can take place at the level of words or phrases or clauses; it can involve grammar and meaning as well as vocabulary. Repetition functions primarily to signal solidarity between women friends. Because women treat talk with friends as a kind of jam session, repetition – that is, saying the same things as each other and using the same linguistic patterns as each other – becomes a powerful symbol of the connection we feel with each other.

The collaborative floor

When speakers choose to establish a collaborative floor rather than a single one-at-a-time floor, they are choosing to do friendship or intimacy. While the single floor prioritizes the individual speaker and the individual speaker's turn, the collaborative floor prioritizes the group and symbolizes connection between speakers.

The collaborative floor in the talk of women friends is characterized by two strategies in particular: the shared construction of utterances and overlapping talk. When friends share in the construction of utterances, they are demonstrating in a very concrete way that they can operate as if they were a single speaker: operating as a single speaker is a powerful way of doing friendship. Further, women friends use overlapping speech as a way of joining in together, of sharing the floor (not as a way of grabbing a turn). When two or more friends speak at the same time, on the same theme, the resulting polyphony is iconic of connection. Women friends also use minimal responses and laughter to assert their presence in the shared conversational space, and to maintain connections between each other.

The work required to establish and maintain a collaborative floor is work that is constitutive of friendship. Every linguistic strategy typical of the collaborative floor serves this purpose – this includes the strategies mentioned already (jointly-constructed utterances and overlapping speech) as well as others such as shorter turns, repetition between speakers, and joking and teasing. The collaborative floor is qualitatively as well as quantitatively different from one-at-a-time turn-taking. Fundamentally this is because the collaborative floor is a shared space: what is said is construed as being the voice of the group rather than of the individual. This emphasis on the connection between speakers makes the collaborative floor a powerful way of doing friendship.

Communicative competence and friendship

This summary of linguistic strategies and their role in doing friendship is potentially misleading. I don't want to give the idea that to accomplish friendship through talk, women speakers just help themselves from a smorgasbord of linguistic features such as stories or hedges or questions. Knowing how to be a friend involves more than this. Knowing how to be a friend is a crucial part of our communicative competence. The phrase communicative competence was coined by Dell Hymes to describe the repertoire of skills that each of us develops as we take our place in a particular speech community.[1] Linguists often restrict their attention to linguistic competence – that is, a native speaker's knowledge of the grammatical structure of their language. But Hymes pointed out that even if you had perfect linguistic competence in a given language, but you didn't know when to join in talk, when to remain silent, when to tell a joke, when to laugh (all crucial aspects of communicative competence), then you would not be judged a competent member of that particular speech community.

The women who are the subjects of this book all demonstrate their communicative competence, both in the broad sense outlined in the previous paragraph, and in the more specialized sense of knowing how to be a friend. One strong piece of evidence for the idea of a specialized competence for 'doing friendship' through talk is that, as competent members of the speech community, we are immediately aware if someone gets it wrong. Many of the women I've talked to about my research, both those I interviewed and others, have spontaneously told me anecdotes about women acquaintances who didn't seem to fully understand the rules.

Getting it wrong

Compulsive completions

The most common mistake seems to occur in relation to the joint construction of utterances. It is part of our communicative competence as women that we learn to construct utterances collaboratively; this is part of our wider competence in the norms of participating in a collaborative floor. But some women seem to think that simply to complete another's utterance is a way of doing friendship (and of doing femininity). Because they fail to grasp that this move is part of a wider strategy – that is, they fail to grasp that this move is part of the joint construction of text in a collaboratively developed floor – they tend to overuse it. This becomes very irritating for other speakers. In particularly serious cases, the compulsive completer will offer a word or words that do not fit what we are trying to say. (This exposes gaps in the assumed shared world.) But even when the completion fits, we may begin to feel that the collaborative floor is being undermined, as over-frequent completions feel intrusive rather than collaborative. So the overuse of this strategy ultimately signals insensitivity and is more likely to function as a barrier to friendship than as a means of establishing friendship. (There were no obvious examples of this in the recordings I analysed: this isn't surprising, since I only recorded well-established friendship groups, that is, groups in which the participants had already established close friendships and who therefore can be assumed to be competent in the rules of how to accomplish friendship through talk.)[2]

False starts and butting in

Another less serious problem arises with speakers who mistime their contributions to talk: overlapping speech results from these over-enthusiastic false starts. This occurred from time to time in the conversations I analysed, but the individuals concerned typically backed down and waited for a more appropriate moment to say what they wanted to say. (Overlapping speech is of course a normal feature of collaborative talk. The problem arises when overlapping speech involves contributions that are not thematically congruent: in a collaborative floor, overlapping speech involves simultaneous contributions to talk which are *on the same theme.*) In the following example, Sally has just added a detail to her anecdote about her neighbour deciding to fly to Australia for his mother's funeral. Mary starts to make a new point – and begins to move the talk on from illustrative anecdote to group discussion – but she realizes that Sally is still talking. As a result she stops and listens, adding a minimal response – *yeah* – to show support for what Sally has said, before making her point.

[Funeral discussion]

- -

SALLY: I said 'But . they'd know, John'/ ((xx)) <LAUGHS>

- -

→ MARY: [but if- yeah/ but if
SALLY: I mean [it's not as if I'm particularly religious/

- -

MARY: you've got a fa- if there's a spouse/ . . .

- -

The next example shows Hannah misjudging the place to come in with a contribution to a round of mirroring anecdotes about premenstrual tension. Becky has told an anecdote about her mother assuming she's having a period whenever she's in a bad mood, and Claire then talks about her own mood swings. Hannah tries to introduce an anecdote about feeling moody in the bath, but mistimes it in relation to Claire's contribution:

[Topic: Periods]

- -

CLAIRE: ((sometimes I'm just sitting there)) [like/ I suddenly feel as
→ HANNAH: [well-

- -

CLAIRE: if I'm going to cry right [((xxx)) suddenly- it just suddenly
JESS: [yes/
→ HANNAH: [I was lying in the bath-

- -

CLAIRE: your eyes like this/

- -

She tries again after Becky and Jess have joined in Claire's description of what her eyes and nose feel like when she's premenstrual, but starts to talk at the same time as Claire, whose contribution is directly relevant to what Becky is saying. Here we can see Claire, Becky and Jessica collaborating in talk about a particular aspect of premenstrual experience, while Hannah wants to move on to talking about a specific episode in her life, a more egocentric move.

CLAIRE: your eyes like this/ if your face goes hot/ and you- and it
BECKY: oh right/ mhm/

CLAIRE: just goes ((xx))/ they su- they just like comes ((like a [heat
BECKY: =yeah [your
JESS: your eyes sting=

CLAIRE: wave))/
BECKY: nose is- it feels like your nose is just sort of . expanding

---

CLAIRE: [it sometimes happens in a lesson/
BECKY: [or something/
→ HANNAH: [well what-

She finally manages to add her mirroring anecdote, after Claire and Becky have rounded off their description of the way their noses feel:

CLAIRE: [it sometimes happens in a lesson/ you're just sort of sitting
BECKY: [or something
→ HANNAH: [well what-

CLAIRE: there going- it goes [hwu: m] <WHOOSHING NOISE>
BECKY: I get that/

CLAIRE: yeah/
BECKY: I got that last time ((xxx))/
→ HANNAH: well what happened to me was-

HANNAH: it was one day this week/ and I was just so hysterical/ and I was

---

HANNAH: lying in the bath/ and I was sobbing/ . . .

This group are the youngest speakers who participated in my research; in this extract, they are fourteen years old. In the conversations they recorded when they were twelve and thirteen years old, they consistently used a single floor and a surprisingly adversarial style of talking. It is only when they reached fourteen that they first demonstrated competence in establishing and maintaining a collaborative floor.[3] In this particular example, we see Hannah struggling to take her place in a collaborative floor, mistiming the opening of her anecdote. But these are young speakers who are still in the process of becoming communicatively competent: it is to be expected that they will not always sustain the norms of conversation typical of adult women friends.

Talking too much

Another aspect of women friends' communicative competence is understanding how much you can talk. Talking too much and talking too little are both problematic. The underlying notion of sharing is critical here: women friends value the pattern they establish of talk alternating between speakers. As Bea said in her interview with me, the normal 'shape' of talk is 'sort of one person talking about themself or their idea or their feeling or whatever, and the other person listening to it and responding to IT but then maybe coming back with something of their own so that it isn't all one-sided'. One-sidedness is definitely frowned upon in friendly talk.

The collaborative floor is characterized by shorter turns than a single or one-at-a-time floor. 'Holding forth' on a subject will tend to be seen as talking too much and is frowned upon because it disrupts the collaborative floor. If one person indulges in a monologue, then the joint voice is lost.[4] As we saw in chapter 6, women friends participate jointly in talk with great skill, whether there are only two or as many as six speakers. The following example, which involves five speakers (and which has already been discussed in chapter 6), demonstrates this very clearly:

[Topic: Apes and language]

MARY:	**I mean they can shuffle words around and**	[**make a different mean-**
BEA:		[draw up a conclusion

MARY:	**ing/**		
BEA:	((xxxxx)) -		
JEN:		**they put two words together**	**to form a compound/**
MEG:			yeah/

MARY:		that's right=
BEA:		=mhm
JEN:	**to mean something that they didn't have a**	**lexical item for/**

MARY:	that's right/		**for**	**a brazil nut/**
BEA:			**a stoneberry for a-**	**a brazil nut/**
JEN:	**which is-**			
HELEN:		right/		

MEG:	**yes/ and**	**lotionberry for vomit/**
HELEN:	mhm/	gosh/

Helen, who had not seen the television programme that prompted this discussion, takes on the role of responding to the account the other four jointly construct. It's striking how the main strand of explication (marked in bold in the transcript) is voiced in turn by Mary, Jen, Bea and then Meg. This means that no speaker takes on the role of expert. It also means that speaking turns are shared and everyone participates.

In a single floor, turns tend to be longer: in informal conversation men prefer to maintain a single floor and often talk at length, particularly when they are playing the expert.[5] Talking too much is certainly one of the things that women object to in men's linguistic behaviour. Rachel, for example, explained in her interview how she had learnt from an early age how to look interested when her father – and later her brothers – talked. Her complaint was not just that they talk at her, but also their assumption that the floor is theirs and that she will listen: she said she didn't, 'like the way they are assuming that anything they have to say is interesting and therefore they just give it to me whether I – whether I really want it or not'. As Barbara said, 'They [men] just brush you off, they say "Yeah, yeah, that's what you said, but this is what I want to say"'.

The one exception to women friends' unspoken rule about not talking too much is story-telling. Story-telling is a valued part of women friends talking practices, and some stories are long: the narrator may hold the floor for a considerable time. A good example is the full story 'Cystitis' (given in appendix A) which lasts eight minutes thirty-nine seconds. I've argued that story-telling gives the speaker privileged access to the floor. One justification for this claim is that in this corpus of conversations between friends there are several examples of long stories, but no examples of women taking long turns at other points in talk. In my experience, women who talk too much cause other women participating in group talk to become uncomfortable – there is a sense that something is wrong, even when it is not understood precisely what this is. Certainly, if one individual talks at length, it will be difficult for other participants to maintain a collaborative floor. It seems that some women are less competent at sustaining a collaborative floor, in particular in understanding how to take their place in the shared floor without monopolizing it. Monopolizing the floor will result in their being read as not doing friendship but as doing individualism and separateness.

Not talking enough

Not talking enough is also problematic. In a collaborative floor, even when a speaker says little of substance, they signal their continuing presence in the collaborative floor by adding minimal responses and laughter. In the following extract, Helen and I (Jen) had both been to the open evening that is being discussed and are enjoying putting together an account of what went on. While I am making the main contribution to discussion here, Helen signals her presence in the collaborative floor with frequent and carefully placed minimal responses.

[Topic: Friends' response to open evening at local school]

JEN: they still didn't like Johnson [the Head]'s talk/ but I mean
HELEN: mhm/

JEN: I said to her that's about the worst thing he ever does/
HELEN: yes/

JEN: and it's not . meant to be for our lot/ . and I think
HELEN: mhm/ mhm/

JEN: he knows it alien ((ates)) . . .
HELEN: mhm/

Similarly, in the following passage, which has already been discussed in chapter 6, Anna and Liz mark their presence in the shared space of the collaborative floor with laughter as well as with side comments.

SUE: he's got this twi- he's got this nervous twitch/

SUE: exactly/ he's got this
ANNA: [I'm not surprised <LAUGHS -
LIZ: [oh <LAUGHS -

SUE: nervous t- <LAUGHS> he's got this real nervous twitch/ and John says
ANNA: ->
LIZ: ->

SUE: John says 'I'm going to ask him about it'/
ANNA: <LAUGHS>
LIZ: <SHRIEKS OF LAUGHTER>

If a woman in a group of women friends remains silent over an extended period, the other women will become uncomfortable. In a group of women friends there is constant (generally unconscious) monitoring going on, to check that talk is reasonably evenly distributed across participants.[6] Questions are used to invite participants to join in if they seem quiet. There's only one example in the conversations I've collected, from a tape involving Hannah, Becky, Claire and Jessica (aged thirteen). Claire hasn't said anything for a while, and this prompts the following exchange:

BECKY: you're very quiet today/.
JESSICA: she's tired/ she's been working

BECKY: h [ave you? ((I'm sorry))/ what did you do?
JESSICA: in the gym/
HANNAH: [have you?

BECKY: oh god/
JESSICA: [for three hours/
CLAIRE: did the rope and ((3 sylls)) [and then- ((there's

CLAIRE: no-)) I hadn't got any equipment/ so I had to borrow somebody

---

CLAIRE: else/ . . .

By the end of this extract, Claire has started to talk, and her account of what she did at the gym dominates the conversation for the next two minutes. It's noticeable how much effort Claire's friends put into encouraging her to talk: Becky and Hannah ask information-seeking questions, while Jessica makes supportive comments, and initially speaks on Claire's behalf. Her utterance *she's tired/ she's been working in the gym* functions as a kind of excuse for Claire's silence, and thus acknowledges that not speaking needs to be explained and so is in some sense against the rules.

I can remember a time when a woman who had recently moved to the area joined the group of women friends that I later recorded (the 'Oxton Ladies'). She seemed rather shy at first – the group has always been very exuberant and outspoken – and I remember experiencing some discomfort as we struggled to give her space in our noisy collaborative floor. She soon got used to us as we did to her and the group developed a new equilibrium. This suggests that our broader competence in 'how to be a friend' has to be fine-tuned to fit the specific context. We do 'being a friend' with specific significant others, not in a vacuum, and who we are with will affect how we do 'being a friend' since it is a dynamic and interactive process.

Challenging

While women friends rely on each other to tell them 'if you were going to make an idiot of yourself', as Liz put it, explicit challenging of a friend's position is not welcome unless invited. Women friends view acceptance of each other as central to what being a friend means. Friends' support is an intrinsic component of friendship: as Meg said to Bea, 'I look to you as someone when particular things go wrong that I can look to for support'. A friend is someone who is 'on your side'.

As we saw in chapter 8, one of the ways women avoid challenge and direct contradiction of each other's points of view is by using questions. Sue responds to Anna's assertion about Saddam Hussein and his troops during the Gulf War *aren't they fanatical? absolute fanatics/* (itself phrased as a rhetorical question) with the question *but are they?*, and goes on *I mean I think . . . there's people like us there who think . . . 'I don't want him to do this'*. Hedges (like *I mean I think* in the utterance above) are another invaluable resource for softening the force of divergent points of view.

In the conversations I've recorded between established friends, there are, not suprisingly, few challenges. Those there are can be divided into two categories: confrontational or supportive. The only examples of confrontational challenges to another speaker come in talk between younger speakers, girls of twelve and thirteen, whose talk contains very few hedges or strategic questions.[7] The following is an example (from a conversation between Hannah, Becky, Jessica and Claire, age thirteen):

BECKY: my Mum says that Safeways is a lot more expensive/
HANNAH: I know/ . so?

BECKY: you always used to say that it wasn't when I said 'it's much more

---

BECKY: expensive'/ and you [said-
HANNAH: [not THAT much more expensive/ like . three p

BECKY: even if it's
HANNAH: more expensive or something/ . %no%
JESSICA: not ten p/

BECKY: three p 'the three ps mount up'/ <MOCK-ADULT VOICE>

In this brief extract, Hannah challenges Becky twice, once with the aggressive challenge *I know/ so?*, and once by interrupting Becky with a contradiction. Becky deflects the challenge by turning her assertion into a joke, a parody of grown-up aphorisms about economy: *the three ps mount up.*

Challenges like these do not appear in the conversations of adult women friends, but there are some examples of what I'm calling supportive challenges. A good example appeared in the last chapter, where Helen challenged me when I said *oh what hubris* about my application for a lectureship at Cambridge University. Her challenge: *oh no but that's TERRIBLE though isn't it/ I mean you can't imagine any men sitting round/ . saying about their applications that it's hubris/* can be described as 'supportive' because Helen very clearly demonstrates that she's on my side – and on the side of women in general. Essentially she is challenging the discourse, not me. We can accept challenges like these because we feel simultaneously supported and validated by them.

Failure to mirror

The mirroring and balance typical of friendly conversation are another aspect of competence which is sometimes lacking. As we saw in chapter 4, the conversations I've recorded are full of mirroring and balance. This aspect of women's talk is highly regarded by women and talked about in a range of terms, including: *mirror, balance, sharing, exchange* and *mutuality*. As Rachel said when interviewed (key words and phrases in bold):

> I think the friendships I've made have always- always been around you know, sort of straight talking, vulnerable talking, and it's **exchanged** vulnerable talking. It's just like you can say whatever you think or whatever you feel, and you do to some extent **expect it back**, I mean, and **it comes back**.

In women's view, friendship is centrally concerned with sharing and with reciprocity, and the mirroring typical of women friends' conversations seems to be symbolic of this.

According to the women who took part in my research, men often fail to do this mirroring work. As Meg said: 'One of the differences is- is that they [men] don't *mirror* it . . . I'm always aware of the kind of *balanced* um- the *balance* that come into conversation between two women, between two friends, and um you just don't get that in my experience with a man.' But it is not only male speakers who sometimes fail to mirror what a woman says: some women do not respond to self-disclosure with matching self-disclosure, but instead change the subject, or (worse) give advice. Failing to respond with matching self-disclosure, with a mirroring turn, will, if it persists, result in the failure of friendship (or will act as a barrier to the establishment of friendship).

A failure to self-disclose, to mirror, may arise in part from a lack of fluency in autobiographical narrative, a basic skill for the purposes of women's friendly talk. Or it may be part and parcel of a more general tendency to prefer information-focused exchange and topics which are impersonal rather than personal (this seems to be the pattern of men's friendly talk). There are no examples of this in the conversations I've collected: even where topics related to work or to politics or to other aspects of the outside world, women friends continually pull them back to the personal, and to feelings and attitudes associated with these situations. The emphasis on the personal, and the preference for person-centred topics, is part of our competence in 'being a friend'.

Taboo topics

A vital aspect of competence in doing 'being a friend' is knowing what to talk about. As the previous section has made clear, our talk is primarily about people, and revolves around women ourselves and those close to us, and around our feelings about what happens in our lives. But there are limits to what can be talked about, and these are negotiated – usually implicitly rather than explicitly – by individual pairs or groups of women friends. The perception of many women is that they feel free to talk about anything: 'I don't think we have any taboo about what we talk about' (Liz), but the reality suggests that there are limits. And ironically it is Liz and her friends who say adamantly that they do not discuss their sexual relationships (so contradicting their claim that they have no taboos): 'I think that he [Sue's husband] thinks that we talk about men and sex, compare sexual experiences and things like that, but then I think that's perhaps a fantasy that men have about women when they're together talking, and we never do' (Anna).

An example of a woman introducing a topic which is *not* acceptable to the group was given at the beginning of chapter 7, where Meg tried to tell a story about a friend she hadn't seen for a long time. The problem arises when she starts to describe the woman's appearance in some detail:

MEG: anyway ((xx)) I think Jean's got a a a a a body hair problem/

OTHERS: <LAUGHTER>

MEG: no-
BEA: well I have quite a lot of body hair/ how much has she got?

MEG: well-
BEA: you mean like it was coming out- . like it was coming
JEN: but where ((xx)) –

MEG: yeah/ . no I saw it on her chest honestly/ and um o-
BEA: out- oh/

MEG: on- I- I do look at this from a- with an objective clinical eye/ er

---

MEG: but I did see what- what amounted to sort of chest hair/ . black/

MEG: she's a very dark- sort of dark skinned and sallow complexion and a

---

MEG: lo- I mean I- I mean I hope I'm just reporting this without any

---

MEG: edge to it/ . you know so I mean I probably-

BEA: you mean you really feel that she's turning into a gorilla?

OTHERS: <LAUGHTER>

This story is greeted with discomfort and disbelief by Meg's friends, and she eventually falls silent and doesn't finish the story. Significantly, no one picks up Meg's theme: there are no mirroring anecdotes. Meg has broken a taboo here: this group of women friends are clearly not prepared to join in discussion of an absent woman which is pejorative about her physical appearance. This is felt to be unsisterly behaviour. Interestingly, Meg takes the risk of trying a further story about Jean, or rather about Jean's son. She does a better job of contextualizing this story in terms of her relationship with this other family and the rivalry between her son and Jean's son, so when her story reaches a triumphant conclusion (involving Jean's son doing badly at university – the story is given in chapter 4, page 87), the group of friends accepts the topic of Schadenfreude (taking pleasure in others' failure), which is certainly not a 'safe' topic. They add mirroring stories of their own, leading into a discussion where they talk about the disturbing nature of such feelings, their sense that such feelings are 'bad', but their recognition that they have all experienced such feelings and have taken pleasure in other's misfortune. In the context of established friendship groups, it is to be expected that speakers are competent at 'being friends'. Meg's lapse here is an isolated example from my corpus of twenty conversations. But it is worth noting that while her story is a failure in one sense, her risk-taking approach to topic-initiation leads eventually to a rich discussion of an important and difficult subject.

Friendship and the development of the 'self'

While it is relatively easy to pinpoint how to get it wrong, getting it right involves a more elusive set of competencies which this book has begun to sketch in. One group of people who consistently 'get it wrong' is the group who suffer from autism. Psychologists have begun to pay attention to friendship as a relationship between people, and to ask what it means to be a friend. This new interest arises in the context of research into autism which suggests that the ability to develop interpersonal relationships may be a vital but relatively ignored aspect of healthy development. The following extract comes from an interview with an intelligent young autistic adult who describes how, in his memory, the first years of his life were empty of people: 'I really didn't know there were people until I was seven years old. I then suddenly realised that there were people. But not like you do. I still have to remind myself that there are people . . . *I never could have a friend. I really don't know what to do with other people, really*'[8] (emphasis added).

This account of himself seems chilling because of the ambiguity of the phrase 'I don't know what to do with other people'. The verb *do with* could mean 'do alongside', but here seems to be used in another sense, a sense that is more appropriate for talking about things, not people (as in 'What shall I do with the left-over pasta'?). It is as if this young man has not grasped the difference between people and things.

Peter Hobson, a developmental psychologist working on autism, describes a 20-year-old man he was involved in caring for at the Maudsley Hospital in London:

> this individual had a number of preoccupations, but foremost amongst these was his inability to grasp what a 'friend' is. He would ask again and again: 'Are you a friend'?, 'Is he a friend'?, and so on. The ward staff made every effort to teach him the meaning of the word 'friend', they even found someone to act as a 'befriender' to accompany him on outings to the local shopping centre. All this was to no avail – he seemed unable to fathom what a 'friend' is.[9]

This experience and subsequent reflection on the nature of friendship and the nature of autism led Hobson to interrogate more closely the concept of 'friend'. How do we come to understand it? What is it that we 'do' in order to be 'friends' with someone? He makes the important point that you can't get to know what a friend is simply by observing – in order to know what it means to be a friend, you have to 'do' friendship, that is, be involved in interpersonal relationships of a particularly close and reciprocal kind. People suffering from autism have difficulty with interpersonal relations of all kinds, but, in Hobson's view, their inability to understand what a 'friend' is fundamentally related to their 'deficient sense of self'.[10]

I have tried to show in this book how much women value friendship and how rich and complex the talk of women friends is. Perhaps we should also make the inference, from these new insights into the nature of autism, that the talk we do with our friends is profoundly important. It seems that 'doing friendship' is vital to development and vital to our becoming well-functioning human beings. Drusilla Modjeska hit the nail on the head when she said that friendships between women 'can offer the terms on which we best learn to be ourselves'[11] (quoted in chapter 2). It is ironic that women's talk has over the centuries been viewed as trivial or self-indulgent. Women's subcultures revolve around talk: this should now be recognized as one of our strengths, not one of our weaknesses.

Women's friendship, women's knowledge

Friendship is a powerful interpersonal relationship which provides us with a safe enough space to talk in ways we might not be able to elsewhere: I mean, to talk in ways that are exploratory and contingent. In our talk with our friends, we both confirm or resist our existing sense of our selves and our world, and also explore new ways of knowing or apprehending the world.[12]

This makes the talk of women friends sound very serious: but exploratory talk is as likely to be playful as serious. Let's look again at Sue, Anna and Liz's talk on the topic 'Relationships' which begins with the story about the obedient husband (see appendix B). This story leads into discussion about marriage and ideas of obedience and rebellion. Although these are talked about in a very playful way, with lots of laughter (see discussion, pages 146–51), there is no doubt that important work is being done here by the three women friends. Discussion is sustained and well focused. The heart of this segment of conversation seems to be the friends' exploration of the meaning of 'obedience', both in terms of its appropriateness in a relationship between two adults and in terms of its congruence with (currently accepted forms of) masculinity. The couple Sue describes are a potent trigger for discussion because the expected pattern, the pattern normalized by dominant discourses, of a 'strong' husband and an 'obedient' wife is reversed here. It is the wife who makes decisions, who says how things are to be, and the husband who obeys. Initially Sue's description of the husband as obedient is challenged:

SUE: but you've got to see it to

SUE: believe it because he's just . obedient/ and she- [and she
LIZ: [WHY did

SUE: just- [what/ obedient?
LIZ: you use that word/ that's a dreadful [word/ obedient/

SUE: yes ((x)) yes but he is/ that's what
LIZ: makes him sound like a pet rabbit/

SUE: he's like/ he's obedient/ [he just does as she says/
ANNA: [oh how aaww-ffuull/

They deal with their horror (*oh how aaww-ffuull*) of this overturning of the 'natural' order by playing with the image of the husband as a pet rabbit, drawing on a theme from an earlier part of the conversation. This leads into a more general discussion of whether partners in a couple are ever equal, and whether living on your own is preferable to being part of a couple. (This passage was analysed as an example of repetition and textual coherence in chapter 9, pages 226–30.) As we saw there their talk becomes less playful; they reflect in a more sombre way on the difficulty of achieving equality in relationships and on the problems of 'coupledom', as Anna calls it.

This extended passage from the talk of these three friends demonstrates how friendship provides an arena where we can explore alternative ideas and forge new understandings of our social world. I want to look at one more example from the talk of a different group of women friends, the Oxton women (an example discussed earlier in chapter 8). This example is more serious in tone throughout: there is none of the laughter or joking found in the talk about the obedient husband. Discussion of the topic 'Child abuse' involves this group of friends in helping each other to work through distressing ideas and to think about the question of abuse in new ways. The collaborative floor plays an important role in providing these friends with a supportive space to take risks in their thinking and to push at the boundaries of existing knowledges.

Meg initiates this section of discussion with her statement *you remember that little boy that was um . in Brighton that was um . carried off and sexually abused*. This leads to the round of questions discussed in chapter 8 (page 197) where the five friends jointly take responsibility for answering Sally's question: *did they ever find the people that did that?*.

MEG:	you remember that little boy that was um . in Brighton that

MEG:	was um . carried off=		=and sexually abused/		everyone was
SALLY:		yes/			yes/	
MARY:	mhm/		=yes=			

MEG:	outraged about	[that=
SALLY:		[did they ever find the people that did that?
BEA:		=mhm/

MEG:	yes they did didn't they?			
SALLY:			yeah/	
MARY:		did they?		yeah/ I remember/ yes/

MEG:			yes/ they
SALLY:			really?
BEA:	did they find them?		
MARY:		they were in France weren't they?	

MEG:	were part of a pornographic set-up/

As I argued in chapter 8, the questions here are used to promote the group voice, and to avoid any one of the women being positioned as an expert. These questions also set up a frame where not knowing and wanting to know are salient. The discussion proceeds as follows:

MEG: yeah/
MARY: but I mean so much research is male-dominated/ I mean it just-

---

MEG: =mhm= ((such see-through
BEA: =but also when you get down to
MARY: it's staggering isn't it?= =I mean ((xx))

MEG: blinkered-))
BEA: it/ . if you began to even have the faintest suspicion that
MARY: that's right/

MEG: mhm/
BEA: your husband . was interfering with . your- the two of

BEA: you's daughter/ . how quickly- . I mean in order to accept

---

BEA: that idea you're having to .
MARY: mhm/ completely review your
JEN: yes/

BEA: [completely change] your view of your husband=
MARY: [view of your husband]= =that's right=
SALLY: =yes/
MEG: yeah/ mhm/

BEA: =and to have him become a person who can do . the undoable=
MEG: mhm/

BEA: =and how easy is it to do that?=
MARY: =that's right= =mhm/

Bea and Mary are the main speakers in this extract: they articulate a series of linked ideas on the topic of child abuse. But the support of the other three women is important in sustaining them through this process, support provided in the form of frequent and well-placed minimal responses. (Through their minimal responses, these three speakers signal their continued presence in the collaborative floor, and thus take joint responsibility for what is said.) There are many linguistic features present which suggest that finding the right words isn't easy. For example, Bea initially says *your* to convey 'belonging to you and your husband', but amends this to *the two of you's daughter,* a nonce form which has the merit of making clear that she intends the possessive pronoun to be plural (*your* is ambiguous between singular and plural). She doesn't complete her rhetorical question *how quickly-,* as she struggles to express herself, and only later does she return to this structure, asking *how easy is it to do that?* (i.e. how easy is it to realize that your husband is capable of doing the undoable?). As she struggles for words, Mary joins in the construction of the key utterance *you're having to completely change your view of your husband.*

Bea's words are punctuated by pauses, indicating the care she is taking in expressing herself. Examples are *if you began to even have the faintest suspicion that your husband was interfering . with your-* and *and to have him become a person who can do . the undoable.* While 'interfering' is a euphemism, and shows there are areas of discussion which the friends find too painful to name directly, Bea's solution to naming what it is the husband does – 'the undoable' – is very powerful. She sets up a tension between the possible and the impossible: her utterance is a semantic contradiction – your husband becomes a person *who can do* – who is capable of doing/who finds it possible to do – *the undoable* – that which it is not possible to do. This moves the talk into a new space: in talking about *the undoable* these women become able to say the unsayable. The women friends move on to a new understanding of why women don't recognize the signs that should tell them their daughter is being abused:

- -

MEG: you don't- you don't assume it's possible/
BEA: and- and your husband has

- -

BEA: become a monster/

- -

Superficially, these two utterances are incoherent: Meg's refers to a world where your husband being an abuser is an impossibility, while Bea refers to a world where *your husband has becomes a monster*. How can these two utterances be joined by *and*? Bea's utterance appeals to our commonsense knowledge that husbands and monsters are two non-overlapping categories – but what she is saying is that the one can become the other. In other words, at a profound level of understanding, these two utterances are totally coherent and express the group's new understanding of the schizophrenic position of the woman married to a child abuser.

Women's friendship: a model of human relationship

When I asked the women I interviewed to describe what women's talk is like (see chapter 3), Rachel characterized it in terms of 'warmth and nurturing and closeness', while Jo gave a list of adjectives: 'intimate, exploratory, provisional – I mean, open-ended'. These two responses focus on two sides of women's talk: its intimacy, the sense of connection between women that it engenders, and also its potential as a collaborative tool for exploring our world. The first of these is what we understand by saying that talking with our friends is constitutive of friendship, because talking with friends accomplishes intimacy and connection. But in an important sense, friendship is equally 'done' in talk which explores ourselves, the world and our place in the world: with our friends we are able to be reflexive in a way which is rarely possible in other, less safe, contexts. Out of these reflexive practices we are able to arrive at new understandings of ourselves and of the world we live in.

We can list the different kinds of talk we do with our friends: 'catching up' talk, playful talk, serious talk. But these superficial categories tell us very little, and fail to capture the truth that we can't separate 'playful' and 'serious' in this simplistic way. Even the most serious discussion has elements of play, in particular because the maintenance of a collaborative floor involves 'playing' in the sense that talk with friends is a kind of jam session: while what we say may be sombre, the music we make together, the patterns we jointly construct, can still give us pleasure. And what seem the most light-hearted moments in conversation are often on closer inspection moments when serious issues are raised: consider, for example, Becky's story 'Knicker stains', or Sue, Liz and Anna's raucous talk about the obedient husband.

In chapter 2, I debated whether women's friendships are a conservative or a liberating force. This simple binary distinction is too crude. Over the centuries, friendship with other women has offered women 'societies of consolation', as Carolyn Heibrun puts it,[13] meaning that women have always provided each other with a space where we can share our everyday experiences and problems as women living under patriarchy. The evidence of my research is that women do talk to each other about our lives and our problems. In part, this makes women's talk a conservative force because, through providing an emotional outlet, women's friendships help to support and sustain the heterosocial order.[14] But there is a great deal of evidence in the conversations and interviews I have collected which suggests that friendship with other women offers us far more than simply 'consolation'. It also offers us the possibility of resistance and change.

Change cannot take place as long as an oppressed group accepts the status quo, that is, accepts the values of the oppressor. But women's friendships with each other provide us with a positive sense of who we are and enable us to develop solidarity. Solidarity with each other is a prerequisite for change. In Janice Raymond's words: 'The empowering of female friendship can create the conditions for a new feminist politics in which the personal is most passionately political'.[15]

And it is the talk that we do with our friends that makes resistance and change possible. Women friends talking are women friends playing: playing provides a context for risk-taking and experimentation. So in the playful conversational practices of women friends, we can try out different discourses, different positions in relation to the world. Subversive discourses can be nurtured and patriarchal discourses can be challenged. Through reflecting on our lives, we come to a greater understanding of ourselves. And through playing with the collaborative strategies which allow us to share the conversational floor, we can jointly move to a new awareness of how things might be, a new understanding of the patterns we observe. In the talk of women friends, new selves are forged and new knowledges are developed.

This is why, in chapter 1, I claimed that this book would be a celebration not just of the ordinary – the everyday speaking practices of women friends – but also of the extraordinary. It is the radical potential of women's friendships that makes them worthy of close investigation. They can be seen as a model of the way relationships should be, of the way relationships might be in the future. My aim has been to celebrate women's friendship, and the way women's friendship is done through talk. This book is a testament to that talk, a celebration of its richness and power, complexity and creativity – in short, its extraordinariness.

Appendices

Appendix A

Cystitis

oh and the worst thing was- I haven't told you this
we- we left London on the Friday
[. . .]
that Friday in the office I wasn't feeling- I was feeling a bit funny
((I just felt weird))
5 I thought that I was getting cystitis
I wasn't sure
I've only had it once before about three years ago and it very familiar
and I thought- and I- and I was in a meeting all afternoon
and Shirley was going to Boots
10 so I said, 'Oh can you just get me something for cystitis
because I think I've got an attack coming on',
and I didn't have time to think more than that.
She brought back that stuff called Cystem which is meant to be fast relief for it,
so I took some of that when we got to the airport,
15 then I thought I remember the last time I had it
the- the- cure was to drink lots of water,
because that flushes the bacteria out of your system.
So while we were waiting at the airport- our plane was delayed- I actually drank three litres of water.
We were there for like an hour and a quarter
20 and I just kept drinking and drinking and drinking.

We got on the plane and of course I couldn't stop going to the loo.
Then it got worse and worse and worse.
I spent the whole plane journey to Ro- to Rome in the toilet.
Three quarters of the way through the plane journey I- I literally couldn't leave I was in such pain
25 Shirley came banging on the door.
'Are you all right? Are you all right'?
She was trying to get the air hostess to come and see to me
and Alitalia I will never fly again
they were just dreadful.
30 And she kept going up to these air hostesses saying, 'My friend's in the toilet and she's ill.
Will you do something',
and they wouldn't do anything.
And finally we were coming in to land,
and by this time I was passing blood,
35 and I was really terrified out of my mind,
cos I'm not a sickly person and I never get ill,
and if something like that happens it just freaks me out.
I was- I didn't know what to do.
So I had to go and sit down because we were about to land,
40 but it was like every two minutes I thought, 'I've got to go to the- the toilet,
I've got to',
so I was hysterical practically.
And finally we sat down coming in to land,
and there's a girl sitting on the other side of the gangway to me,
45 quite a pretty Italian girl,
and this air steward is bending down talking to her,
a male air steward chatting her up basically,
and he looks across at me.
He says, 'What's the matter with you? are you not very well?',
50 and I thought, 'Finally getting through here',
and I said, 'Yes I'm not'.
And he said- and he said, 'What's wrong?',
and he can hardly speak a word of English,
so I've got to try and explain,
55 and all the passengers are listening.
So I told the girl,
and she translated for him,
and he said to me, 'Would you like to see a doctor when we land?
I can arrange for that if you want'.
60 So I said, 'Well OK,

but I don't want to be taken away in an ambulance or anything like that,
but yes, if you can arrange and radio ahead and and arrange for me to see a doctor,
that'd be great'.
He said, 'Yes no problem'.
65 He said, 'There won't be an ambulance or anything'.
Three minutes later we land,
and there are men running down the gangway towards me.
They- they bodily lift me out of my seat,
and there's the blue flashing light outside the plane.
70 I couldn't believe it.
Shirley followed me down the steps.
I had my- my hand luggage with me.
They literally pushed Shirley away,
grabbed my bag from me,
75 bundled me into this ambulance
and off I was taken,
and they wouldn't let her come with me
and she doesn't speak a word of Italian.
I speak faltering Italian,
80 I- I know how to say, 'It's a nice day' or 'The boys in classroom are not behaving as they should' or whatever.
So they take me to this first aid place
and I've literally- they shoved me out of the ambulance
and treated me like a criminal.
One says, 'Where's your passport', you know, snatch snatch,
85 and they take-
I was in so much pain, honestly,
it was just awful.
I wanted to cry.
They took me to this first aid place
90 and there's a female doctor there who speaks English, thank god,
so I tell her what's wrong,
thinking she's going to examine me.
No examination,
'Here's a prescription.
95 This drug- this drug will cure it within two or three hours.
It's nothing, it's nothing,
it's nothing to worry about',
and I thought, 'If you were passing blood you wouldn't say it's nothing to worry about'.
She said, 'We'll call you a- a taxi,

100 it'll stop by a pharmacy.
You're going to an address in Rome aren't you'?
and I said, 'Yes'.
Meanwhile Shirley's somewhere I don't know where.
'We'll call you a taxi.
105 It'll take you and your friend to the pharmacy, all night pharmacy,
you can get the prescription and go to your apartment'.
She said, 'Wait in this room here',
which is like a hospital bedroom,
'and I'll just be out here if you want me'.
110 So I go in to the room.
Twenty minutes later and I'm thinking, 'Well where's Shir-'.
'Oh,' she said, 'the Alitalia staff will bring your friend to you'.
Twenty minutes go by and no Shirley
so I think I'll go and look for the doctor.
115 Go outside, look for the doctor –
the doctor's nowhere to be seen.
Only people around are orderlies and the night watchman.
None of them speak a word of English
and I'm desperately trying to think what is the Italian for 'where is my friend?'.
120 Get out my dictionary, <LAUGHS>
'dove mi amici?',
and they just say, 'Shut up', basically.
They say- the only Italian they- I managed to understand,
'The Alitalia staff will bring her to you,
125 she'll be here in a minute,
don't worry',
and at this stage I wasn't worried.
It was only twenty minutes.
Go back in to the cubicle thinking, 'Oh I feel so ill,
130 god I wish Shirley was here, I wonder where she is',
meanwhile feeling guilty –
she's got my suitcase, her suitcase, everything,
she can't speak Italian.
Another twenty minutes go by.
135 I go out again –
no sign of the doctors,
everybody speaks Italian.
This goes on for an hour and a half
and by this time it is midnight,
140 I've spent all day at work,
I've got chronic cystitis,

I'm in a lot of pain,
I don't know where Shirley is,
and I just cried.
145 I sat down in the reception and I cried.
In fact the night watchman comes up puts his arm around me,
says, 'Don't worry we'll find your friend',
starts ringing all over the Rome airport,
gets the Alitalia desk who tell him to get lost,
150 say it's none- none of their business where-
they're not concerned where Shirley is,
I'm nothing to do with them,
why doesn't he just get on with his job blah blah blah.
Eventually about twenty minutes later the phone rings
155 and it's someone who's found Shirley.
She's on the other end of the phone, she's furious.
'Where are you?',
and I said- and I was just crying,
I said, 'Where are you? they told me you were coming'.
160 She said, 'I don't know where you are',
and I said, 'Well I don't know where YOU are, how can I tell them where to-'
and it was just awful,
and she'd finally found erm-
she'd gone to the Alitalia desk and they'd turned her away.
165 She'd gone to find a taxi rank
and the taxi driver wouldn't take her to the pharmacy
because it was only like two minutes taxi ride and he wanted a good fare,
and he didn't realize she wanted to go in to Rome afterwards,
and eventually she found a car park attendant who'd managed to speak a little bit of English
170 and understood that she wanted the phone number of the pharmacy to ring me, the first aid place.
Anyway we eventually met up and we'd-
oh I just cried and cried and cried
and Shirley just was stony faced.
She's not the most sympathetic of people at all.
175 We got in to Rome.
The taxi fare says like thirty-five quid,
we were charged forty-five quid ((because of)) the luggage,
and we'd been warned about it,
and I was all prepared to argue my case,
180 but I was feeling so ill I couldn't.

And so we got up to the steps to Ted's apartment.
oh the taxi driver was so aggressive and unpleasant I didn't feel we could even ask him where the nearest pharmacy was,
'cos that'd probably cost us another ((xx))
[...]
By this time it was one o'clock in the morning.
185 Ted's apartment is up five flights of stairs in a huge villa which has no lift.
We get up there and I've got all these instructions which he'd sent us about how to get in with the burglar alarm,
which involves turning the key three times, waiting thirty seconds, putting another key in the lock,
and he said in his memo, 'If you set the alarm off it's really serious, the police arrive, security guards arrive',
190 and I thought, 'The next thing is we're going to set the alarm off'.
Well we didn't.
We got in to the flat
and I just thought, 'All I want to do is go to bed', and I-
I didn't know what to do I was in such a state.
195 We went to bed.
got up the next morning,
it was four o'clock the next day before I got to a pharmacy and got what I wanted,
and I was- I was cured within hours,
but I've had another attack since I came back and I'm on ti- antibiotics now,
200 but it was just the most awful thing
[...]
and I just wanted to go home,
and we laughed about it afterwards,
and Shirley said, 'I'm not coming on holiday with you again,
you're a real liability',
205 but I thought well if I'd been in her- if she'd been in my position I think I'd have been a bit more sympathetic.
I couldn't help it and ((xx)) you know,
but she's just not very good at dealing with illness,
[...]
so anyway that was that.
And we had a fairly nice time in Rome
but Rome wasn't at all what I was thinking it would be...

Appendix B

Obedient husband

- -

SUE: I told you I went round to a friend's who had ((a)) guitar/

- -

2 SUE: oh it was lovely/ the wife right
LIZ: I know you enjoyed that/

- -

SUE: his wife would not let him have a guitar/ . she said no and

- -

4 SUE: he's so obedient= she's- she said you're not having a guitar/
ANNA: =<SUBDUED LAUGH>
LIZ: <LAUGH>

- -

SUE: so he didn't have one/ he just didn't play it ever/ and then for

- -

6 SUE: christmas she allowed him to have a guitar/ as long as he didn't

- -

SUE: play it in front of her=
LIZ: =((y'know)) John would have an

- -

8 SUE: =yes=
ANNA: [how- I can't understand- [how can people live
LIZ: electric [one= =cos it's got to be [raunchy/

- -

SUE: well- she's ((xx))
ANNA: lives like that though/ if someone said to me I couldn't have
LIZ: ((xxx)) you can't-

- -

10 SUE: =this couple you've got to
ANNA: something I'd just go out and b[uy it=
LIZ: [buy it out of sheer-

- -

SUE: see it to believe it/ he thinks that she is .
ANNA: this isn't the

- -

12 SUE: no/
ANNA: couple that used to look after Helena sometimes is it?

- -

[. . .]

- -

	SUE:	I like him so much= =he's jus- he's really really nice/
	ANNA:	=yeah=
	LIZ:	

14	SUE:	and . if I was her I would think . oh I wouldn't
	ANNA:	
	LIZ:	cos he's laid back/

	SUE:	like to say that to him/ cos he's just . too nice/ and he goes
	ANNA:	
	LIZ:	

16	SUE:	'oh OK Ginny'= ='OK Ginny' . and like . he's not allowed to
	ANNA:	oh
	LIZ:	=aaah=

	SUE:	play/ =no you wouldn't . he's just so .
	ANNA:	I think I'd kill him= I couldn't bear to live with someone
	LIZ:	

18	SUE:	he's just so nice/ he thinks she's wonderful/ and I
	ANNA:	like that/
	LIZ:	

	SUE:	would be worried if I was her . you know= to- to push him-
	ANNA:	
	LIZ:	=what? that you weren't

20	SUE:	she- she pushes him to [the abs-
	ANNA:	[he'll probably stab her with
	LIZ:	matching up?

	SUE:	[she pushes him to the limit/ yeah I
	ANNA:	the bread knife one [day= she'll wake
	LIZ:	=yeah ggrrr <VICIOUS NOISE>

22	SUE:	think he will/ . I think he'll rebel= <LAUGHS>
	ANNA:	up dead= <LAUGHS ----------------------
	LIZ:	='here you are Ginny' <LAUGHS -------> =have a s-

	SUE:	<LAUGHS -------------------------------->
	ANNA:	--->
	LIZ:	have a cut throat <CUTTING NOISE> <LAUGHS ------------------

24	SUE:	but that- this particular night she let him play the guitar/
	ANNA:	<SNORT> <LAUGHS --------------------->
	LIZ:	-------------------->

	SUE:	and it was so nice you know/ and she like she bans him= this
	ANNA:	
	LIZ:	<LAUGHS---> =<CACKLES>
26	SUE:	is what I f-=
	ANNA:	=I wouldn't put up with it I'm sorry
	LIZ:	=he'll probably pick it up one day and go
	SUE:	=I wouldn't/ no/ but you've got to see it to
	ANNA:	though/ would you?=
	LIZ:	[ckxxx] <MIMICS BREAKING NOISE>
28	SUE:	believe it because he's just . obedient/ and she- [and she
	ANNA:	
	LIZ:	[WHY did
	SUE:	just- [what/ obedient?
	ANNA:	
	LIZ:	you use that word? that's a dreadful [word/ obedient/
30	SUE:	yes ((x)) yes but he is/ that's what
	ANNA:	
	LIZ:	makes him sound like a pet rabbit/
	SUE:	he's like/ he's obedient/ [he just does as she says/ . if she
	ANNA:	[oh how aaww-ffuull/
	LIZ:	
32	SUE:	says it it must be right/=
	ANNA:	=if I lived with someone who did
	LIZ:	
	SUE:	
	ANNA:	everything I said/ I would go off them in about . a matter of
	LIZ:	
34	SUE:	actually I must admit I'm quite ((a
	ANNA:	a fortnight/
	LIZ:	yeah/ I would as well/
	SUE:	fu-)) – she's a very very strong personality/ and I'm surprised it
	ANNA:	
	LIZ:	
36	SUE:	doesn't irritate/ but she likes to test . what she can do
	ANNA:	
	LIZ:	yeah/

SUE: to him/ and you watch her do it/ and she like pushes him/ pushes
ANNA:
LIZ: yeah but maybe-

SUE: him <SINGSONG> [John says-
ANNA:
LIZ: maybe- you're not there all the time/ maybe [there's a s-

---

SUE: [John says at home he [must- he must rebel/ he [must/
ANNA:
LIZ: [there's a limit- yeah/ [must be/ [yeah he must/

SUE: John can't bear to think-
ANNA: [John probably wants to help him
LIZ: ((cos)) John- <LAUGHING> [John can't bear-

SUE: [d'you know what
ANNA: rebel/ 'Come [round for lessons in rebelling'
LIZ: [he gives him- yeah [give him-

SUE: the funny thing is- yeah
LIZ: 'Buy a saxophone – I'll give you the number

SUE: [yeah he would/ he's got this twi- he's got this
LIZ: where you [buy one'/

SUE: nervous twitch/ exactly/ he's got this
ANNA: [I'm not surprised <LAUGHS---------------------
LIZ: [oh <LAUGHS-------------------------------

SUE: nervous t- <LAUGHS> he's got this real nervous twitch/and John says
ANNA: --------------------->
LIZ: ----------------------------->

SUE: 'I'm going to ask him about it'/
ANNA: <LAUGHS>
LIZ: <SHRIEKS OF LAUGHTER> I can

SUE: [ask- you can't-
LIZ: imagine [John saying 'Why- is that- why do you do that

SUE: [but listen when he's not with her he hasn't got it/
LIZ: all [the time?'/ .hh

SUE: he hasn't got it when he's not with her/

Notes

Notes on the transcription of the conversations

1 See Elinor Ochs 'Transcription as theory'.
2 Carole Edelsky discusses transcription systems at some length in her groundbreaking article 'Who's got the floor?'.

Chapter 1 'This is on tape you know'

1 Vera Brittain *Testament of Friendship*, page 117.
2 'Anna' and 'Liz' are pseudonyms. The names of all participants – and of the people they talk about – have been changed throughout the book. The only names which have not been changed are those of me and my family. Place names have also been changed where they might serve to identify an individual.
3 I should point out that the surreptitious recording of conversation for the Survey of English Usage was carried out in the 1950s and 60s, long before the advent of Ethics Committees. (A selection of these transcribed conversations was published in 1980 in the influential volume edited by Jan Svartvik and Randolph Quirk *A Corpus of English Conversation*.)
4 See William Labov *Sociolinguistic Patterns* and Peter Trudgill *The Social Differentiation of English in Norwich*.
5 William Labov had also pioneered the use of participant observation in his work on the language of Black adolescent males, a method which was far more suggestive of the way to go about getting at everyday talk. See Labov *Language in the Inner City*.
6 Lesley Milroy discusses this issue in *Observing and Analysing Natural Language*.
7 This extract has been slightly simplified for ease of reading.
8 John Wilson 'The sociolinguistic paradox: data as a methodological product'.
9 I am extremely grateful to Christine Cheepen and John Wilson who were so generous about giving me access to their data, and allowing me to include it in my corpus. (Cheepen's transcripts have since been published as an appendix to Cheepen & Monaghan *Spoken English*.) I have also had the benefit

of listening to tapes and looking at transcripts of all-female conversations collected by Karen Atkinson as part of her work on intergenerational talk (Atkinson *The Talk of Elderly Women*), and by Shan Wareing as part of her research into gender differences in the oral component of Scottish public examinations (Wareing 'Cooperative and competitive talk').

10 Details are as follows.

Number of speakers involved	*Number of sessions*	*Length of session*	
		Mean (in minutes)	*Range (in minutes)*
2	4	40	25–45
3	4	110	15–180
4	8	45	20–90
5	2	68	45–90
6	2	33	20–45

11 The question of whether friendship between women – and the language women friends use – is affected by sexual orientation is addressed in the paper 'Que(e)rying friendship' which I co-wrote with Mary Ellen Jordan.

12 For an exploration of the issues involved in this kind of friendly interview as a method of collecting data, see Wendy Hollway *Subjectivity and Method in Psychology*, and Ann Oakley 'Interviewing women'.

13 I would like to record my thanks here to Noni Geleit, for allowing me to use her recordings of her brother and his friends (collected for an undergraduate sociolinguistic project, Geleit 'Men talking to men'), and to Janis Pringle who gave me access to her recordings of groups of men friends talking in the pub (data which was the basis of her MA dissertation; see Pringle 'Is cooperative talk possible among men?').

14 Keith Brown, Andrew Rosta (they both provided (partial) transcriptions of these tapes too!).

15 The following table gives details of the corpus:

Number of	*Women*	*Men*	*Total*
Conversations	20	20	40
Speakers	26	26	52
Hours of talk	19 hrs 45 mins	17 hrs 30 mins	37 hrs 15 mins

16 Rayna Green ' "It's okay once you get it past the teeth" and other feminist paradigms for folklore studies', page 4.

17 Dell Hymes 'The ethnography of speaking' and *Foundations in Sociolinguistics*. See also John Gumperz & Dell Hymes (eds) *Directions in Sociolinguistic;* Richard Baumann & Joel Sherzer *Explorations in the Ethnography of Speaking;* Muriel Saville-Troike *The Ethnography of Communication.*

18 Apart, that is, from the sign languages of the deaf, which need to be

videotaped, not audiotaped. The original term for this field of research – 'the ethnography of speaking' – exposes our 'audist' assumption that all languages are spoken, when this is not the case: there are many sign languages in the world, and ethnographers of communication are interested in all kinds of language, whether signed or spoken. The term *audist* comes from Harlan Lane *The Mask of Benevolence.* (I'm grateful to Pip Cody for alerting me to this issue.)

19 Peter Trudgill, in Foreword to Muriel Saville-Troike *The Ethnography of Communication.*

20 Muriel Saville-Troike *The Ethnography of Communication,* page 2.

21 Diane Bell *Daughters of the Dreaming,* page 285. For further discussion of this issue, see Deborah Cameron *Feminism and Linguistic Theory;* Donna Haraway 'Situated knowledges'; Sandra Harding *The Science Question in Feminism;* Nancy Hartsock 'The feminist standpoint'.

22 Teresa de Lauretis 'The essence of the triangle or taking the risk of essentialism seriously'.

23 Diane Bell, *Daughters of the Dreaming,* page 298.

Chapter 2 'She's just a very very special person to me'

1 The point I want to emphasize is that the dominant view of women stresses our domestic roles, and positions women as belonging in the home rather than in the public domain.

2 For further discussion of this point, see Pat O'Connor *Friendships between Women.* Lilian Rubin calls women's friendships 'the most neglected relationship of our time' (Rubin, *Just Friends,* page 191).

3 This notion achieved its most forceful expression in Lionel Tiger's popular, pseudoscientific book *Men in Groups.*

4 See Lillian Faderman *Surpassing the Love of Men,* and Carroll Smith-Rosenberg 'The female world of love and ritual'.

5 See in particular Janice Raymond *A Passion for Friends,* and Mary E. Hunt *Fierce Tenderness.*

6 See, for example, Helena Wulff on teenage girls growing up in South London, *Twenty Girls;* Pat O'Connor on elderly women and their friends in chapter 5 of her book *Friendships between Women;* Gilda O'Neill *A Night out with the Girls,* a light but informative account of what women do with each other for fun, based on interviews with a wide range of women; Gouldner & Strong *Speaking of Friendship,* based on interviews with seventy-five middle-class American women aged 30–65; chapter 8 of Lillian Rubin *Just Friends,* on lesbian women and friendship.

7 See Robinette Kennedy's chapter on women in contemporary Crete: 'Women's friendships on Crete', Annette Hamilton's paper on Aboriginal women, 'A complex strategical situation', and Diane Bell's book on Aboriginal women, *Daughters of the Dreaming.*

8 See the various papers in the collection edited by Rosan Jordan & Susan Kalcik *Women's Folklore, Women's Culture.*

9 The phrase 'gender identity' is the term normally used in psychology, while

'gendered subjectivity' comes from post-structuralist theory. 'Subjectivity' is not strictly synonymous with 'identity', however, referring to 'the conscious and unconscious thoughts and emotions of the individual, her sense of herself and her ways of understanding her relation to the world' (Weedon, *Feminist Practice and Poststructuralist Theory*, page 32).

10 The earliest example of someone using this kind of methodology as far as I know is Wendy Hollway in her (1982) PhD thesis (see her book *Subjectivity and Method in Psychology*). She used as data for her PhD a series of unstructured interviews with people who were friends of hers. She describes how this felt wrong at first 'because enjoying myself talking to people who wanted to talk to me did not feel like data-gathering'. But she suggests that what she succeeded in doing was to forge a new way of doing research, which was 'to talk with people in such a manner that they felt able to explore material about themselves and their relationships, past and present, in a searching and insightful way'. She asserts that this is 'a valuable method' and 'good research practice'. (All quotations are from *Subjectivity and Method in Psychology*, page 11.)

11 The extracts in this chapter and the next are presented verbatim, using a transcription style that minimizes problems for the reader. I've indicated where cuts have been made with the following symbol: [. . .]. I've also in most cases cut out my own brief contributions to the talk (i.e. where I say *yes* or *mhm* or *oh god*).

12 For example, the interview with Margaret Atwood on the BBC Radio 4 programme 'Bookshelf', broadcast on 10 October 1991, and her novels, e.g. *The Edible Woman, Cat's Eye.*

13 This story, like others in the following chapter, is set out in lines which correspond roughly to the speaker's breath-groups. See chapter 5 (page 114) for further details about the transcription of stories.

14 S.P. Schacht & Patricia Atchison 'Heterosexual instrumentalism', page 121.

15 See Valerie Hey *The Company She Keeps*, Helen Gouldner & Mary Symons Strong *Speaking of Friendship*; Fern Johnson & Elizabeth Aries 'The talk of women friends'; Robinette Kennedy 'Women's friendships on Crete'; Janice Raymond *A Passion for Friends*; Lilian Rubin *Just Friends.*

16 See Janice Raymond *A Passion for Friends*; Lillian Faderman *Surpassing the Love of Men*; and Carroll Smith-Rosenberg 'The female world of love and ritual'.

17 Adrienne Rich 'It is the lesbian in us . . .' in *On Lies, Secrets and Silence*, pages 200–1.

18 Janice Raymond *A Passion for Friends*, page 9.

19 See, for example, Dorothy Jerrome 'Good company'; Tamsin Wilton, 'Sisterhood in the service of patriarchy'.

20 The friendship that develops between Celie and Shug, in Alice Walker's novel *The Color Purple*, for example, enables Celie to talk about the terrible things that have happened in her life: through expressing her grief over these things, she is able to move on, to escape the grip of the past, and to move out of the power of men. See also Alison Lurie *The War between the Tates*; Michele Roberts *A Piece of the Night.*

21 Shere Hite *The Hite Report.*

22 Gouldner & Strong, *Speaking of Friendship*, page 150.

23 I am grateful to Norma Grieve for the phrase 'ethic of reciprocity'.
24 Pat O'Connor, *Friendships between Women*, page 8.
25 Drusilla Modjeska, *Poppy*, page 309.

Chapter 3 'We never stop talking'

1 Hannah's answer is framed in the past tense because at the time I interviewed her and Becky, she had won a place at an International School in Italy, while Becky continued at school in London, so they could only see each other in school holidays.
2 Woman quoted in Lilian B. Rubin, *Just Friends*, page 61.
3 Helena Wulff, *Twenty Girls*, page 137.
4 T. McCabe 'Girls and leisure', page 129.
5 Valerie Hey, 'The company she keeps', page 392.
6 Helen Gouldner & Mary Symons Strong, *Speaking of Friendship*, page 59.
7 Fern Johnson & Elizabeth Aries, 'The talk of women friends', page 235.
8 See Penelope Eckert 'Cooperative competition in adolescent "girl talk"'; Donna Eder '"Go get ya a french"; Marjorie Goodwin *He-Said-She-Said*; Deborah Tannen 'Gender differences in topical coherence'.
9 Janice Raymond *A Passion for Friends*, page 181.
10 For a well-argued critique of the (stultifying) links between masculinity and rationality, see Victor Seidler *Rediscovering Masculinity*.
11 By chance, there are some brief moments in the conversations I've recorded between women friends where a man intrudes – usually a husband or a brother. In the following example, Anna's brother Mark arrives home and comes in to say hello to his sister's friends. He and Anna start arguing about rice: note the (X + notX) pattern of this brief dialogue.

ANNA: wild rice is nice/ you've never tasted it so-
MARK: well the Indians don't eat it so why the bloody hell should you?
ANNA: they probably do/
MARK: they don't/

This extract will be discussed again in chapter 7.
12 Nancy Chodorow *The Reproduction of Mothering*, page 169.
13 '"Personally speaking": experiencing a men's group', ch. 3 in Victor Seidler (ed.) *The Achilles Heel Reader*, page 53.
14 For further discussion of the idea of talk as social action, see Penelope Eckert & Sally McConnell-Ginet 'Think practically and look locally'.

Chapter 4 'We talk about everything and anything'

1 For discussion of the notion of topic (and of criteria for identifying topics), see Wolfram Bublitz *Supportive Fellow-Speakers and Cooperative Conversations*, pages 16–26; Wallace Chafe *Discourse, Consciousness and Time*, pages 120–45; Anna-Brita Stenstrom *An Introduction to Spoken Interaction*.

2 One reason for the disparity between what was said in the interviews and what is talked about in the recorded conversations is that many women had returned to paid work by the time I carried out the interviews in 1993. The conversations were recorded in the period 1983–91, and during this time many of the women involved were based at home, looking after children.
3 The silence on the part of women about our sexual experience is endorsed by Marilyn Frye, who writes: 'The experience of others has for the most part . . . been opaque to me; they do not discuss or describe it *in detail* [sic] at all'. She claims that in the Western world, the words and meanings associated with the sexual encode men's but not women's experience. This means that we cannot discuss or describe our experience because we haven't got the tools: we have been excluded from the formulation of meaning: 'Most of my lifetime, most of my experience in the realms commonly designated as "sexual" has been pre-linguistic, non-cognitive. I have, in effect, no linguistic community, no language, and therefore in one important sense, no knowledge'. See Frye, 'Lesbian "sex"'.
4 In this respect, women's conversation is unlikely to differ markedly from any informal conversation between equals. There has been little analysis of informal conversation in terms of its basic components: as Christine Cheepen comments, 'it has been generally assumed that they [i.e. friendly conversations between equals] are without an overall structure of any kind, and there has been no attempt to analyse them at any level higher than the conversational turn' (Cheepen, *The Predictability of Informal Conversation*, page 47). Cheepen proposes four components: Introduction; Speech-in-action; Story; Closing. One linguist who has looked at the structure of informal conversation is Wallace Chafe, who works with the distinction monologic–polyphonic, which corresponds roughly to my own story-discussion distinction. (See Chafe *Discourse, Consciousness and Time*, pages 120–36.) Others working in this field, but with a particular interest in oral narrative, implicitly work with two main components: Story and non-Story (see Erickson 'The social construction of discourse coherence'; Ochs & Taylor 'Family narrative as political activity').
5 For a detailed analysis of this topic, see my 1989 paper 'Gossip revisited'.
6 I said in 'Gossip revisited': 'This pattern of topic development is typical of the material I have transcribed' (page 99), but having now transcribed a great deal more material I think this claim needs modifying.
7 The research evidence is that all-male conversation is characterized by abrupt topic shift, while all-female conversation is characterized by more gradual, progressive topic shift. See Elizabeth Aries 'Interaction patterns and themes of male, female and mixed groups'; Bruce Dorval *Conversational Organization and Its Development*; Deborah Jones 'Gossip'; Susan Kalcik '". . . like Ann's gynaecologist or the time I was almost raped"'; Amy Sheldon 'Pickle fights'; Deborah Tannen *You Just Don't Understand*.
8 According to research into normal conversational practice, disagreement is avoided as far as possible: in other words, speakers work on the principle 'Try to agree'. See Anita Pomerantz 'Agreeing and disagreeing with assessments'; Geoffrey Leech *Principles of Pragmatics*.
9 I have discussed this topic at some length in a paper on the talk of teenage girls, 'Gender, discourse and subjectivity'.

Chapter 5 'D'you know what my mother did recently?'

1 All quotations from Ursula Le Guin come from her essay 'Some thoughts on narrative' published in the collection *Dancing at the Edge of the World.*
2 William Labov 'The transformation of experience in narrative syntax' in *Language in the Inner City,* page 396.
3 See Wallace Chafe 'The deployment of consciousness in the production of a narrative'.
4 These terms all come from Labov 'The transformation of experience in narrative syntax'.
5 Barbara Johnstone *Stories, Community, and Place,* page 68.
6 Diane Bell *Daughters of the Dreaming,* page 298. As Margaret Yocom argues, in 'Woman to woman: fieldwork and the private sphere', the home is the context for women's story-telling, and story-telling often takes place while women work together. Yocom compares the competitive public arena where men's story-telling occurs with the private sphere 'with its intimacy and bonding' (page 52), which is the setting for women's story-telling.
7 See Roger Abrahams *The Man-of-Words in the West Indies;* Richard Baumann *Story, Performance and Event;* Labov 'The transformation of experience in narrative syntax'; Johnstone *Stories, Community, and Place* and 'Community and contest'. Baumann describes the first-person narratives about practical jokes which he collected in Texas, USA, as 'a ludic exercise in dominance, control and display' (page 36).
8 Labov 'The transformation of experience in narrative syntax', page 354. But it's interesting to note that Peter Trudgill had to to alter this part of his sociolinguistic interview when he carried out fieldwork in Norwich, England, because 'most Norwich people seemed to have lived rather more peaceful and uneventful lives . . . than the inhabitants of New York City' (Trudgill *The Social Differentiation of English in Norwich,* page 52). He substituted a question which asked interviewees if they'd ever been in an amusing situation. So the topics of stories relate to local culture as well as to social categories such as gender.
9 Rosan Jordan and Susan Kalcik argue (in their introduction to *Women's Folklore, Women's Culture*) that folklorists have concentrated on male, public performance, 'ignoring folklore that is more collaborative and enacted in the privacy of the domestic sphere or as part of ordinary conversation' (page ix).
10 This story was also told by Anna. While all the women I recorded told stories, some women told more stories than others, and each group had its key story-teller or story-tellers. Anna was one of these.
11 Livia Polanyi 'Literary complexity in everyday storytelling', page 155.
12 Johnstone *Stories, Community, and Place,* page 66.
13 Christine Cheepen *The Predictability of Informal Conversation,* page 54.
14 Johnstone *Stories, Community, and Place,* page 66.
15 Labov *Language in the Inner City,* pages 363–4.
16 Johnstone *Stories, Community, and Place,* page 5.
17 J. Hillis Miller, 'Narrative', pages 69 and 70.

Chapter 6 'The feminine shape . . . is more melding in together'

1 Following normal linguistic practice, I shall use the term *utterance* to refer to chunks of talk produced by speakers in conversation. The word *sentence* is inappropriate in the description of spoken language, since it refers essentially to that unit of written language which begins with a capital letter and ends with a full stop. The phenomenon I am calling *jointly constructed utterances* has been variously described as 'collaborative completion' (John Rae 'Collaborative completions in advisory exchanges'), 'collaborative sentence construction' (Gene Lerner 'On the syntax of sentences-in-progress') and 'mutual sentential completion' (Felix Diaz 'Collective formulation in problem-oriented talk', chapter 4). For further discussion of this phenomenon, see also my 1994 paper, 'No gap, lots of overlap'.

2 Married couples also talk in a more melded way (see Jane Falk 'The conversational duet'; Anthony Johnson *Couples Talking*), as do friends in mixed groups (see Wolfram Bublitz *Supportive Fellow-Speakers and Cooperative Conversations;* Carole Edelsky 'Who's got the floor'?). There is virtually no research evidence of all-male groups talking in this way: what little evidence there is suggests men friends prefer a one-at-a-time floor (see Coates 'One-at-a-time').

3 POLYPHONY: '[MUSIC] The simultaneous combination of a number of parts, each forming an individual melody, and harmonizing with the others' (*Shorter Oxford English Dictionary*). This metaphor is also used by Wallace Chafe to describe talk where there are 'separate voices articulating different melodies at once'. See Chafe 'Polyphonic topic development' and *Discourse, Consciousness and Time*, pages 120–36.

4 Most linguists accept the model of turn-taking devised by Harvey Sacks (see Sacks *Lectures*) and developed by Sacks, Emmanuel Schegloff and Gail Jefferson – see in particular their famous paper 'A simplest systematics for the organisation of turn-taking in conversation', published in 1974.

5 Carole Edelsky, 'Who's got the floor'?.

6 This is also the model of conversation assumed by linguists, formalized in Sacks, Schegloff & Jefferson 'A simplest systematics for the organisation of turn-taking in conversation'.

7 The assumption that all talk involves a single floor (perhaps more accurately, the lack of knowledge about collaborative floors) means that examiners in the newly established oral component of public examinations in English have problems rewarding girls who use conversational strategies typical of a collaborative floor. See Cheshire & Jenkins/ Jenkins & Cheshire 'Gender issues in the GCSE oral English examination', parts 1 and 2; Shan Wareing, 'Cooperative and competitive talk'.

8 See Jane Falk 'The conversational duet'.

9 See, for example, Don Zimmerman & Candace West 'Sex roles, interruptions and silences in conversation'; Pamela Fishman 'Conversational insecurity'.

10 See Jennifer Coates 'Gossip revisited', pages 105–7. Zimmerman & West, in their paper 'Sex roles, interruptions and silences in conversation', argue that male speakers delay – that is, deliberately mis-time – minimal responses in order to signal lack of interest in what is being said.

11 I am grateful to participants (especially Jenny Cheshire and Peter Trudgill)

at the postgraduate seminar on Gender and Discourse Analysis, Schloss Munchenwiler, Switzerland, November 1993, who refined my understanding of the role of laughter in this particular piece of talk.

12 See, for example, A. Haas 'Sex-associated features of spoken language by four-, eight- and twelve-year old boys and girls'.

13 In a small-scale study of talk between female intimates, Joanne Scheibman found that 76 per cent of all turns involved overlap (including laughter as well as speech). See Scheibman 'Two-at-a-time'.

14 See Fern Johnson & Elizabeth Aries 'Conversational patterns among same-sex pairs of late-adolescent close friends'; Stuart Miller *Men and Friendship*; Joseph Pleck 'Man to man'; Victor Seidler *Rediscovering Masculinity*; Drury Sherrod 'The bonds of men'.

Chapter 7 'You know so I mean probably'

1 See Janet Holmes 'Hedging your bets and sitting on the fence', and chapter 3 of *Women, Men and Politeness*; Bent Preisler *Linguistic Sex Roles in Conversation*; Jennifer Coates 'Epistemic modality and spoken discourse' and 'Gossip revisited'.

2 See M.J.K. Halliday *Explorations in the Functions of Language*.

3 The use of the word *face* as a technical term in the social sciences originates with Erving Goffman (see his *Interaction Ritual*). The idea of face needs has been extensively developed by Penelope Brown and Stephen Levinson, and it is their work I draw on here (see in particular Brown & Levinson *Politeness*).

4 For example, in my 1987 paper, 'Epistemic modality and spoken discourse', I compare two 45-minute stretches of conversation, one involving three men, the other five women. The men discuss three main topics (home-made beer making, hi-fi systems, showing a film in class) which correspond to their own areas of expertise, whereas the women talk about a wide range of topics, from child abuse and fear of men to trains and ships in the docks, which draw on the personal experience of everyone present. (For a detailed account of the topics discussed by the Oxton women in this 45-minute stretch of talk, see the beginning of chapter 4.)

5 Robin Lakoff *Language and Woman's Place*.

6 Ibid, page 54.

7 See note 1.

8 See Fern Johnson & Elizabeth Aries 'The talk of women friends' and 'Conversational patterns among same-sex pairs of late-adolescent close friends'; Stuart Miller *Men and Friendship*; Joseph Pleck 'Man to man'; Janis Pringle 'Is cooperative talk possible among men'?; Victor Seidler *Rediscovering Masculinity*.

9 But see Sally Johnson & Ulrike Meinhoff (eds) *Language and Masculinity*.

10 See Margaret Deuchar, 'A pragmatic account of women's use of standard speech'.

Chapter 8 'It was dreadful wasn't it?'

1 Analysts using a CA (Conversation Analysis) approach would argue that this is the way to identify a question; in other words, they argue that a

question is part of a two-part structure (or 'adjacency pair'): Question–Answer. However, as the material in this chapter will demonstrate, in women's friendly talk, questions (that is, constructions that I am calling questions) often receive no reply, and thus would not qualify as questions by this test.

2 A count of a subsection of my conversational material established that roughly 16 per cent of all tag questions can be described as information-seeking, while the remaining 84 per cent have other functions.

3 See Janet Holmes 'Hedging your bets and sitting on the fence'; *Women, Men and Politeness* chapter 3; Deborah Cameron et al. 'Lakoff in context'.

4 See Dede Brouwer et al. 'Speech differences between women and men'; Pamela Fishman, 'Conversational insecurity'; Victoria DeFrancisco 'The sounds of silence'.

5 Robin Lakoff *Language and Woman's Place*, page 17.

6 For research on question use in magistrates' courts, see Sandra Harris 'Questions as a mode of control in magistrates' courts'; in doctor–patient interaction, see Alexandra Todd 'A diagnosis of doctor–patient discourse in the prescription of contraception'; Candace West *Routine Complications;* Cameron et al. 'Lakoff in context'; in teacher–pupil interaction, see Douglas Barnes 'Language and learning in the classroom'; Janet Holmes 'Stirring up the dust'; Michael Stubbs *Discourse Analysis;* Cameron et al. 'Lakoff in context'; in the talk of TV presenters see Cameron et al. 'Lakoff in context'.

7 Research is still sparse in this area, but my analysis of the conversations of male friends shows unequivocally that men use questions less frequently, and that when they do use them they prefer information-seeking questions. See Coates *Women, Men and Language*, pages 122–4, 189, 'One-at-a-time'.

8 See chapter 3, page 62, and Nancy Chodorow *The Reproduction of Mothering*. Subsequent feminist research has shown that women's sense of morality can be characterized as connected rather than separate (see Carol Gilligan *In a Different Voice;* Gilligan et al. *Mapping the Moral Domain*) as can our preferred ways of learning and dealing with knowledge (see Belenky et al. *Women's Ways of Knowing*).

9 Other commentators use the term *addressee-oriented* (e.g. Holmes 'Hedging your bets' and *Women, Men and Politeness* chapter 3; Cameron et al. 'Lakoff in context') but I hope to capture a wider generalization with the term *other-oriented.*

10 Ironically, questions are also a key linguistic strategy in conversations which encourage speakers to play the expert, but the sort of questions which encourage expertism are *information-seeking* questions, often with rising intonation, used in conjunction with a strictly observed single (one-at-a-time) floor. (For an analysis of such questions, see Janet Holmes 'Women's talk in public contexts'.)

Chapter 9 'I just kept drinking and drinking and drinking'

1 Repetition is also an important aspect of textual cohesion. *Cohesion* refers to the way linguistic elements tie up with other linguistic elements in a text. Analysts using a cohesion approach focus on the text as *product* rather than *process;* they do not take account of those factors which constrain the production

and interpretation of texts. See Michael Halliday and Ruqaiya Hasan *Cohesion in English.*

2 For discussion of this point, see Michael Stubbs *Discourse Analysis,* page 179.

3 The terms *planned* and *unplanned discourse* originate in Elinor Ochs' paper 'Planned and unplanned discourse'.

4 The label *redundant* would apply if we used a strict Wittgensteinian approach – see Talmy Givon 'Coherence in text vs. coherence in mind' (and see also my response paper – Jennifer Coates 'The negotiation of coherence in face-to-face interaction'). More worryingly, this is the view taken by some teachers and examiners involved in the assessment of the oral component of Scottish Standard Grade English (a public exam taken in Scotland at about age 16) – see Shan Wareing 'Cooperative and competitive talk'.

5 It has been argued that the 'yes but' strategy is a key feature of good psychotherapeutic practice: see Senta Troemel-Ploetz ' "She's just not an open person" ' and 'The construction of conversational differences in the language of women and men'.

6 What seems to count in determining whether an instance of overlapping speech is interpreted as an interruption (a bid for the floor, where the floor is singly developed) or as a supportive move (part of a collaborative floor) is the polarity of next speaker's move. Polarity can be defined as 'a system of positive/negative contrastivity found in language' (David Crystal *A First Dictionary of Linguistics and Phonetics,* page 274). Where two chunks of talk occur one after the other or simultaneously, chunk B will be said to have positive polarity in relation to chunk A where chunk B agrees with, confirms, repeats or extends the proposition expressed in chunk A, or makes a point on the same topic that demonstrates shared attitudes or beliefs. Chunk B will be said to have negative polarity when it denies, disagrees with or ignores chunk A. (See Coates 'No gap, lots of overlap'.)

7 See Deborah Tannen *Talking Voices.*

8 It's estimated that over 6,000 languages are spoken in the world today (see Tove Skutnabb-Kangas & Jim Cummins *Minority Education*). Of these, 'only around 106 have been committed to writing to a degree sufficient to have produced literature', according to Walter J. Ong (*Orality and Literacy,* page 7).

9 See Roman Jacobson 'Linguistics and poetics'; Dell Hymes, *'In Vain I Tried to Tell You'*; Deborah Tannen, 'Repetition in conversation'.

10 For further discussion of women and connection, see Terri Apter *Altered Loves;* Carol Gilligan *In a Different Voice;* Carol Gilligan et al. (eds) *Mapping the Moral Domain;* Fern Johnson & Elizabeth Aries 'The talk of women friends'.

Chapter 10 'Thank god I'm a woman'

1 The term discourse is particularly associated with the work of Michel Foucault. For further discussion of Foucault's theories of discourse, see Norman Fairclough *Discourse and Social Change;* Chris Weedon *Feminist Practice and Poststructuralist Theory.*

2 For further discussion of these ideas, see David Lee *Competing Discourses,* Nicola Gavey 'Feminist poststructuralism and discourse analysis'.

3 Wendy Hollway 'Heterosexual sex', page 131.

4 The analysis of linguistic texts in terms of discourse is associated with the branch of linguistics known as critical linguistics and with the work of Norman Fairclough – see in particular Fairclough *Discourse and Social Change*.
5 Simone de Beauvoir *The Second Sex* (transl. H. M. Parshley).
6 At the time this conversation was recorded, Sue had gone back to college as a mature student to train as a primary school teacher.
7 The term *subject* as used here pulls together three different strands of thought, one more political (we are not free but *subject to* the power of others), one more philosophical (we are thinking *subjects*, sites of consciousness) and one more grammatical (sentences have *subjects* – they are what the sentence is about). (See Tim O'Sullivan *Key Concepts in Communication*.) The word also gains meaning from its opposition to *object*, even though, ironically, the two words are often very close in meaning. Here, for example, it would be equally true to say 'our talk about men does powerful work in our construction of ourselves as feminine objects'. Showing how women are *objectified* in patriarchal discourses has been one of the goals of feminist discourse analysis.
8 I can say this with confidence about Hannah and her friends, since I have recordings of them since they were twelve. But although I knew Emily when she was twelve, I only recorded her with her friends when they were sixteen, so I have no definite proof that her language changed.
9 There are few good example of positive talk about significant males in the conversational data. This could be because one of the chief functions of women's friendly talk is to allow us to talk about our anxieties and problems, and about our triumphs in the outside world. Ongoing good relationships do not seem to be a salient topic of conversation.
10 It had not crossed my mind that I might have to leave the room during recording. On this particular occasion I had to go and answer the phone, and my friends started to talk about me after I had left the room. I have only listened to the first few seconds of this talk, as it seems to me that I have absolutely no right to know what they said in my absence.
11 I am grateful to David Lee (personal correspondence) for alerting me to the slipperiness of this phrase.
12 Weedon *Feminist Practice and Poststructuralist Theory*, page 98.
13 Fairclough *Discourse and Social Change*, pages 3–4.

Chapter 11 'Talk's absolutely fundamental': Being a friend

1 Dell Hymes, 'On communicative competence'.
2 There are, however, occasional disfluencies in collaborative talk, as in the following example from the Oxton group:

[Topic = Yorkshire Ripper murders]

SALLY: I just thought if the car breaks down on the way home/

SALLY: I mean I'll DIE of FEAR/ <LAUGHS> I'll never get out/ <EXAGGERATED>

- -

SALLY: and I'll just- . because . everyone – was TERRified of
→ MARY: just sit here and die/

- -

SALLY: the whole- you know the whole thing/
MEG: yes/

- -

This is an example of how one speaker's predilection to leave utterances unfinished can be uncomfortable for speakers who prefer utterances to be completed. It seems clear that Sally and three of the four other women taking part in this conversation are quite happy with *and I'll just-*, an incomplete clause which very much fits the pattern of unfinished but unproblematically understood utterances typical of the collaborative floor (see the section on incomplete utterances, chapter 6, page 122). Mary's completion of Sally's incomplete chunk begins *after* Sally has started a new chunk, the clause *because everyone was TERRified of the whole- you know the whole thing,* Sally seems momentarily disconcerted by Mary's contribution – she pauses after *everyone* before continuing with the rest of the clause. Such an example is rare, and does not disrupt the collaborative floor. What it throws into relief is the (unnoticed) skill which is involved in our normal successful participation in collaborative talk.

3 For a detailed comparison of the linguistic strategies used by the girls at different ages (from twelve to fifteen years of age), see my paper 'Discourse, gender and subjectivity'.

4 The issue of friendship and talking too much was the subject of an episode of the American series *Northern Exposure*: a man who has spent twenty years living alone as a fire prevention officer in Alaska returns to civilization, but alienates people by talking at length on abstruse topics. The man becomes depressed because he has no friends. In the end, the local doctor, Fleischmann, takes him on one side and gives him a lesson in 'friendly talk', a lesson which consists chiefly in teaching him not to talk endlessly, but to pay attention to the other person(s) present.

5 See Coates *Women, Men and Language*, pages 188–92; Deborah Tannen *You Just Don't Understand*.

6 See Elizabeth Aries 'Interaction patterns and themes of male, female and mixed groups' and Susan Kalcik '"... like Ann's gynaecologist or the time I was almost raped" – personal narratives in women's rap groups'.

7 See note 3.

8 Donald Cohen quoted in R. Peter Hobson *Autism and the Development of Mind*, page 3. (My thanks to Moira Gommon for pointing out the relevance of this work.)

9 Hobson *Autism and the Development of Mind*, page 5. This patient was diagnosed as having Asperger's syndrome, 'a condition with a typical developmental history closely allied to that of autism'.

10 Hobson *Autism and the Development of Mind*, page 3.

11 Drusilla Modjeska *Poppy*, page 309.

12 See Chris Weedon *Feminist Practice and Poststructuralist Theory*, chapter 4 'Language and subjectivity'. The significance of friendship in women's lives

also enables women to make perceptual leaps. The following is a compelling example of a woman scientist understanding natural phenomena in a new way because of having access to the metaphor of friendship. Barbara McClintock, a cytogeneticist, writes about her work with chromosomes as follows: 'I wasn't outside, I was down there. I was part of the system. It surprised me because I actually felt as if I was right down there *and these were my friends*' (emphasis added) (Keller quoted in Hollway *Subjectivity and Method in Psychology*, page 120).

13 Carolyn Heilbrun, *Writing a Woman's Life*, page 100.

14 Tamsin Wilton has argued forcefully (in 'Sisterhood in the service of patriarchy') that 'bonding between heterosexual women acts to shore up the heteropatriarchy' (page 507).

15 Janice Raymond *A Passion for Friends*, pages 9–10.

Bibliography

Abrahams, Roger (1983) *The Man-of-Words in the West Indies: Performance and the Emergence of Creole Culture*. Baltimore: Johns Hopkins University Press.
Apter, Terri (1990) *Altered Loves: Mothers and Daughters during Adolescence*. London: Harvester Wheatsheaf.
Aries, Elizabeth (1976) 'Interaction patterns and themes of male, female and mixed groups', *Small Group Behaviour* 7, 7–18.
Atkinson, Karen (in press) *The Talk of Elderly Women*. London: Longman.
Atwood, Margaret (1989) *Cat's Eye*. London: Bloomsbury Press.
Barnes, Douglas (1971) 'Language and learning in the classroom', *Journal of Curriculum Studies* 3.
Bauman, Richard (1986) *Story, Performance, and Event*. Cambridge: Cambridge University Press.
Bauman, Richard & Sherzer, Joel (eds) (1974) *Explorations in the Ethnography of Speaking*. Cambridge: Cambridge University Press.
Belenky, Mary, Clinchy, Blythe, Goldberger, Nancy & Tarule, Jill (1986) *Women's Ways of Knowing*. New York: Basic Books.
Bell, Diane (1993) *Daughters of the Dreaming* (2nd edition). St Leonards, NSW: Allen & Unwin.
Bergvall, Victoria, Bing, Janet & Freed, Alice (eds) (1996) *Language and Gender Research: Theory and Method*. London: Longman.
Bing, Janet & Bergvall, Victoria (1996) 'The question of questions: beyond binary thinking', in Victoria Bergvall, Janet Bing & Alice Freed (eds) *Language and Gender Research: Theory and Method*. London: Longman.
Brittain, Vera (1981) *Testament of Friendship*. London: Fontana.
Brouwer, Dede, Gerritsen, Marinel & de Haan, Dorian (1979) 'Speech differences between women and men: on the wrong track?', *Language in Society* 8, 33–50.
Brown, Penelope & Levinson, Stephen (1987) *Politeness*. Cambridge: Cambridge University Press.
Bublitz, Wolfram (1989) *Supportive Fellow-Speakers and Cooperative Conversations*. Amsterdam: John Benjamins.
Cameron, Deborah (1992) *Feminism and Linguistic Theory* (2nd edition). London: Macmillan.
Cameron, Deborah, McAlinden, Fiona & O'Leary, Kathy (1989) 'Lakoff in context: the social and linguistic functions of tag questions', pages 74–93 in Jennifer

Coates & Deborah Cameron (eds) *Women in Their Speech Communities*. London: Longman.

Chafe, Wallace (1980) 'The deployment of consciousness in the production of a narrative', pages 9–50 in Wallace Chafe (ed.) *The Pear Stories: Cognitive, Cultural and Linguistics Aspects of Narrative Production*. Norwood, N.J.: Ablex.

Chafe, Wallace (1994) *Discourse, Consciousness and Time: The Flow and Displacement of Conscious Experience in Speaking and Writing*. Chicago: University of Chicago Press.

Chafe, Wallace (1995) 'Polyphonic topic development'. Paper presented at the Symposium on Conversation, University of New Mexico, 14–16 July.

Chan, Grace (1992) 'Gender, roles and power in dyadic conversations', pages 55–67 in Kira Hall, Mary Bucholtz & Birch Moonwomon (eds) *Locating Power: Proceedings of the 2nd Berkeley Women and Language Conference*. Berkeley: Berkeley Women and Language Group, University of California.

Cheepen, Christine (1988) *The Predictability of Informal Conversation*. London: Pinter Publishers.

Cheepen, Christine & Monaghan, James (1990) *Spoken English: A Practical Guide*. London: Pinter Publishers.

Cheshire, Jenny & Jenkins, Nancy (1991) 'Gender issues in the GCSE oral English examination, part 2', *Language and Education* 5, 19–40.

Chodorow, Nancy (1978) *The Reproduction of Mothering: Psychoanalysis and the Sociology of Gender*. Berkeley: University of California Press.

Coates, Jennifer (1987) 'Epistemic modality and spoken discourse', *Transactions of the Philological Society*, 110–31.

Coates, Jennifer (1989) 'Gossip revisited: language in all-female groups', pages 94–122 in Jennifer Coates & Deborah Cameron (eds) *Women in Their Speech Communities*. London: Longman.

Coates, Jennifer (1993) *Women, Men and Language* (2nd edition). London: Longman.

Coates, Jennifer (1994) 'No gap, lots of overlap: turn-taking patterns in the talk of women friends', pages 177–92 in David Graddol, Janet Maybin & Barry Stierer (eds) *Researching Language and Literacy in Social Context*. Clevedon, Avon: Multilingual Matters.

Coates, Jennifer (1995) 'The negotiation of coherence in face-to-face interaction: some examples from the extreme bounds', pages 41–58 in Morti-Ann Gernsbacher & Talmy Givon (eds) *The Negotiation of Coherence*. New York: John Benjamins.

Coates, Jennifer (1996) 'Discourse gender, and subjectivity: the talk of teenage girls' to appear in Mary Bucholtz, A.C. Liang, Laurel Sutton & Caitlin Hines (eds) *Cultural Performances: Proceedings of the 3rd Berkeley Women and Language Conference*. Berkeley Women & Language Group, University of California Berkeley.

Coates, Jennifer (in press) 'One-at-a-time: the organization of men's talk', in Sally Johnson & Ulrike Hanna Meinhof (eds) *Language and Masculinity*. Oxford: Blackwell.

Coates, Jennifer & Cameron, Deborah (eds) (1989) *Women in Their Speech Communities*. London: Longman.

Coates, Jennifer & Jordan, Mary Ellen (in press) 'Que(e)rying friendship: discourses of resistance and the construction of gendered subjectivity', in Anna Livia & Kira Hall (eds) *Queerly Phrased: Language, Gender and Sexuality*. Oxford: Oxford University Press.

Crystal, David (1980) *A First Dictionary of Linguistics and Phonetics*. London: Andre Deutsch.
de Beauvoir, Simone (1988) *The Second Sex* (translated by H.M. Parshley). London: Picador.
DeFrancisco, Victoria L. (1991) 'The sounds of silence: how men silence women in marital relations', *Discourse & Society* 2, 413–24.
de Lauretis, Teresa (1989) 'The essence of the triangle or taking the risk of essen tialism seriously: feminist theory in Italy, the US and Britain', *Differences* 1, 1–37.)
Deuchar, Margaret (1989) 'A pragmatic account of women's use of standard speech', pages 27–32 in Jennifer Coates & Deborah Cameron (eds) *Women in Their Speech Communities*. London: Longman.
Diaz, Felix Martinez (1994) 'Collective formulation in problem-oriented talk'. PhD thesis, Lancaster University.
Dorval, Bruce (ed.) *Conversational Organization and Its Development*. Norwood, N.J.: Ablex.
Eckert, Penelope (1990) 'Cooperative competition in adolescent "girl talk"', *Discourse Processes* 13, 5–31. (Reprinted, pages 32–61, in Deborah Tannen (ed.) *Gender and Conversational Interaction*. Oxford: Oxford University Press, 1993.)
Eckert, Penelope & McConnell-Ginet, Sally (1992) 'Think practically and look locally: language and gender as community-based practice'. *Annual Review of Anthropology* 21, 461–90.
Edelsky, Carole (1981) 'Who's got the floor?', *Language in Society* 10, 383–421. (Reprinted, pages 189–227, in Deborah Tannen (ed.) *Gender and Conversational Interaction*. Oxford: Oxford University Press, 1993.)
Edelsky, Carole & Adams, Karen (1990) 'Creating inequality: breaking the rules in debates', *Journal of Language and Social Psychology* 9, 171–90.
Eder, Donna (1993) '"Go get ya a french": romantic and sexual teasing among adolescent girls', pages 17–31 in Deborah Tannen (ed.) *Gender and Conversational Interaction*. Oxford: Oxford University Press.
Erickson, Frederick (1990) 'The social construction of discourse coherence', pages 207–38 in Bruce Dorval (ed.) *Conversational Organization and its Development*. Norwood, N.J.: Ablex.
Faderman, Lillian (1985) *Surpassing the Love of Men*. London: Women's Press.
Fairclough, Norman (1992) *Discourse and Social Change*. Cambridge: Polity Press.
Falk, Jane (1980) 'The conversational duet', *Proceedings of the 6th Annual Meeting of the Berkeley Linguistics Society* 6, 507–14.
Fishman, Pamela (1980) 'Conversational insecurity', pages 127–32 in Howard Giles, Peter Robinson & Philip Smith (eds) *Language: Social Psychological Perspectives*. Oxford: Pergamon Press.
Frye, Marilyn (1990) 'Lesbian "sex"', pages 305–15 in Jeffner Allen (ed.) *Lesbian Philosophies and Cultures*. New York: State University of New York Press.
Gavey, Nicola (1989) 'Feminist poststructuralism and discourse analysis', *Psychology of Women Quarterly* 13, 459–75.
Geleit, Noni (1988) 'Men talking to men: the back-channel response in all-male discourse'. BA dissertation, Roehampton Institute.
Gilligan, Carol (1982) *In a Different Voice*. Cambridge, Mass.: Harvard University Press.

Gilligan, Carol, Ward, Janie Victoria & Taylor, Jill McLean (eds) (1988) *Mapping the Moral Domain*. Cambridge, Mass.: Harvard University Press.

Givon, Talmy (1995) 'Coherence in text vs. coherence in mind', pages 59–115 in Morti-Ann Gernsbacher & Talmy Givon (eds) *The Negotiation of Coherence*. New York: John Benjamins.

Goffman, Ervin (1967) *Interaction Ritual*. New York: Anchor Books.

Goodwin, Marjorie Harness (1990) *He-Said-She-Said: Talk as Social Organization among Black Children*. Bloomington, Ind.: Indiana University Press.

Gouldner, Helen & Strong, Mary Symons (1987) *Speaking of Friendship*. New York: Greenwood Press.

Graddol, David & Swann, Joan (1989) *Gender Voices*. Oxford: Blackwell.

Green, Rayna (1993) ' "It's okay once you get it past the teeth" and other feminist paradigms for folklore studies', prologue to Susan Tower Hollis, Linda Pershing & M. Jane Young (eds) *Feminist Theory and the Study of Folklore*. Urbana, Ill.: University of Illinois Press.

Gumperz, John & Hymes, Dell (eds) (1972) *Directions in Sociolinguistics: The Ethnography of Communication*. New York: Holt, Rinehart and Winston.

Haas, A. (1978) 'Sex-associated features of spoken language by four-, eight-, and twelve-year old boys and girls'. Paper presented at the 9th World Congress of Sociology, Uppsala, Sweden, 14–19 August.

Halliday, M.A.K. (1973) *Explorations in the Functions of Language*. London: Edward Arnold.

Halliday, M.A.K. & Hasan, Ruqaiya (1976) *Cohesion in English*. London: Longman.

Hamilton, Annette (1981) 'A complex strategical situation: gender and power in Aboriginal Australia', pages 69–85 in Norma Grieve & Patricia Grimshaw (eds) *Australian Women: Feminist Perspectives*. Melbourne: Oxford University Press.

Haraway, Donna (1988) 'Situated knowledges: the science question in feminism and the privilege of partial perspective', *Feminist Studies* 14, 575–99.

Harding, Sandra (1986) *The Science Question in Feminism*. Ithaca, N.Y.: Cornell University Press.

Harding, Sandra (1990) 'Starting thought from women's lives: eight resources for maximizing objectivity', *Journal of Social Philosophy* 21, 140–9.

Harris, Sandra (1984) 'Questions as a mode of control in magistrates' courts', *International Journal of the Sociology of Language* 49, 5–27.

Hartsock, Nancy M. (1983) 'The feminist standpoint: developing the ground for a specifically feminist historical materialism', pages 283–310 in Sandra Harding & M.B. Hintikka (eds) *Discovering Reality*. Dordrecht: D. Reidel.

Heilbrun, Carolyn G. (1988) *Writing a Woman's Life*. New York: Ballantine Books.

Herring, Susan, Johnson, Deborah & Dibenedetto, Tamra (1992) 'Participation in electronic discourse in a "feminist" field', pages 250–62 in Kira Hall, Mary Bucholtz & Birch Moonwomon (eds) *Locating Power: Proceedings of the 2nd Berkeley Women and Language Conference*. Berkeley: Berkeley Women and Language Group, University of California.

Hey, Valerie (1996) *The Company She Keeps: An Ethnography of Girls' Friendship*. Buckingham: Open University Press.

Hite, Shere (1989) *The Hite Report: Women and Love*. Harmondsworth: Penguin Books.

Hobson, R. Peter (1993) *Autism and the Development of Mind*. Hove: Lawrence Erlbaum Associates.

Hollway, Wendy (1983) 'Heterosexual sex: power and desire for the other', pages 124–40 in Sue Cartledge & Joanna Ryan (eds) *Sex and Love: New Thoughts on Old Contradictions*. London: Women's Press.
Hollway, Wendy (1989) *Subjectivity and Method in Psychology*. London: Sage Publications.
Holmes, Janet (1984) 'Hedging your bets and sitting on the fence: some evidence for hedges as support structures', *Te Reo* 27, 47–62.
Holmes, Janet (1989) 'Stirring up the dust: The importance of sex as a variable in the ESL classroom'. *Proceedings of the ATESOL 6th Summer School Sydney*, vol. 1, 4–39.
Holmes, Janet (1992) 'Women's talk in public contexts'. *Discourse & Society* 3, 131–50.
Holmes, Janet (1995) *Women, Men and Politeness*. London: Longman.
Hunt, Mary E. (1991) *Fierce Tenderness: A Feminist Theology of Friendship*. New York: Crossroad.
Hymes, Dell (1962) 'The ethnography of speaking', pages 13–53 in T. Gladin & W.C. Sturtevant (eds) *Anthropology and Human Behaviour*. Washington, D.C.: Anthropological Society of Washington.
Hymes, Dell (1971) 'On communicative competence', pages 269–93 in J.B. Pride & Janet Holmes (eds) *Sociolinguistics*. Harmondsworth: Penguin Books.
Hymes, Dell (1974) *Foundations in Sociolinguistics: An Ethnographic Approach*. Philadelphia: University of Pennsylvania Press.
Hymes, Dell (1981) *'In Vain I Tried to Tell You': Essays in Native American Ethnopoetics*. Philadelphia: University of Pennsylvania Press.
Jacobson, Roman (1960) 'Linguistics and poetics', pages 350–77 in Thomas A. Sebeok (ed.) *Style in Language*. Cambridge, Mass.: MIT Press.
James, Deborah & Clarke Sandra (1993) 'Interruptions, gender & power', pages 231–80 in Deborah Tannen (ed.) *Gender and Conversational Interaction*. Oxford: Oxford University Press.
Jenkins, Nancy & Cheshire, Jenny (1990) 'Gender issues in the GCSE oral English examination, part 1', *Language and Education* 4, 261–92.
Jerrome, Dorothy (1984) 'Good company: the sociological implications of friendship', *Sociological Review* 32, 696–715.
Johnson, Anthony (in press) *Couples Talking*. London: Longman.
Johnson, Fern & Aries, Elizabeth (1983a) 'The talk of women friends', *Women's Studies International Forum* 6, 353–61.
Johnson, Fern & Aries, Elizabeth (1983b) 'Conversational patterns among same-sex pairs of late-adolescent close friends', *Journal of Genetic Psychology* 142, 225–38.
Johnson, Sally & Meinhoff, Ulrike (in press) *Language and Masculinity*. Oxford: Blackwell.
Johnstone, Barbara (1990) *Stories, Community, and Place*. Bloomington, Ind.: Indiana University Press.
Johnstone, Barbara (1993) 'Community and contest: Midwestern men and women creating their worlds in conversational storytelling', pages 62–80 in Deborah Tannen (ed.) *Gender and Conversational Interaction*. Oxford: Oxford University Press.
Jones, Deborah (1980) 'Gossip: notes on women's oral culture', pages 193–8 in Cheris Kramarae (ed.) *The Voices and Words of Women and Men*. Oxford: Pergamon

Press. (Reprinted, pages 242–50, in Deborah Cameron (ed.) (1990) *The Feminist Critique of Language*. London: Routledge.)
Jordan, Rosan & Kalcik, Susan (eds) (1985) *Women's Folklore, Women's Culture*. Philadelphia: University of Pennsylvania Press.
Kalcik, Susan (1975) '". . . like Ann's gynaecologist or the time I was almost raped": personal narratives in women's rap groups', *Journal of American Folklore* 88, 3–11.
Kennedy, Robinette (1986) 'Women's friendships on Crete: a psychological perspective', pages 121–38 in Jill Dubisch (ed.) *Gender and Power in Rural Greece*. Princeton: Princeton University Press.
Labov, William (1972a) *Sociolinguistic Patterns*. Philadelphia: University of Pennsylvania Press.
Labov, William (1972b) 'The transformation of experience in narrative syntax', pages 354–396 in *Language in the Inner City*. Philadelphia: University of Pennsylvania Press.
Labov, William (1972c) *Language in the Inner City*. Philadelphia: University of Pennsylvania Press.
Lakoff, Robin (1975) *Language and Woman's Place*. New York: Harper & Row.
Lane, Harlan (1993) *The Mask of Benevolences: Disabling the Deaf Community*. New York: Vintage Books.
Le Guin, Ursula (1989) *Dancing at the Edge of the World*. London: Victor Gollancz.
Lee, David (1992) *Competing Discourses: Perspective and Ideology in Language*. London: Longman.
Leech, Geoffrey (1983) *Principles of Pragmatics*. London: Longman.
Lerner, Gene (1991) 'On the syntax of sentences-in-progress'. *Language in Society* 20, 441–58.
Maltz, Daniel & Borker, Ruth (1982) 'A cultural approach to male–female miscommunication', pages 195–216 in John Gumperz (ed.) *Language and Social Identity*. Cambridge: Cambridge University Press.
McCabe, Trisha (1981) 'Girls and leisure', pages 123–33 in Alan Tomlinson (ed.) *Leisure and Social Control*. Brighton Polytechnic: Chelsea School of Human Movement.
Miller, J. Hillis (1990) 'Narrative', in F. Lentricchia & T. McLaughlin (eds) *Critical Terms for Literary Study*. Chicago: University of Chicago Press.
Miller, Stuart (1983) *Men and Friendship*. San Leandro, Calif.: Gateway Books.
Milroy, Lesley (1987) *Observing and Analysing Natural Language*. Oxford: Blackwell.
Modjeska, Drusilla (1990) *Poppy*. Ringwood, Victoria: McPhee Gribble.
Oakley, Ann (1981) 'Interviewing women, a contradiction in terms', pages 30–61 in Helen Roberts (ed.) *Doing Feminist Research*. London: Routledge.
Ochs, Elinor (1979) 'Transcription as theory', in Elinor Ochs & Bambi Schieffelin (eds) *Developmental Pragmatics*. New York: Academic Press.
Ochs, Elinor (1983) 'Planned and unplanned discourse', pages 129–57 in Elinor Ochs & Bambi Schieffelin *Acquiring Conversational Competence*. London: Routledge.
Ochs, Elinor & Taylor, Carolyn (1992) 'Family narrative as political activity', *Discourse & Society* 3, 301–40.
O'Connor, Pat (1992) *Friendships between Women: A Critical Review*. London: Harvester Wheatsheaf.
Ong, Walter J. (1982) *Orality and Literacy: The Technologising of the Word*. London: Methuen.

O'Neill, Gilda (1993) *A Night out with the Girls*. London: Women's Press.

O'Sullivan, Tim (1983) *Key Concepts in Communication*. London: Methuen.

Pleck, Joseph (1975) 'Man to man: is brotherhood possible'?, in N. Glazer-Malbin (ed.) *Old Family, New Family*. New York: Van Nostrand.

Polanyi, Livia (1982) 'Literary complexity in everyday storytelling', pages 155–70 in Deborah Tannen (ed.) *Spoken and Written Language: Exploring Orality and Literacy*. Norwood, N.J.: Ablex.

Pomerantz, Anita (1984) 'Agreeing and disagreeing with assessments', pages 152–63 in J.M. Atkinson & John Heritage (eds) *The Structure of Social Action*. Cambridge: Cambridge University Press.

Preisler, Bent (1986) *Linguistic Sex Roles in Conversation*. Berlin: Mouton de Gruyter.

Pringle, Janis (1991) 'Is cooperative talk possible among men?' MA dissertation, University of London.

Rae, John (1990) 'Collaborative completions in advisory exchanges'. Poster presented at the International Pragmatics Association Conference, Barcelona, July.

Raymond, Janice (1986) *A Passion for Friends: Towards a Philosophy of Female Affection*. London: Women's Press.

Reisman, Karl (1974) 'Contrapuntal conversations in an Antiguan village', pages 110–24 in Richard Bauman & Joel Sherzer (eds) *Explorations in the Ethnography of Speaking*. Cambridge: Cambridge University Press.

Rich, Adrienne (1980) 'It is the lesbian in us . . .', pages 199–202 in *On Lies, Secrets and Silence: Selected Prose, 1966–1978*. London: Virago.

Rubin, Lilian (1985) *Just Friends: The Role of Friendship in Our Lives*. New York: Harper Row.

Sacks, Harvey (1992) *Lectures*. Oxford: Blackwell.

Sacks, Harvey, Schegloff, Emanuel A. & Jefferson, Gail (1974) 'A simplest systematics for the organisation of turn-taking in conversation', *Language* 50, 696–735.

Sadker, Myra & Sadker, David (1990) 'Confronting sexism in the college classroom', pages 176–87 in Susan Gabriel & Isaiah Smithson (eds) *Gender in the Classroom: Power and Pedagogy*. Urbana, Ill.: University of Illinois Press.

Saville-Troike, Muriel (1989) *The Ethnography of Communication* (2nd edition). Oxford: Basil Blackwell.

Schacht, S.P. & Atchison, Patricia (1993) 'Heterosexual instrumentalism: past and future directions', pages 120–35 in Sue Wilkinson & Celia Kitzinger (eds) *Heterosexuality*. London: Sage.

Scheibman, Joanne (1995) 'Two-at-a-time: the intimacy of simultaneous speech in sister talk'. *LGSO Working Papers 1995*. University of New Mexico Linguistics Department.

Sherrod, Drury (1987) 'The bonds of men: problems and possibilities in close male relationships', pages 213–39 in Harry Brod (ed.) *The Making of Masculinities*. Boston: Allen & Unwin.

Seidler, Victor (1989) *Rediscovering Masculinity: Reason, Language and Sexuality*. London: Routledge.

Seidler, Victor (ed.) (1991) *The Achilles Heel Reader*. London: Routledge.

Sheldon, Amy (1990) 'Pickle fights: gendered talk in pre-school disputes', *Discourse Processes* 13, 5–31. (Reprinted, pages 83–109, in Deborah Tannen (ed.) *Gender and Conversational Interaction*. Oxford: Oxford University Press, 1993.)

Skutnabb-Kangas, Tove & Cummins, Jim (eds) (1988) *Minority Education: From Shame to Struggle*. Clevedon, Avon: Multilingual Matters.

Smith-Rosenberg, Carroll (1975) 'The female world of love and ritual: relations between women in nineteenth-century America', *Signs: Journal of Women in Culture and Society* 1, 1–29.

Stenstrom, Anna-Brita (1994) *An Introduction to Spoken Interaction*. London: Longman.

Stubbs, Michael (1983) *Discourse Analysis*. Oxford: Blackwell.

Svartvik, Jan & Quirk, Randolph (eds) (1980) *A Corpus of English Conversation*. Lund: Gleerup.

Swann, Joan (1989) 'Talk control: an illustration from the classroom of problems in analysing male dominance in conversation', pages 123–40 in Jennifer Coates & Deborah Cameron (eds) *Women in Their Speech Communities*. London: Longman.

Tannen, Deborah (1987) 'Repetition in conversation: towards a poetics of talk', *Language* 63, 574–605.

Tannen, Deborah (1989) *Talking Voices: Repetition, Dialogue, and Imagery in Conversational Discourse*. Cambridge: Cambridge University Press.

Tannen, Deborah (1990) 'Gender differences in topical coherence: creating involvement in best friends' talk', *Discourse Processes* 13, 73–90.

Tannen, Deborah (1991) *You Just Don't Understand: Women and Men in Conversation*. London: Virago.

Tannen, Deborah (ed.) (1993) *Gender and Conversational Interaction*. Oxford: Oxford University Press.

Tiger, Lionel (1969) *Men in Groups*. London: Nelson.

Todd, Alexandra Dundas (1983) 'A diagnosis of doctor–patient discourse in the prescription of contraception', pages 159–87 in Sue Fisher & Alexandra D. Todd (eds) *The Social Organization of Doctor–Patient Communication*, Washington, D.C.: Center for Applied Linguistics.

Troemel-Ploetz, Senta (1982a) ' "She's just not an open person": a linguistic analysis of a restructuring intervention in family therapy'. *Family Process* 16, 339–52.

Troemel-Ploetz, Senta (1982b) 'The construction of conversational differences in the language of women and men'. Talk given at the 10th World Congress in Sociology, Mexico City, 18 August. (Published in German translation in Senta Troemel-Ploetz (ed.) (1984) *Gewalt durch Sprache*. Frankfurt: Fischer.)

Troemel-Ploetz, Senta (1992) 'The construction of conversational equality by women', pages 581–9 in Kira Hall, Mary Bucholtz & Birch Moonwomon (eds) *Locating Power: Proceedings of the 2nd Berkeley Women and Language Conference*. Berkeley: Berkeley Women and Language Group, University of California.

Trudgill, Peter (1974) *The Social Differentiation of English in Norwich*. Cambridge: Cambridge University Press.

Wareing, Shan (1994) 'Cooperative and competitive talk: the assessment of discussion at Standard Grade'. PhD thesis, University of Strathclyde.

Weedon, Chris (1987) *Feminist Practice and Poststructuralist Theory*. Oxford: Blackwell.

West, Candace (1984a) 'When the doctor is a "lady" ': power, status and gender in physician–patient encounters', *Symbolic Interaction* 7, 87–106.

West, Candace (1984b) *Routine Complications: Troubles with Talk between Doctors and Patients*. Bloomington, Ind.: Indiana University Press.

West, Candace & Zimmerman, Don (1983) 'Small insults: a study of interruptions in cross-sex conversations between unacquainted persons', pages 103–18 in

Barrie Thorne, Cheris Kramarae & Nancy Henley (eds) *Language, Gender and Society*. Rowley, Mass.: Newbury House.

Wilson, John (1987) 'The sociolinguistic paradox: data as a methodological product', *Language and Communication* 7, 161–77.

Wilson, John (1989) *On the Boundaries of Conversation*. Oxford: Pergamon Press.

Wilton, Tamsin (1992) 'Sisterhood in the service of patriarchy: heterosexual women's friendships and male power', *Feminism & Psychology* 2, 506–9.

Wodak, Ruth (1981) 'Women relate, men report: sex differences in language behaviour in a therapeutic group', *Journal of Pragmatics* 5, 261–85.

Woods, Nicola (1989) 'Talking shop: sex and status as determinants of floor apportionment in a work setting', pages 141–57 in Jennifer Coates & Deborah Cameron (eds) *Women in Their Speech Communities*. London: Longman.

Wulff, Helena (1988) *Twenty Girls: Growing up, Ethnicity and Excitement in a South London Microculture. Stockholm Studies in Social Anthropology 21*.

Yocom, Margaret R. (1985) 'Woman to woman: fieldwork and the private sphere', pages 45–53 in Rosan Jordan and Susan Kalcik (eds) *Women's Folklore, Women's Culture*. Philadelphia: University of Pennsylvania Press.

Zimmerman, Don & West, Candace (1975) 'Sex roles, interruptions and silences in conversation', pages 105–29 in Barrie Thorne & Nancy Henley (eds) *Language and Sex: Difference and Dominance*. Rowley, Mass.: Newbury House.

Index

(Items in ***bold italics*** are the names of particular topics from the conversations.)